A Research Agenda for Global Crime

Elgar Research Agendas outline the future of research in a given area. Leading scholars are given the space to explore their subject in provocative ways, and map out the potential directions of travel. They are relevant but also visionary.

Forward-looking and innovative, Elgar Research Agendas are an essential resource for PhD students, scholars and anybody who wants to be at the forefront of research.

Titles in the series include:

A Research Agenda for Shrinking Cities
Justin B. Hollander

A Research Agenda for Women and
Entrepreneurship
*Edited by Patricia G. Greene and Candida
G. Brush*

A Research Agenda for Entrepreneurial
Cognition and Intention
*Edited by Malin Brännback and Alan L.
Carsrud*

A Research Agenda for Entrepreneurship
Education
Edited by Alain Fayolle

A Research Agenda for Service Innovation
Edited by Faïz Gallouj and Faridah Djellal

A Research Agenda for Global
Environmental Politics
Edited by Peter Dauvergne and Justin Alger

A Research Agenda for New Institutional
Economics
*Edited by Claude Ménard and Mary M.
Shirley*

A Research Agenda for Regeneration
Economies
Reading City-Regions
*Edited by John R. Bryson, Lauren Andres
and Rachel Mulhall*

A Research Agenda for Cultural Economics
Edited by Samuel Cameron

A Research Agenda for Environmental
Management
*Edited by Kathleen E. Halvorsen, Chelsea
Schelly, Robert M. Handler, Erin C. Pischke
and Jessie L. Knowlton*

A Research Agenda for Creative Tourism
*Edited by Nancy Duxbury and Greg
Richards*

A Research Agenda for Public
Administration
Edited by Andrew Massey

A Research Agenda for Tourism
Geographies
Edited by Dieter K. Müller

A Research Agenda for Economic
Psychology
*Edited by Katharina Gangl and Erich
Kirchler*

A Research Agenda for Entrepreneurship
and Innovation
*Edited by David B. Audretsch, Erik E.
Lehmann and Albert N. Link*

A Research Agenda for Financial Inclusion
and Microfinance
*Edited by Marek Hudon, Marc Labie and
Ariane Szafarz*

A Research Agenda for Global Crime
*Edited by Tim Hall and Vincenzo
Scalia*

A Research Agenda for Transport Policy
*Edited by John Stanley and David A.
Hensher*

A Research Agenda for Tourism and
Development
*Edited by Richard Sharpley and David
Harrison*

A Research Agenda for Global Crime

Edited by

TIM HALL

University of Winchester, UK

VINCENZO SCALIA

University of Winchester, UK

 Edward Elgar
PUBLISHING

Cheltenham, UK • Northampton, MA, USA

Published by
Edward Elgar Publishing Limited
The Lypiatts
15 Lansdown Road
Cheltenham
Glos GL50 2JA
UK

Edward Elgar Publishing, Inc.
William Pratt House
9 Dewey Court
Northampton
Massachusetts 01060
USA

A catalogue record for this book
is available from the British Library

Library of Congress Control Number: 2019930687

This book is available electronically in the **Elgar**online
Social and Political Science subject collection
DOI 10.4337/9781786438676

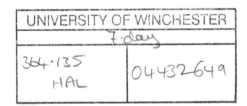

MIX
Paper from
responsible sources
FSC
www.fsc.org   FSC® C013056

ISBN 978 1 78643 866 9 (cased)
ISBN 978 1 78643 867 6 (eBook)

Typeset by Servis Filmsetting Ltd, Stockport, Cheshire

Printed and bound in Great Britain by TJ International Ltd, Padstow, Cornwall

Contents

Contributors

Rosalba Altopiedi is Assistant Professor in Sociology of Deviance at DIGSPES, University of Eastern Piedmont, Italy. She is a sociologist with a particular interest in corporate and green crimes, environmental and health activism, legislation and social policies on doping and drug abuse. In her studies she combines different approaches and methodologies: quantitative data and ethnographic analysis (surveys, collections of life stories, mapping of the research field and the use of 'snowball' sampling strategies for the achievement of hidden populations) to explore different fields of research.

Matt Clement lectures in criminology at the University of Winchester. He has written *A Peoples History of Riots, Protest and the Law: The Sound of the Crowd* (2016) and is co-founder of the new open-source *Journal of Riot and Protest Studies*. He has also published on various themes including knife crime in the UK, the impact of austerity, contemporary social movements and the rise of populism. He is currently researching a history of state crime and terrorism with Vincenzo Scalia, titled 'Strategies of Tension: State Deviance, Labelling and Double Binds'.

Nicholas Groombridge is a retired senior lecturer in criminology and sociology. He taught at St Mary's University, Twickenham, London for 20 years and is now a visiting and guest lecturer and consultant. Nic also spent 20 years in administrative/policy positions in the UK Home Office. His work has always sought to examine 'mundane' or overlooked crimes and harms. His doctoral thesis examined joyriding but placed it in the context of the wider, but accepted, harms of 'car culture'. His book *Sports Criminology* (2016) seeks to unpick the many harms of sport and examines the claims that it encourages crime but may also prevent it. He has published on green criminology, surveillance, and sexuality and criminology. His journal articles 'Masculinities and Crimes against the Environment', *Theoretical Criminology* (1998), 'Crime Control or Crime Culture TV', *Surveillance and Society* (2002) and 'Perverse Criminologies: the Cabinet of Doctor Lombroso', *Social & Legal Studies* (1999) are regularly cited as foundational.

Tim Hall is Professor of Interdisciplinary Social Studies at the University of Winchester, UK. He is a human geographer with interests in urban geography, pedagogy and higher education research. His recent research, however, has sought to open up spaces for the discussions of organized crime and the illicit within the contemporary global economy from an economic geography perspective. He is the author and editor of a number of books including *The Entrepreneurial*

City (1998, edited with Phil Hubbard), *Urban Geography* (fifth edition 2017, with Heather Barrett), *The Illicit and Illegal in Regional and Urban Governance and Development: Corrupt Places* (2018, edited with Francesco Chiodelli and Ray Hudson) and *The Economic Geographies of Organized Crime* (2018). His work has appeared in a number of edited collections and international journals including *Area, Geography, Progress in Human Geography* and *Transactions of the Institute of British Geographers.*

Dick Hobbs is a part-time Professor of Sociology and Criminology at Western Sydney University. Before retiring from full-time employment Dick held Chairs at the universities of Essex and Durham and the London School of Economics. He is an Associate Fellow of the Royal United Services Institute. His books include *Doing the Business* (1988), *Bad Business* (1995) and *Lush Life* (2013). He is also the co-author of *Bouncers* (2004, with Philip Hadfield, Stuart Lister and Simon Winlow), *Securing the Olympic Site* (2011, with Jon Coaffee, Gary Armstrong and Pete Fussey) and *Policing the Olympics: London 2012* (2016, with Gary Armstrong and Richard Giulianotti). In 2016 he received the Outstanding Achievement Award presented by the British Society of Criminology.

Ray Hudson is Professor of Geography at Durham University. He holds the degrees of BA, PhD and DSc from Bristol University and DLitt from Durham University. A political-economic geographer, he has a particular interest in geographies of economies and the uneven and combined development of capitalist economies. He has published widely. His books include *Producing Places* (2001), *Economic Geographies: Circuits, Flows and Spaces* (2005), *Approaches to Economic Geography: Towards a Geographical Political Economy* (2016), *The Illicit and Illegal in Regional and Urban Governance and Development: Corrupt Places* (2018, edited with Francesco Chiodelli and Tim Hall), *Co-Produced Economies: Capital, Collaboration, Competition,* (2019). His research has been recognized by election to the Fellowship of the British Academy, the Academy of the Social Sciences and Academia Europaea and by the award of the Victoria Medal by the Royal Geographical Society and the Sir Peter Hall Award by the Regional Studies Association.

Jo Large is Lecturer in Criminology in the School for Policy Studies, University of Bristol, UK. Jo's research focuses on the connections between consumption and harm. This includes analysis of counterfeit markets and the overlapping nature of illicit and licit economies. Jo is the author of the forthcoming book *The Consumption of Counterfeit Fashion* (Palgrave Macmillan) and a co-author of *Fake Goods Real Money: The Counterfeiting Business and its Financial Management* (2018, with Georgios Antonopoulos, Alex Hall, Anqi Shen, Michael Crang and Michael Andrews). More recently, Jo's interests have extended to examining the relationship between charity-based tourism and harm.

John Lea is Visiting Professor at Goldsmiths, University of London, UK. He is one of the founders of the Left Realist school of criminology and has written widely in the areas of criminological theory and criminal justice. His publications include *What is to be Done About Law and Order?* (1984 with Jock Young) and *Crime and Modernity* (2002). His work has appeared in a number of edited collections, including *Criminology and War: Transgressing the Borders* (2015), *The Palgrave Handbook on Criminology and War* (2017) and journals including *Theoretical Criminology* and *The Howard Journal of Criminal Justice*. Several of his publications have been translated into German, Italian and Spanish.

Craig Martin is a Reader in Design Cultures at the University of Edinburgh. He is a cultural geographer and design theorist whose research examines the social complexity of design, including the dissolution of traditional boundaries between good and bad design, as well as licit and particularly illicit forms of social practice such as smuggling. He has published widely in a range of edited collections and international journals. His most recent book is *Shipping Container*, part of the Object Lessons series by Bloomsbury Academic. He is currently finishing his next book, also for Bloomsbury Academic, entitled *Deviant Design: The Ad Hoc, the Illicit, the Controversial*.

Daniel Mitchell is Lecturer in Criminology in the Department of Social Policy, Sociology and Criminology at the University of Birmingham. He received his PhD, titled 'Criminology and War', from the University of Lincoln. His research interests involve the exploration of responsibility and accountability in the context of war crimes and genocide, informal and formal mechanisms of punishment as a response to crimes against humanity, and the role of victim-offender dualities in the commission of human rights abuses and state crime. He is currently working on a journal article addressing violence and empowerment in the context of public support for, and involvement in, acts of war and genocide.

Vincenzo Scalia is Reader in Criminology at the University of Winchester. He was previously Senior Lecturer in Criminology at Anglia Ruskin University. Born and bred in Palermo, Sicily, where he gained his PhD, he graduated in Bologna, Italy, and received an MA in Social and Political Theory from the University of East Anglia, Norwich. He has taught in Italy, the UK, Mexico and Argentina. His works, focused on penology, juvenile justice, organized crime and urban security, have been translated also into Spanish and Turkish, making Vincenzo a global criminologist for global crimes. His most recent book is *Crime, Networks and Power: The Structural Transformation of Sicilian Cosa Nostra* (2016).

Svetlana Stephenson is Reader in Sociology at London Metropolitan University. Her research addresses the social organization of marginal and criminal groups in Russian society, and the intersection of formal and informal social control. She is the author of *Gangs of Russia: From the Streets to the Corridors of Power* (2015) and *Crossing the Line: Vagrancy, Homelessness and Social Displacement in Russia* (2006), and has had articles published in *Current Sociology, The Sociological Review, Europe-Asia Studies, Work, Employment and Society* and other peer-reviewed journals.

Majid Yar is Professor of Criminology at Lancaster University, having previously held positions at the universities of Kent, Keele and Hull. He has researched and written widely across the areas of criminology, sociology, media and culture, and social and political thought. His books include *Criminology: The Key Concepts* (with Martin O'Brien, 2008), *The Handbook of Internet Crime* (with Yvonne Jewkes, 2010), *Cybercrime and Society* (2013), *Crime, Deviance and Doping* (2014), *The Cultural Imaginary of the Internet* (2014) and *Crime and the Imaginary of Disaster* (2015).

Acknowledgements

Many thanks to Katy Crossan and Harry Fabian from Edward Elgar for approaching us with the initial idea for this volume, to the contributors for responding with such enthusiasm and for their support of the project, and to Cath Hall for her thorough copy-editing of the first draft of the manuscript.

1   Thinking through global crime and its research agendas

Tim Hall and Vincenzo Scalia

What do we mean when we talk about global crime?

Approximately 11:45, Thursday 24 August 2017, Naples central train station. One of us (Tim) is travelling from Rome to his brother's wedding which is taking place near Reggio Calabria in southern Italy the next day. The train waits at Naples for approximately 15 minutes before it is scheduled to move on to its next stop. The scene on the train is noisy and chaotic, a contrast to the tranquillity of the journey from Rome. Large numbers of passengers have departed the train at Naples and a larger number are boarding. Many are talking loudly, some are shouting into mobile phones as they struggle to find their seats. One woman standing near his left shoulder is particularly loud. At one point she shouts at top volume into her mobile phone. He turns around in annoyance. A couple of seconds later he glances up at the luggage rack above the carriage windows. The black bag he had placed there as the train left Rome is gone. He turns around immediately and the woman on the phone has disappeared. He looks back up the carriage in the opposite direction but sees no one exiting the carriage with his bag. On the platform a whistle is blown and the train begins to depart. The bag contained his passport, and that of his wife who is travelling with him, his mobile phone, his bank and credit cards, house keys and travel documents which gave his home address and dates of travel. There is much panic, then considerable sympathy and kindness from the other passengers in the carriage as the realization that he has been robbed sinks in.

When the train pulled into Reggio Calabria some hours later the long process of unpicking the consequences of the robbery began. His Italian sister-in-law took him to the local Carabinieri station so that a report of the robbery could be obtained. Banks and credit card companies were telephoned to cancel cards. The British Embassy in Rome was contacted, and an appointment was booked so that he could obtain emergency travel documents to return to the UK a few days later. Alternative travel and accommodation arrangements were booked to get him and his wife back to Rome in time for their Monday morning appointment at the British Embassy. His mobile telephone company was reached to cancel the stolen phone. Initial contact with travel insurance companies was made. The subsequent untangling of the consequences of this momentary encounter in a Naples train station took over two months and enrolled spaces in many different countries.

A simple mapping of the actors connected to this crime illustrates the transnational dimensions of a crime that would be classed, within a classical criminological reading, as nothing more than an example of an everyday, local, volume crime. The banks who provided the debit cards that were stolen on the train were Lloyds and National Westminster (NatWest). Lloyds Bank is a British bank, one of the largest retail banks in the UK. Lloyds has extensive international operations, although dealing with the theft of the debit card fell within the remit of its UK banking operation and involved contact with one of Lloyds' 18 UK call centres. NatWest is also a UK bank and again the stolen card was dealt with through its UK call centre network. His credit card was provided by John Lewis, a UK retail company, but was a Mastercard, a company that describe itself as a 'leader in global digital payment' (https://www.mastercard.co.uk/en-gb.html). Mastercard is an American multinational headquartered in New York and St Louis Missouri with operations worldwide. Mastercard is a key player in facilitating the global credit card payment network that has become a mundanely routine part of life for many today. His mobile phone was provided by O2, the trading name of Telefónica UK, which is headquartered in Slough in southern England but is part of the Spanish multinational Telefónica which operates globally. Telefónica's headquarters are in Madrid and cancelling the mobile phone took (numerous) calls to its call centres that appeared to be located in South Africa, although the actual locations of O2's call centres are somewhat opaque, as entering +O2 +"call centre" +locations into an internet search engine will reveal. It is likely that these call centres were managed by a company called Capita, headquartered in London. Tim eventually had to contact the CEO of O2 at the Slough head office to address the inconsistencies and payment problems he experienced after trying to cancel his stolen phone. The insurance policy through which he attempted to claim the losses he had suffered as a result of the robbery was provided by Worldwide Internet Insurance Services Ltd, trading as Cover For You, which is licensed in Gibraltar, a common tactic for UK companies seeking to take advantage of its low corporate tax rate, although Cover For You has a head office in London. The policy was underwritten by AXA UK which has a head office in London but which is part of AXA, a French multinational headquartered in the 8th arrondissement of Paris. His insurance claim was dealt with by Rightpath Claims whose head office is in Rochford, a town in Essex in southeast England. Finally, Trenitalia, the Italian national train company he used to get back to Rome earlier than originally planned for the meeting at the British Embassy, is headquartered in Rome, while UNA Hotels and Resorts, which he used for additional nights of accommodation in Rome, has its head office in Milan. All of these companies were enrolled, albeit in small ways, in the event of Tim being robbed in Naples.

Beyond being struck by the irony of a supposed expert in organized crime being robbed in Naples, this incident highlights something about the complexities of concepts of crime in a global age. The robbery described above was, at first glance, a classic example of local crime. There appears to have been no obvious connections between the gang who took the bag and any organized crime groups in Naples. There have been, for example, no repercussions in terms of identity theft, and the house keys that were in the stolen bag were not immediately Fed Ex'd to London so that the house could be broken into and the new car, that was sitting on the driveway, stolen. However, many aspects of its consequences crossed national boundaries and had international connections. What, then, does the example above tell us about the notion of global crime? Viewing crime as it has tended to be viewed traditionally as a discrete event and through local-global binaries offers only truncated perspectives. The robbery Tim experienced was over in minutes within the spatial confines of a busy railway carriage but had a hinterland that was networked across many countries.

Thinking of this event in relational terms ties together a number of spatially distant places through the networks of connections that are now typical of the daily lives and interactions of many, although it should be stressed not all, in the Global North. A map of the connections from this event, and one which does not even access the more obscure connections that underlie many of the actors involved, for example, to offshore banking sites beyond Gibraltar, would destabilize the notion that this was simply a case of local crime. It suggests actually that few crimes now can be thought of purely as local, discrete events and that perhaps traditional ways of thinking through crime in a global age need some critical re-evaluation. This task – and the contributors to this collection approach it in many different ways and from a number of perspectives – is the key aim of this book.

Thinking through global crime – academic debates

Discussions about global crime, particularly in relation to organized crime, have developed only in recent times. The reason at the heart of this late development might be that the label 'global' started being used only after the fall of the Berlin Wall, in 1989. The collapse of the Eastern Bloc is supposed to have brought about a boost in the internationalization of economic and cultural exchange, as well as a higher degree of cultural hybridization. Following these crucial worldwide changes, Anthony Giddens, in 1991, in his book *The Consequences of Modernity*, forged the term *globalization* to refer to five specific dimensions: the world capitalist economy; the transformation of nation states; the world military order; the international labour division; and culture. The dimensions of globalization prove valid theoretical lenses to focus on globalized crime: how do criminal organizations draw advantage from this global integration of economy and culture?

The debate about global crime is as recent as that about globalization. There are three main reasons for such a late development. Firstly, the existence of criminal organization has been doubted for many years. On the one hand, it was denied in those areas where organized crime was most likely to exist, such as in Sicily (Santino, 2000). On the other hand, it was not clear what a criminal organization was, how it differed from a gang, a brotherhood, or groups like the Freemasons. Anthropologists such as Anton Blok (1974) defined the mafia not as an organization but as a cluster of independent individuals (the Mafioso) who acted as brokers between the local and the global community. The interpretation of organized crime provided by Blok, though trying to analyse 20 years before Giddens the relationships between local and global communities, did not acknowledge the existence of criminal organizations, and did not articulate the concept of mediation as it did not specify what sort of role the Mafioso played within the global economy. Secondly, when the existence of organized crime was recognized it followed a judicial interpretation fraught with ethnic prejudices. We are referring to the definition of organized crime as an *alien conspiracy*, fuelled by the Kefauver US Congress Committee in 1952. This view, on the one hand, admitted that a phenomenon such as organized crime existed, but on the other hand provided an ethnically biased interpretation: that of the same old ethnic groups, such as Italians, Irish and Jews, being labelled as the ones who swelled the ranks of criminal organizations, acting as an internal threat to the free and democratic American post-World War II society. An updated version of the Kefauver Committee's view is provided by Loretta Napoleoni, an Italian-born journalist based in London. According to Napoleoni (2005), there is an overlap between terrorist and criminal organization, which share the aim of destroying the Western social fabric by carrying out their illegal activities.

The third reason for this belated development relates to globalization: only since 1989 have both public opinion and academics become widely aware of the fact that criminal organizations can pass national borders and create a wide-ranging network of activities, thus drawing advantage from the liberalization of exchanges, deregulations of finance, and, finally, from technological advancement. The debate on global crime developed out of the sociological concept of globalization and most of the authors who covered this topic, and who we will be mentioning in the following pages, are sociologists. Their work has been influential also for criminologists. The only criminologists who have provided an original interpretation of organized crime and globalization are David Nelken (1998) and Vincenzo Ruggiero (1996).

In order to reach a definition of organized crime, and to reflect upon the possibilities of its global expansions, we have to wait until 1993. This is the year when Diego Gambetta, an Italian-born researcher who was then a full professor in Oxford, published his study about the Sicilian Mafia, a book which proved to be influential among all scholars who have worked on organized crime. This book, despite its many theoretical and empirical flaws that have been explored elsewhere (Scalia, 2010, 2016), provided academics with two important conceptual tools. The first one concerns the definition of organized crime, which Gambetta envisages as an *industry of private protection*, with criminal organizations operating like companies in legal markets to make profits by enhancing their reputation through the use of a specific *brand*. This latter aspect relates to the second tool Gambetta has provided: the relationship between organized crime and its expansion outside its original contexts. The brand of private protection, Gambetta argues, can be used only in those contexts where its reputation has been established for a long time. Consequently, it is not possible for organized crime to expand outside its *natural* boundaries; in other words, outside those contexts where the lack of public trust requires the supply of private protection. When public trust is high, both on a horizontal level (that is, between social actors) and on a vertical level (between society and the central government), there is no need for private protection, and it will be difficult for crime to grow to a transnational or global scale. How is it possible to explain, then, the expansion of the Sicilian Mafia, the Calabrian 'Ndrangheta and the Neapolitan Camorra in northern Italy? Or the presence of Latin American Narcos and Russian Solncevo in London? Gambetta uses a medical metaphor, suggesting that it is a matter of *contagion*. Healthy societies, where a market economy provides a reasonable allocation of resources and the state grants a minimum acceptable degree of security to every citizen, will resist the infiltration of organized crime. As a consequence of this, criminal organizations can transplant their own activities through the use of violence, as well as by spreading their illegal activities, such as drug trafficking, within an uncorrupted social fabric. Gambetta's view sound like an updating of Kefauver's *alien conspiracy*, but this is the minimum flaw such a view denotes. The economic, cultural and social trends of recent years have brought about a blending of legal and illegal worlds, sometimes making it difficult to draw a line between the two (see Hudson, Chapter 2 this volume, for example). Moreover, coercion has been but marginal, as investments by criminal organizations have often proved to be profitable for the legal market.

Federico Varese (2011) has attempted to reshape the theory of private protection to fit it into a global perspective. In Varese's view, mafias are *on the move*. As their business grows, criminal organizations seek other opportunities to expand their illegal profitable activities. It is a matter of a *transplant* rather than one of contagion, as the creation and development of illegal activities where they did not exist before means to introduce something external to the social pattern of the areas where new mafias try to expand. Criminal transplants can be successful only under some specific local conditions: limited public attention to the issue of organized crime; a weak penal legislation which makes it easier for criminal organizations to dodge both controls and repression; weak organized crime groups (or strong, but inclined to make deals); and vacuums in the social fabric caused by economic or political crisis. To cut a long story short, the analysis of global crime provided by Federico Varese, unlike Gambetta, accepts the possibility that globalization can bring about the expansion of organized crime in areas where it was unthinkable until recently. Moreover, Varese, does not regard this process as the result of an imposed colonization, but rather as the consequence of the ability that criminal organizations have to calculate and plan their operational strategies. Finally, Varese enhances the importance of *local* elements for the migration and transplant of mafias to be successful. The more global the world grows, the more local dimensions matter.

In exploring the importance of local and global variables for the reproduction of criminal organization, it is crucial to explore such dimensions as local culture, politics and economics. How instrumental is the globalization of organized crime? How relevant are such factors as local culture as well as utilitarian interests? These questions are crucial if one wants to understand how it is possible that such social phenomena as organized crime can expand outside their local context without 'forcing' the new social environment into their acceptance.

Rocco Sciarrone (2011), a sociologist teaching at the University of Turin, draws on the category of social capital developed by Mark Granovetter (1983) to shed a light on the ways in which criminal organizations expand their activities from *traditional areas*, that is their areas of origin, to *non-traditional areas*, or the new places into which they move. The definition of social capital refers to the relational network that shapes either individual or collective lives. It is made of strong ties, which refer to family, kinship, territory-based bonds, and weak ties, a domain encompassing professional, recreational and all the functional bonds. Sciarrone, in analysing the growth of the Calabrian 'Ndrangheta both in northern Italy and abroad, shows how whereas strong ties matter in traditional areas – as kinship, territory and family allow criminal organizations to tighten those bonds, allowing them to hold their areas of origin in a firm grasp – weak ties are more suitable for expansion in non-traditional areas. For example, accountants or lawyers who tell the Mafioso the names of local firms who are experiencing hardship, so as to require a 'helping hand' from these criminal organizations, are the kind of weak tie needed to expand the range of activities of the Mafioso. Moreover, professionals also help the mobs to disguise themselves as legal actors, by setting up apparently legal firms whose official owners are bogus individuals found in the local context. All the parties draw advantage from such interactions: professionals who act as consultants and can claim a payment from their clients, entrepreneurs whose activity is rescued by the investment provided by criminal organizations, and, of course, the mobs themselves. Legal actors, in the event that they might be questioned by the police, might argue that they did not know the real activity of the client, and that they were acting either as consultants or as partners.

Sciarrone calls the areas of interaction between legal and illegal actors the *grey area*, to be distinguished from the *white area*, i.e. the entirely legal context, and the *black area*, i.e. the domain of entirely criminal interactions. An important point made by Sciarrone is that the actors who, in non-traditional areas, operate in grey areas are *local* actors who seek advantage by their interactions with criminal organizations. The idea of contagion proposed by Diego Gambetta is, by this token, ruled out. Moreover, Sciarrone widens the theoretical perspective proposed by Federico Varese: whereas the latter proposes a view that is based on the *weakness* of local society, focusing his analysis on the point of view of the Mafioso, the former proposes an interpretation based on the advantage local societies foresee in accepting the investments of criminal organizations to increase their gains. Sciarrone's analysis of global crime is therefore more focused on the *strengths* of local society. As a consequence of this, global crime can expand in every local context, regardless of the social fabric. All the local actors who consider it profitable to run businesses with criminal organizations will be keen to welcome them.

In moving from sociology to criminology, discussion on global crime revolves around two approaches. Vincenzo Ruggiero (1996, 2016) argues that it does not make sense to differentiate between *clean* and *dirty* economics. Firstly, because illegal actors provide legal actors with the wide range of goods and services they demand: drugs, prostitution, labour market control, gambling are demanded by 'clean' society. Secondly, because the organization of illegal economics marches at pace with legal spheres. The same organization, the same aim (profits), make the legal and the illegal two faces of the same coin. Finally, money gained in illegal markets is invested, recycled and spent in the legal markets, regardless of its origin. Globalization makes the borders between legal and illegal activities more and more blurred. Deregulation, as well as the increasing globalization of markets, provides more room for the increase of crime on a global scale, as there are more and more opportunities for investments, as well as for money laundering. Global crime also keeps pace with global markets through the creation of network-based organizations, involving both legal and illegal actors, which is typical of contemporary capitalism. Further, David Nelken (1998), though agreeing with Ruggiero on the expansion of global crime in relation to the globalization of markets, does not agree with the idea that worldwide economic integration brings about the shrinking of the role of states. National governments are always the focal point of penal policies, and still have a military force. Since globalization cannot completely overcome states as locally specific entities, as well as the local economic peculiarities, Nelken suggests a strategy to fight global crime inspired by the old ecologist slogan 'think globally, act locally'.

The approaches we have discussed here denote some common peculiarities: (1) the issue of the relation between the legal and illegal worlds appears to be crucial. Most of the sociologists, as well as Nelken, take up this point, with Ruggiero proposing a critical approach. (2) Can crime become global? Whereas Sciarrone, Nelken and Ruggiero are positive about it, Gambetta is sceptical, and Varese tries to suggest some specific conditions under which crime can expand. (3) What is the role of the state? Most of the authors agree with Gambetta that the more the role of central states shrinks, the more crime becomes global. Sciarrone oversees this problem, as he focuses on the *grey area*; Nelken thinks that states will never lose their prerogatives, and this can help in forging anti-crime politics. These are some of the points which make up the discussion about global crime that follows. Of course, discussions about global crime are not restricted to those of organized crime. As well as organized crime, this volume explores some of the wider complexities of global crime, and highlights both the acts and the actors involved and the contexts that sustain these activities.

Key themes in thinking through global crime

If there is a defining feature of the chapters in the volume it is their diversity. The study of global crime as it is currently practised spans multiple disciplines. This is something we were keen to capture in this volume, so you will find material here from disciplines including criminology, geography, legal studies and sociology, for example. Similarly, we were keen not to impose any theoretical or methodological restrictions on the authors of individual chapters collected here. We feel that the chapters in this book can then reflect the range and richness of perspectives that critical scholars, writing broadly from a social science perspective, are currently bringing to questions and issues of global crime.

However, despite this diversity there are a number of strong common themes and concerns that emerge across these chapters. The first theme, and one that is common to all of the chapters, is the complex relationships between legal and illegal, licit and illicit and the role of space in shaping these contingencies (see also Chiodelli et al., 2017). These are questions fundamental to the study of any crime but they are especially prescient where crime is now routinely networked across international spaces characterized by, at times, radically different regulatory, legal and social contexts. What might be considered illegal in one space might be legal, if perhaps illicit, in others. These questions form a central aspect of the chapter by Ray Hudson but are also explored explicitly in different contexts by Rosalba Altopiedi, Craig Martin and Majid Yar among others. A key aspect of the complex relationships between the legal and illegal and the licit and illicit is their inter-twining through circuits of circulation within contemporary capitalism and the exploitation of these circulatory infrastructures, physical and virtual, by both licit and illicit actors, although such blunt categorizations are themselves problematic. Again, Ray Hudson and Craig Martin explore these issues in their chapters, as does Jo Large through her discussion of transnational markets in counterfeit goods (see also Gregson and Crang, 2017; Nordstrom, 2007).

There has been a tendency within discussions of globalization generally, and par-ticularly of transnational crime in a global age, to produce overly globalist renditions of these processes and relations (see for example Jamieson, 1995; Robinson, 2002; Shelley, 2006; Sterling, 1994 and critical reactions to in Hall, 2018: 7; Wright, 2006: 159–160) inattentive to their local contours, the enduring grounded-ness of criminal actors and to the continued presence of the state within all this. This is something that Dick Hobbs has long been critical of (1998, 2013) and something he returns to in his chapter in this volume. Within this volume, then, we are also reminded of the enduring importance of the state in, for example, maintaining power asymmetries exercised in the normative definitions of legality and illegality, in exercising vio-lence and practising criminality (explored in the chapters by Matt Clement, Daniel Mitchell and Svetlana Stephenson in very different contexts) and in the creation of multiple 'black sites', spaces beyond the law and in the discursive power of official constructions of crime (see the chapters by Daniel Mitchell and John Lea). In their chapters, Rosalba Altopiedi and Majid Yar also explore the significances of the state in the contexts of environmental crime and cyber-crime. The chapters here ground us in some of the realities of globalization and remind us not to get caught up in some of its weightless and frictionless fantasies. Mention of the state also raises questions of the challenges of the governance, surveillance, regulation, policing and securitization of transnational spaces in times of hyper-circulation and the limita-tions of extant models of doing so. These are themes considered here by authors such as Ray Hudson, Dick Hobbs, Majid Yar, Craig Martin and Jo Large. Further, as

John Lea and Daniel Mitchell remind us in their chapters, these are processes prone to politicalization in pursuit of the interests of the powerful.

A number of authors in this volume – Rosalba Altopiedi, Jo Large and Daniel Mitchell, for example – advocate that we embrace the notion of harm in our discussions of many of the processes this book explores, as this raises ontological questions about what we should consider criminal. Harm is a concept that has gained increasing purchase within criminological discourse in recent years, and it captures the consequences of acts that are not formally criminal but that produce significant negative externalities, typically highly uneven in their social impacts. These include incidents of state and corporate crime (scandals such as the disaster at the Union Carbide Plant in Bhopal, India, in which 500,000 people, most of whom were housed in the informal settlements around the plant, were exposed to a leak of methyl isocyanate gas in December 1984, for example, are discussed by Rosalba Altopiedi) but also include the more routine operations of states and economies that generate social and environmental harm. The concept of harm as explored by Altopiedi and other authors here highlights the centrality of the illegal and illicit, which is woven into, and indeed even constitutive of, the political and economic mainstream, and debunks the myth that harm and crimes are purely external threats. This is particularly significant in the current age where much political discourse about globalization is suffused with imagined threats from various geographically or discursively externally located others.

The final point that we would like to make about all of the chapters here is that they show the value of adopting a critical, rather than a technical, legalistic or administrative, approach to understanding global crime. These points are made explicitly by some authors such as Rosalba Altopiedi, Matt Clement, Nicholas Groombridge, Dick Hobbs, Jo Large, John Lea and Daniel Mitchell, and they are inherent in all of the chapters within the volume. Critical perspectives highlight to us questions of power and the challenges of theorizing crime, harm and transnationality, which are central to much of the analysis advanced by the authors in this volume.

A final hope is that this volume invigorates discussion about global crime beyond its traditional disciplinary homes and across disciplinary boundaries. We very deliberately invited authors from disciplines that have traditionally said little about transnational and global crime to contribute to this volume. We encouraged contributors from different disciplines to engage in dialogue as they developed and wrote their chapters. Many of the issues that are discussed in this volume, we feel, are simply too significant and too pressing to be the preserve of a singular discipline. The disciplinary make-up of this volume reflects this belief.

References

Blok, A. (1974). *The Mafia of a Sicilian Village, 1860–1960: A Study of Violent Peasant Entrepreneurs*, Cambridge: Waveland Press.

Chiodelli, F., Hall, T., Hudson, R. and Moroni, S. (2017). 'Grey governance and the development of cities and regions: the variable relationship between (il)legal and (il)licit', in Chiodelli, F., Hall, T. and Hudson, R. (eds) *The Illicit and Illegal in the Development and Governance of Cities and Regions: Corrupt Places*, Abingdon: Routledge, pp. 1–19.

Gambetta, D. (1993). *The Sicilian Mafia: An Industry of Private Protection*, Harvard, MA: Harvard University Press.

Granovetter, M. S. (1983). 'The strength of weak ties', *The American Journal of Sociology*, 78 (6), 1360–1380.

Gregson, N. and Crang, M. (2017). 'Illicit economies: customary illegality, moral economies and circulation', *Transactions of the Institute of British Geographers*, 42 (2), 206–219.

Hall, T. (2018). *The Economic Geographies of Organized Crime*, New York: Guilford.

Hobbs, D. (1998). 'The case against: there is not a global crime problem', *International Journal of Risk, Security, and Crime Prevention*, 3 (2), 139–146.

Hobbs, D. (2013). *Lush Life: Constructing Organized Crime in the UK*, Oxford: Oxford University Press.

Jamieson, A. (1995). 'The transnational dimension of Italian organized crime', *Transnational Organized Crime*, 1 (2), 151–172.

Napoleoni, L. (2005). *Terror Incorporated: Tracing the Dollars Behind the Terror Networks*, New York: Seven Stories Press.

Nelken, D. (1998). Globalizzazione del Crimine e Giustizia Penale, *Dei Delitti e delle Pene*, 2/3, 64–77.

Nordstrom, C. (2007). *Global Outlaws: Crime, Money, and Power in the Contemporary World*, Berkley, CA: University of California Press.

Robinson, J. (2002). *The Merger: The Conglomeration of International Organized Crime*, Woodstock and New York: The Overlook Press.

Ruggiero, V. (1996). *Organized and Corporate Crime in Europe*, London: Routledge.

Ruggiero, V. (2016). *Crimes of the Powerful*, Oxford: Oxford University Press.

Santino, U. (2016). *Mafia and Antimafia*, London: IB Tauris.

Santino, U. (2000). Storia del Movimento Antimafia. Dalla Lotta di Classe all'Impegno Civile, Rome: Editori Riuniti.

Scalia, V. (2010). 'From the octopus to the spider's web. The structural transformation of the Sicilian Cosa Nostra', *Trends in Organized Crime*, 13 (4), 283–297.

Scalia, V. (2016). *Crime, Network and Power: The Structural Transformation of the Sicilian Cosa Nostra*, Basingstoke: Palgrave Macmillan.

Sciarrone, R (2011). *Alleanze nell'Ombra*, Rome: Donzelli.

Shelley, L. (2006). 'The globalization of crime and terrorism', *eJournal USA*, 11 (1), 42–45.

Sterling, C. (1994). *Crime Without Frontiers: The Worldwide Expansion of Organised Crime and the Pax Mafiosa*, London: Warner Books.

Varese, F. (2011). *Mafias on the Move*, Princeton, NJ: Princeton University Press.

Wright, A. (2006). *Organised Crime*, Cullompton, UK: Willan.

2 Economic geographies of the (il)legal and the (il)licit

Ray Hudson

Introduction

There is a voluminous literature in economic geography which seeks to explain the reasons for and processes underlying the varied multi-scalar geographies of economies that characterize the historical geography of capitalism. The diverse contributions to this literature vary in their approaches to explanation and in the processes and scales that they emphasize, ranging from macro-scale political economies that prioritize the socio-spatial, the systematic and the structural in understanding the uneven and combined development of economic actors, classes and places, to more micro-scale approaches that emphasize individual decisions and institutions and the nodal, the near and the network (see Hudson, 2001, 2005, 2016; Peck, 2016). Despite these deep differences in theoretical approach, however, they do share one feature in common: that is, with rare exceptions (for example, see Allen, 2005; Hall, 2013; Rengert, 1996) they exhibit a preoccupation with the geographies of the economies of the legal, implicitly conceiving the economy as made up of legitimate activities performed and regulated in a series of legal markets. Expressed slightly differently, the 'norm' in capitalist economies is typically represented as economic actors behaving within markets according to the rules and regulations of the formal legal economy. There certainly are activities that in practice are carried out and regulated in this way. On the other hand, there are activities (such as deliberately contaminating food products, drug and narcotics production and sale, the sale of human body parts and organs, prostitution and the trafficking of migrants and refugees, often as modern slaves) that in many if not all territorial jurisdictions are illegal (for an example of where cannabis is deemed legal, see Polson, 2017). In those places where all stages in their production, circulation and sale in markets are, by definition, illegal they continue to flourish precisely because they can be very profitable (for example, see Latza Nadeau, 2018). More generally, however, there is a third case on which economic geography is also largely silent. For it may be the case that economic activities are constituted via a hybrid mix of legal and illegal activities, with a variety of ways of conjoining the legal and illegal within them that problematizes the conceptions of legal and illegal (Hudson, 2005, 2013). Put another way, it may be the case that capitalist economies constituted solely via wholly legal activities are the exception rather than the rule, especially in particular spaces of the global economy, and that in contrast links between the illegal and legal are endemic in such economies. As a result, markets may be structured in particular and varying ways, with a competitive advantage conferred on those who avoid legal regulation.

There is, however, one more general and important though still partial exception to this silence about the illegal and legal and relationships between them in a body of literature that focuses upon 'informal economies': that is, economies in which illegal activities are regarded as licit and/or legal activities are performed by actors who are not legally entitled nor sanctioned to do so but whose behaviour in this way is seen as licit, as socially accepted. Although there are exceptions (for example, Hadjimichalis and Vaiou, 1990), much of the literature dealing with informal economies and the constitutive processes of informalization is located beyond the disciplinary boundaries of economic geography (for example, see Castells, 2000; Portes et al., 1989). Recognizing this, in this chapter I will be concerned to fill this gap and explore the territory of economic geographies of the illegal and illicit, including those that have been referred to as 'informal economies', and their links with the legal in constituting economies.

Conceptualizing relations between the (il)licit and (ill)legal

In order to explore these relationships, building on earlier work (Hudson, 2013; see also Chiodelli et al., 2017) I will conceptualize economic activities as located within conceptual spaces defined by two dimensions: first, those activities that are legal or illegal and, second, those that are licit or illicit. The former binary refers to activities defined in relationship to the formal legal system of regulation in operation in a given time and place, typically but not exclusively the territory of a national state; the latter to the definition of activities as socially sanctioned – or not – as legitimate and socially acceptable. Critically, both definitions of (il)legal and (il) illicit are specific to particular times and places; these are spatially and temporally variable relational attributes, with specific historical geographies. This approach allows for the construction of a simple but time/space variable fourfold classification of activities, depending upon the particular combination of the (il)legal and (il) licit. Those activities that are both legal and licit – that is, those activities and their constituent spaces that implicitly at least form the subjects of the vast majority of theoretical approaches within economic geography – are not the focus of my concern here. Indeed, although the centre of most theoretical concerns, the wholly legal and licit formal economy and its regulatory mechanisms provided via state policies and laws, with emphasis upon the national state as the sovereign actor, is in practice a rather rare and unusual form of economic organization. Of rather more, but still relatively minor, interest here are those activities that are legal but seen as illicit (such as aggressive corporate tax avoidance; excessive salaries for senior corporate executives and university Vice Chancellors; transfer pricing to shift profits to low taxation jurisdictions; or legally enforced and legitimated land grabs, especially in parts of the (so-called) Global South). While they are not the prime focus of interest here, they are nonetheless practically important and far from unusual in capitalist economies. They are enabled as a result of governance via systems of formal regulation and law that leave space for such practices because they facilitate accumulation, including a resurgence of accumulation via dispossession in neo-liberalizing regimes (for example, see Baka, 2017; Harvey, 2003; Liberti, 2013; Springer, 2013), and allow powerful economic and political actors and interest groups to benefit and prosper. As a result, they are also integral to the expanded reproduction of inequality, not least because of the vast sums that are denied to elected governments that could otherwise be used for more socially progressive purposes (see Zucman, 2015). The recent revelations in the Panama and Paradise Papers reveal the extent to which tax avoidance via super-rich individuals, financial elites and major corporations such as Apple are now routine and the norm (for example, see Palan, 2017) while illegal insider trading on the London stock market would seem to be rife (Elison, 2018) and such practices are unlikely to be confined to London. Rather than the legal, however, the focus in this chapter is upon those activities that are illegal, both those regarded as illicit and those seen as licit (and so encompassing those seen as part of 'informal economies'), and also on the resultant constitutive relationships between illegal and legal economies.

I will therefore be concerned with relationships between (il)legal and (il)lict, the spaces in which these activities are performed, and the varying ways in which they are governed. Their governance combines elements of formal regulation via state policies, both directly through the actions of elements of the state apparatus and indirectly through relationships between individuals and organizations that they sanction and regulate, with informal institutions ranging from kinship ties and trust to the threat, or reality, of physical force and violence, and in extremis death (Gambetta, 2011). Furthermore, I will consider the relationships between these diverse activities as not so much performed 'in' the economy and accumulation process but rather as constitutive *of* the economy and accumulation, especially the crossovers and linkages between the circuits of legal capital accumulation and those of illegal economies, both licit and illicit (see also Gregson and Crang, 2016). There are important connections and flows that are integral to the workings of capitalist economies between the circuits of capital accumulation in legal economies and those in illegal economies, not least in enabling flows of money capital from the latter to the former. Consequently, circuits of capital (Palloix, 1977) are routinely constituted via a hybrid mix of legal and illegal activities, with many of the latter regarded as licit, and with a resultant variety of ways of conjoining the legal and illegal within and between them and in the process of capital accumulation, in part depending upon what is regarded as licit and what is regarded as illicit.

As such, the economy is thus seen as routinely constituted via varying mixes of and connections among (il)legal and (il)licit practices, as commodities, money and people are fixed in place for varying times and as they flow between places in the routine performance of the economy. They constitute one aspect of the dialectical relationship between fixity and fluidity in the economy of capital (Harvey, 1982). Many, if not all, commodities in their passage along a circuit of commodity production may, and routinely do, pass through a variety of legally and illegally regulated spaces and may involve illegal activities and practices that are nonetheless seen as licit. Seen in this way capitalist economies are always some mix of the (il)legal and (il)licit, conjoined in varying moral economies, with wholly legal activities the exception rather than the rule, especially in particular spaces of the global economy. In summary, illegal activities and practices that are customarily regarded as licit are integral to the constitution of the economic geographies of capitalism.

The illegal but licit in commodity production

As suggested above, it is important to distinguish between two distinct types of the illegal but licit activities in capitalist economies, and more specifically here in commodity production. First, there are those activities that are illegal but, for a variety of reasons, are socially sanctioned as acceptable. Second, there are those activities that are legal but are performed by a variety of people who, for diverse reasons – for example because they are children or because they are illegal migrants, often working under conditions of 'modern slavery' in both the Global South and North (for example, see National Crime Agency, 2017) – are not legally entitled to perform them. Nevertheless, their performance of these activities is sanctioned as socially acceptable. There is an important caveat in that while regarded as socially acceptable by some, this may often be contested by other social groups within a population. For example, trades unions may contest the presence of illegal migrants who are prepared to undercut other workers on the labour market in terms of wages and working conditions. Other groups in civil society may be supportive of the presence of such migrants but may challenge the conditions under which they live and work. Bearing in mind this distinction between different forms of relationship between the illegal and licit, it is possible to make some further elaboration of the links between them.

First, consider those activities which are themselves legal but are performed by people not legally entitled to do so and which are nonetheless regarded as licit and socially acceptable. People who provide labour illegally (for example, as illegal migrants, as indentured labourers, or as under-age child workers) provide labour-power that is not legally purchased on formally regulated labour markets, or even purchased at all. Although they are not legally authorized to perform as workers, they are then put to work by the owners and managers of capital, carrying out a variety of tasks in activities that are legal and part of the mainstream economy, but with all that their illegal status implies about minimal wages, degraded working conditions, and reduced costs of production (for example, see Gatti, 2006; National Crime Agency, 2017). Labour is always produced as a fictive commodity and indeed has to be in order that the commodity labour-power can come into existence. But the conditions under which labour is reproduced, and the issue of who bears the costs of that reproduction (be it family, community, or state, or some combination of the three), has important implications for the value of labour-power and so for the price that capital has to pay to secure the commodity labour-power. Clearly, however, in circumstances in which capital can purchase labour-power from illegal migrants or others who have no legal status and so minimal bargaining power, the costs of acquiring workers to provide labour-power can be radically reduced, often falling below their costs of reproduction.

Labour-power acquired from illegal labour is thus vulnerable to super-exploitation, cutting the costs to capital of its acquisition and deployment, altering the balance of class forces in the labour market, and so providing considerable scope for capital to realize super-profits. For example, various mafia groups in Italy have become increasingly involved in people trafficking as it is more profitable than drug smuggling (Latza Nadeau, 2018). As noted above, illegal labour is not necessarily provided only by illegal migrant workers. If it is provided via illegal migrant workers, however, it can have a doubly downward effect on labour costs. First, as is the case for migrant labour within legal systems of both intranational (notably China in recent years) and international migrant labour flows (for example, to the USA from Mexico or to West Germany from Turkey in 1960s), the costs of reproduction of such labour would have been already displaced elsewhere in time and space (for example, see Nadiruzzaman and Shewly, 2017). Second, and in addition however, illegal migrant labourers by definition lack citizenship and legal rights, and as a result they are particularly vulnerable to further exploitation since they lack any form of legal protection (Mingione, 1999). Furthermore, such labourers serve to displace members of the indigenous population in the labour market and so further help create labour reserves and a reserve army of labour, intensifying further downward pressure on wages and on the value of labour-power, and thereby enhancing the rates of exploitation, profit and accumulation more generally. National states may turn a blind eye to such illegal migration and employment practices as a way of further intensifying labour market competition as one strand of broader neo-liberal strategies in labour markets that have already been deregulated (Evans et al., 2006: 61).

In some cases, migrant workers who initially had legal status may lose their jobs and so become illegal migrants as their work permits cease to be valid. Often, in these circumstances, they are unable to return to their country of origin because of indebtedness incurred in fees paid to agents in order to become migrants in the first place. As a result, they become particularly vulnerable to recruitment as illegal labourers with a very precarious and risky existence. In other instances, especially those involving agency contract workers, agencies deliberately arrange for people to become illegal immigrants in order that they can be employed on inferior conditions and lower wages (for example, see SOMO, 2009).

Second, there are those activities which are illegal but considered licit as a result of custom and practice. There is an important distinction to be made here, however. First, there are those illegal activities which have been seen as licit and a legitimate part of informal economies. Illegality is accepted as licit in the absence of alternative ways of 'getting by'. Such illegal activities therefore may be pivotal elements of 'survival strategies' in what has long been known as the 'informal economy' and present in both the Global North and South. In many parts of the Global South, 'informal economies' spring up to sustain life on marginal terms in low-cost accommodation in shacks, shanty towns and favelas. The unemployed eke out a living in whatever ways they can in the urban slums, in the process defining a way and standard of life and, 'even more importantly for capital, a cost of living that defines a lower bound for wages in the formal sector' (Harvey, 2014: 175). Much of the literature refers to informal economies as endemic over much of the Global South, but they are by no means confined there. In parts of deindustrialized and marginalized regions in the global North there may be acceptance of practices of selling stolen goods around the back of the pub on a Friday night; or of illegal and untaxed casual work in agriculture or on building sites, resulting in small-scale tax avoidance by working 'off the books' or failing to declare casual earned income (for example, Evans et al., 2006). Such illegal activity becomes a normalized part of quotidian existence in places that have suffered severe economic decline as a consequence of their location in the political economy of market-dominated neo-liberalism (for example, see Hobbs, 2013). Thus, in a range of places which have either never been part of mainstream capitalist economies, or once were but have become marginal to, or totally excluded from, the dominant circuits of capital, engaging in illegal economic activities can be seen as licit, as a necessary and socially acceptable element in strategies of survival and 'getting by', by many of those who live there.

In addition, however, and more fundamentally in relation to wider processes of capital accumulation, there are illegal activities that are seen as licit as a result of custom and practice in the wider, 'allegedly' legal mainstream economy. At one end of a spectrum, these relate to evidence of widespread tolerance of petty pilfering from paid work in the formal legal economy (for example, see Ditton, 1977; Hobbs, 1988). More significantly in relation to processes of capital accumulation, there is a plethora of evidence of a wide range of illegal business practices – *inter alia*, fraud, embezzlement, theft, bribery, commission kickbacks, insider trading, front running, market rigging, false trade invoicing, transfer mispricing, making illicit political donations and tax evasion – in the mainstream economies in many cities and regions (for example, see Durand, 2017: 9–18; Elison, 2018). This is particularly important in emphasizing the hybrid character of economic activities, as the illegal becomes central to the constitution of the legal, the two genetically intertwined in the DNA of capitalist economic practices.

Counterfeiting and the theft of IPR

An increasing number and range of products have become counterfeited and illegally copied, with counterfeit goods accounting for an estimated 7 per cent of global trade, as 'today nearly every consumer and industrial product is subject to counterfeiting' (Chaudhry and Zimmerman, 2010: 26, citing the OECD, 2007), with consequent problems for their purchasers in terms of quality assurance and provenance (see Large, Chapter 8 this volume). Furthermore, in relation to pharmaceutical products and electronic consumer goods, there are issues in terms of health and safety. Counterfeiting thus encompasses both the production of commodities for final (consumer) markets and the production of components and parts that form part of the preceding circuit of commodity production. There is a distinct macro-geography to the production of counterfeits, with particular countries in which such practices are widely tolerated as part of 'customary illegality'. China alone is the origin of two-thirds of counterfeit production (Glenny, 2008; Phillips, 2005). Russia and some other South Asian and Latin American countries are also major sources of counterfeit production (Chaudhry and Zimmerman, 2010). It is likely that the extent of counterfeit production has increased subsequent to 2007, given the effects of the economic crisis and the policy response to this in terms of austerity.

As well as the production of illegal copies of branded goods, there is the widespread production of 'knock-offs', that is goods that may appear to be the same as branded products, with only very slight and barely noticeable visual differences in appearance, but with enough of a difference that, as a result, they do not abuse the legally enforceable IPR of any brand owner or manufacturer. In all these cases, counterfeiting and the production of knock-offs, goods may be produced by workers who are legitimate and legal (Phillips, 2005). However, they may also be produced by illegal workers, resulting in products that are indistinguishable from the authentic brand, 'a sort of true fake' (Saviano, 2008: 39) being produced at very low labour cost. In addition, illegally produced goods may be packed and distributed by legal businesses, often specialized logistics companies, further blurring the boundary between legal and illegal.

In recent years, there has been a growth in markets in the European Union specializing in the sale of illegally imported consumer goods from China, including Aubervilliers, near Paris; the Barras in Glasgow; Cheetham Hill, in Manchester; Fuenlabrada, near Madrid; Prato, in the Arno valley near Florence; Neuss, near Düsseldorf; and Wolka Kosowska, between Krakow and Warsaw in Poland (O'Neill, 2017). There are also notorious examples of more established markets in which specifically counterfeit goods are openly traded, bought and sold at a fraction of the price of the genuine branded article, including Xiushui Market in Beijing and Harco Glodok in Jakarta (Chaudhry and Zimmerman, 2010: 42−43) as well as street markets in major global cities such as London, Los Angeles, New York and Paris. Such markets enable consumers to acquire the symbolic value and prestige of premium brands at a fraction of the price of the genuine article, undercutting the latter in the market while to all intents and purposes appearing to be that genuine article.

Illegality in the core of the commodity production process

There are numerous examples of the illegal mining of key minerals (for example, see Erman, 2007; Nordbrand and Bolme, 2007), illegal working conditions in agriculture (for example, see Kiezebrink, 2017) and illegal production of manufactured goods that then compete in a range of mainstream legal markets. While the commodities themselves may be legal, the conditions under which they are produced are not. Thus, while legitimate commodities may be produced by workers who are legally entitled to employment, there are many instances of people working in conditions that violate labour laws and flaunt health and safety legislation, unprotected against dangerous chemicals or machinery – the disaster at Bhopal is simply one of many examples (see Hudson, 2010). Furthermore, labour-power that is legally purchased on the labour market can be illegally employed in other ways – for example as a result of companies withholding wages and workers being forced to work beyond the legal limit for overtime, violating both national legislation and international agreements such as the ILO's Hours of Work Convention, thereby increasing the production of absolute surplus-value. Often workers have little choice but to work excessive and illegal overtime because their legal basic wage is below the level of a 'living wage' or because they are coerced to work 'voluntary' unpaid overtime, often under the threat of losing their jobs, to meet demanding production targets that otherwise cannot be met (for example, see Nordbrand and de Haan, 2009). Many workers in the new industrial zones of Southeast Asia are migrants from poor rural areas, often young and female, with no previous experience of factory work, working to send remittances back to their families and home areas. As such, they are particularly vulnerable and susceptible to pressure from managers and owners to work illegally.

Such employment practices are often facilitated by the absence of trades unions (for example in the 'no union no strike' Export Production Zones of the Philippines) or the presence of unions that are effectively under state control and/or the influence of employers. Such practices are rife. They are widespread in China, parts of India, Myanmar, over much of the rest of Southeast Asia, and in central, eastern and parts of southern Europe, typically in sectors such as clothing as well as consumer electronics and IT in which production is commonly represented as 'high-tech' and 'clean' (for example, see Barbu et al., 2013; Chan et al., 2008; Ferus-Comelo and Pöyhönen, 2011; Lan, 2014; Mackay, 2004; Pöyhönen and Wan, 2011; SACOM, 2011). Major original equipment manufacturing multinationals that outsource production may have corporate social responsibility (CSR) policies in place that prescribe legal working practices and define required standards in the workplace. However, these frequently come into conflict with competitive pressures at the point of production to cut costs. As a result, local managers ignore the requirement to comply with the CSR policies and deliberately falsify employment records to disguise illegal overtime and underpayment of wages (Ruwanpura and Wrigley, 2011; Sum and Ngai, 2005). Furthermore, '. . . the pressures of keeping prices competitively low encouraged manufacturers to enter into sub-contracting relationships with smaller workshops on the edge of illegality' (Tokatli et al., 2011: 1206). Commodities produced under these circumstances can then compete with and undercut legitimately produced commodities, reducing the market share and profits of those producers operating legally and conforming to the requirements of labour legislation. This, however, creates systemic pressures for all companies to seek to produce in these ways. It is also important to acknowledge that such illegal working practices are also prevalent in activities such as ship breaking and waste recycling, linked to the growing international trade in wastes, which are more commonly seen as 'dirty' and less desirable, in peripheral locations in the global North as well as South (for example, see Buerk, 2006; Frandsen et al., 2011; Gregson et al., 2012; Nordbrand, 2009).

Illegality in the circulation of commodities

The illegal trading and sale of legitimate commodities and/or the trading of illegal commodities can be of great significance. In part, this is because the legal and illegal can be conflated in distribution and sale. While some commodities – for example, narcotics – are simply illegal, others such as cigarettes and tobacco may be produced illegally as well as legally (Shen et al., 2009) and it can be unclear as to which were produced legally, and which illegally, as they move from sites of production to sites of consumption. While illegally produced commodities are by definition traded illegally, there is also money to be made as a result of commodities that are legally produced, ranging from cigarettes, food and consumer electronics to weaponry, avoiding customs duties or trade restrictions by smuggling (for example, see O'Neill, 2017), thereby underpinning the creation of 'grey markets'. This confers a competitive advantage to those companies that follow such a strategy vis-à-vis those companies that do pay such duties, and denies (territorially bounded) state taxation revenues that they would otherwise receive and could deploy in social and economic development projects (for example, see Nordbrand and Bolme, 2007). Illegal trade often flourishes precisely because it is focused on ports that lack the capacity to cope with the volume of goods passing through them, above all because of the growth and prevalence of containerized trade (Guerrero and Rodrigue, 2014), and the very low probability that illegal goods in containers will be detected (Glenny, 2008; Nordstrom, 2007). However, it is important to note that illegality in trade may also be accepted as licit in the absence of alternative ways of 'getting by' in particular places (for example, in relation to drug trafficking see Raineri, 2017).

From 'dirty money' to clean money capital: flows of money, spaces of sanitization and disguise

While I will focus here on specific spaces in which dirty money acquired through illegal activities is sanitized to become available as money capital in the legal economy, it is important to emphasize the way in which corruption has become endemic in contemporary capitalism. While fraud and corruption have ever been the companions of capitalism, with the emergence of financialization and the rise to dominance of the finance sector over the last four decades they have become pervasive as a result of the 'deep empathy on the part of the legal system with the competitive pressure on financial institutions to break the law in order to make a profit' (Streeck, 2017: 31). Indeed,

> [f]inance is an industry where innovation is hard to distinguish from rule-bending or rule-breaking; where the payoffs from semi-legal and illegal activities are particularly high; where the gradient in expertise and pay between firms and regulatory authorities is extreme; where revolving doors between the two offer unending possibilities for subtle and not-so-subtle corruption. (Streeck, 2017: 70)

He continues: 'After Enron and World Com, it was observed that fraud and corruption had reached an all-time high in the US economy. But what came to light after 2008 beat everything.' This included: rating agencies being paid by the producers of toxic securities to award them top grades; insider trading on a large scale; offshore shadow banking, money laundering and assistance in large-scale tax evasion as the normal business of the biggest banks with the best addresses; the sale to unsuspecting customers of securities constructed so that other customers could bet against them; and the leading banks worldwide fraudulently fixing interest rates and the price of gold. These were not activities carried out in murky locations on the margins of the economy, nor in tax havens on exotic islands, but in the financial districts of major world cities, including London and New York, in the heart of the capitalist economy where corruption is endemic, and tolerated if not actually encouraged by national states (Christensen, 2011; Garcia-Bernardo et al., 2017; Norfield, 2017; Penna and O'Brien, 2017; Unger and Rawlings, 2008: 348–349).

Money laundering and the flow of money from the illegal economy to become money capital in the legal economy has become of particular importance in relation to capital accumulation. While some money from illegal activities is used to support consumption and livelihoods – often in circumstances in which other sources of money are absent – and some remains as capital reinvested in the illegal economy, a much greater proportion finds its way into the circuits of the legal economy as legitimate money capital, invested in legal activities in mainstream markets. An estimated minimum of two-thirds of the money earned in the illegal economy finds its way into the legal economy (Schneider and Enster, 2000). This crossover between the circuits of the illegal and legal is of great significance, and the inflow of money capital contributes both to enhancing the competitive position of those who own it and to the overall expanded reproduction of capital and its geography. At the same time, money which remains within the circuits of illegal activity can finance activities that compete with those that are legally compliant. Furthermore, because these links and activities around circuits of capital necessarily are performed in specific places, money from illegal activities invested in the legal mainstream raises the question of the places and spaces in which illegally acquired profits become 'clean' money.

This cleansing typically occurs in one or two types of spaces. First, in legal jurisdictions, notably tax havens – both offshore in places such as Bermuda, the Cayman Islands and Jersey and onshore in the financial districts of cities in the heart of the globalizing economy. As well as facilitating legal activities, these 'secrecy spaces' (Christensen and Hampton, 1999; Murphy, 2017) also provide an interface between the legal and illegal economies (Hampton, 1996) and one that is permissive of illegal flows of money. Tax havens, originally established as spaces in which perfectly legal (though what many people would see as ethically and morally dubious and so illicit) activities of tax avoidance were and still are permissible, have subsequently become the sites of many of the major financial transactions of the global economy. What has also become clear is that such activities are also rife in the financial centres of the allegedly legal economy. As a result of the existence of such places, transactions and flows that in other times and places would be deemed illegal and/ or illicit are deemed to be licit. They exemplify the way in which illegal practices have become regarded as a customary and licit feature of the mainstream economy that is constituted through enmeshed and genetically encoded conjoined legal and illegal practices.

As a result, profits generated from illegal activity – from, *inter alia*, fraud, embezzlement, theft, bribery, commission kickbacks, narcotics trafficking, illegal arms dealing, counterfeiting, insider trading, market rigging, false trade invoicing, transfer mispricing, making illicit political donations and tax evasion – are routinely sanitized and recycled into the circuits of the legal via secretive instruments intended for legal tax avoidance. Tax havens encourage and enable grand-scale corruption by providing an operational base used by legal and financial professionals and their clients to exploit gaps in tax legislation and regulation. Whether intentionally or not, the very complexity of legal tax avoidance schemes creates space for illegal practices. Elaborate schemes are devised to 'weave dirty money' (Christensen, 2011: 183) into commercial transactions and to disguise the proceeds of crime and tax evasion using complex multi-jurisdictional structures that exploit the asymmetries among regulatory spaces. Precisely because they involve activities on the fringes of or beyond the boundaries of formal legal regulation, such financial activities require a high degree of trust to enable them to function successfully in tax havens that form key nodes in global financial networks (Hudson, 1998).

Revealingly, national states and multilateral agencies consistently downplay concerns about 'dirty money' and money laundering except, significantly, in relation to drugs and terrorism, which form only a small proportion of illegal cross-border flows (Baker, 2005: 269). This discursive selectivity is highly significant, symptomatic of a tacit recognition of the prevalence of illegality and systematic and large-scale laundering of 'dirty money'. Money laundering is accepted as a licit activity, recognizing the intimate relationships between legal and illegal activities in the constitution of capitalist economies and the pivotal role of tax havens as spaces in which these financial flows and transfers take place (Christensen, 2011: 181–184; Murphy, 2017). The servicing of illegal economic activities is focused on these tax havens precisely because of the lack of transparency that surrounds transactions carried out in and through them, either because of banking secrecy laws or through *de facto* judicial arrangements and banking practices.

The second type of space in which dirty money is cleansed lacks the formal status of tax havens. These spaces are found in jurisdictions in which local circumstances and institutions enable particular illegal activities to become licit. Such spaces are disproportionately concentrated in the (so-called) transitional and developing economies but are by no means limited to them as neo-liberal economic policies and practices have sharpened socio-spatial inequalities and created fertile breeding grounds for illegality in the core areas of capitalism as well as in its peripheries. This often involves the entanglement of elements of the legal state and its officials in illegal activities, either directly or indirectly, sanctioning them by turning a 'blind eye' (often in return for a financial consideration) to their existence: for example, see Pöyhönen and Simola (2007). Well-known examples include the spaces controlled by Cosa Nostra in Sicily, the 'Ndrangheta in Calabria, the Camorra in Naples, the Chinese Triads, the Japanese Yakuza and the Russian Mafia (for example, see Allum and Allum, 2008; Castells, 2000; Glenny, 2008; Hill, 2005; Saviano, 2008). All these organizations are involved in illegal flows of labour, the illegal trade of people and things, the illegal production of goods and the laundering of the resultant money by various mechanisms into the mainstream economy for private gain. State officials may also turn a 'blind eye' to such illegal practices not for personal gain but because of a desire to encourage economic growth in their area – or simply to enable people to subsist – in a situation in which there seems no alternative to engagement with the illegal (for example, see CIVIDEP, 2009; Kynge, 2009; Raineri, 2017). One consequence of systematically turning a blind eye to illegal activities, however, is a loss – often considerable – of revenue to the state that potentially could be used for progressive developmental purposes.

Conclusions

Clearly there is a very diverse range of activities and commodities that are illegal but that, for varying reasons, are as seen as licit, though not necessarily by all members of a society, as the revelations in the Panama and Paradise Papers have made clear. Definitions of the boundaries of the (il)licit may be, and often are, socially contested. Nonetheless, (il)legal and (il)licit activities are in practice woven together, entangled in complex ways to *constitute* the economy; it increasingly makes little sense (if it ever did) to think of neatly partitioned legal and illegal economies, licit and illicit activities. Criminal networks – and one might add illegal activities more generally – are 'woven into the texture of ordinary social life, where criminal conducts intermesh with habitual social patterns' (Raineri, 2017: 22). The progressive embeddedness of the illegal and the criminal economy into the 'normal(-ized)' economy deconstructs the fiction that locates illegal economies as an independent, isolated sphere of social relations. In contrast, they are integral to, enmeshed within, and constitutive of the mainstream economy. This is a conclusion that has far-reaching implications for the ways in which economic geographers understand economic geographies, both methodologically – given the difficulties that by definition exist in researching the illegal and investigating activities that are intended to remain hidden – and theoretically.

Not least, this is the case in relation to theorizing the relationship between national states and economies. The creation by national states of specific legal spaces for non-citizens – such as tax havens and export-processing zones – 'amounts to the creation of "islands" within the generality of national law' (Gerstenberger, 2012: 78) within which states accept, even encourage, the possibility of conducting business beyond the reach of national taxes, national banking legislation and national labour regulations in spaces in which the boundaries between the legal and illegal could be blurred, or even wholly abolished. Since by definition such illegal activities are located in 'spaces of exception' beyond the regulatory reach of national states and international organizations, their governance and regulation necessarily depend upon a range of social mechanisms ranging from kinship and friendship relations, trust and tolerance to bribery, extortion, physical force and fear of violence (and, in extremis, death), working around or simply ignoring legal regulation. They are not unregulated, but rather differently regulated in quite specific ways. This regulation can be facilitated by the 'blind eyes' of the state, with states at varying spatial scales ignoring or condoning such activities and regulatory practices for a variety of reasons, ranging from individual self-interest to wider societal concerns with the survival strategies of marginalized groups or more equitable forms of economic and social development. Alternatively, in circumstances of weak or non-existent formal state governance and regulatory mechanisms (for example, in so-called 'failed states'), illegal organizations may fill the resultant vacuum and are at least tolerated as licit – with examples ranging from gangs in Russia (Stephenson, 2015; Stephenson and Zakharova, 2017; and Stephenson, Chapter 9 this volume) to gangs in East Timor (Scambary, 2017) and various mafias in parts of Italy. The key issue here is the way in which illegality and its associated systems of governance and regulation, in the absence of any alternative, are routinely ignored, condoned or simply accepted so that the illegal and its associated governance processes come to be seen as licit and extend their influence beyond their initial formative spaces.

In summary, there is a chronic interweaving of economic activities and regulatory processes that routinely cross the binary divides of (il)legal and (il)licit. As a result, the illegal becomes genetically encoded in the economy and the relationships between legal and illegal are a common – and maybe even defining – feature of economic and social organization in capitalist economies. Moreover, the relationships between the illegal and (il)licit are variable over time and space – they too have variable geographies. Given all this, it makes little sense to continue to conceptualize economies as either legal or illegal; rather, they are dialectically related in ways that vary over time and space. Recognition of this, and the inherent spatiality of relationships between the (il)legal and (il)licit, poses a major challenge not just for economic geographers but for social scientists more generally who seek to understand the structure and developmental trajectories of contemporary capitalist economies. The extent to which illegal and illicit practices deprive national states of tax revenues that could be used to tackle problems of poverty, to provide health and social care, to promote legitimate economic development and more generally to tackle issues of inequality and uneven development further emphasizes the need to understand the relationships between the (il)licit and (il)legal and have practical as well as theoretical significance.

References

Allen, C. M., (2005), *An industrial geography of cocaine*, Routledge, New York.

Allum, F. and P. Allum, (2008), 'Revisiting Naples: clientelism and organised crime', *Journal of Modern Italian Studies*, 13, 340–365.

Baka, J., (2017), 'Making space for energy: wasteland development, enclosures, and energy dispossessions', *Antipode*, 49, 977–996.

Baker, R., (2006), *Capitalism's Achilles heel*, Wiley, New Jersey.

Barbu, M., M. Dunford and L. Weidong, (2013), 'Employment, entrepreneurship, and citizenship in a globalised economy: the Chinese in Prato', *Environment and Planning A*, 45, 2420–2441.

Buerk, R., (2006), *Breaking ships: how supertankers and cargo ships are dismantled on the beaches of Bangladesh*, Penguin, London.

Castells, M., (2000), *End of millennium*, Blackwell, Oxford.

Chan, J., E. de Haan, S. Nordbrand and A. Torstensson, (2008), *Silence to deliver: mobile phone manufacturing in China and the Philippines*, SOMO and Swedwatch, Amsterdam.

Chaudhry, P. and A. Zimmerman, (2010), *The economics of counterfeit trade: governments, consumers, pirates and intellectual property rights*, Springer, Berlin.

Chiodelli, F., T. Hall, R. Hudson and S. Moroni, (2017), 'The grey governance and development of cities and regions: the variable relationship between (il)legal and (ill)licit', in F. Chiodelli, T. Hall and R. Hudson (eds), *The illicit and the illegal in regional and urban governance and development*, Routledge, London, 1–19.

Christensen, J., (2011), 'The looting continues: tax havens and corruption', *Critical Perspectives on International Business*, 7, 177–196.

Christensen, J. and M. Hampton, (1999), 'A legislature for hire: the capture of the state in Jersey's Offshore Finance Centre', in M. Hampton and J. Abbott (eds), *Offshore finance centres and tax havens: the rise of global capital*, Macmillan, Basingstoke, 166–191.

CIVIDEP, (2009), *Corporate geography, labour conditions and environmental standards in the mobile phone manufacturing industry in India*, SOMO – Centre for Research on Multinational Corporations, Amsterdam.

Ditton, J., (1977), *Part-time crime: ethnography of fiddling and pilferage*, Macmillan, London.

Durand, C., (2017), *Fictitious capital*, Verso, London.

Elison, A., (2018), 'City traders getting away with abuse of markets', *The Times*, 19 January, 1–2.

Erman, E., (2007), *Rethinking legal and illegal economy: a case study of tin mining in Gangka Island*, available at http://globetrotter.berkeley.edu/GreenGovernance/papers/Erman2007.pdf (accessed 14 January 2012).

Evans, M., S. Syrett and C. Williams, (2006), *Informal economic activities and deprived neighbourhoods*, Department of Communities and Local Government, London.

Ferus-Comelo, A. and P. Pöyhönen, (2011), *Phony equality: labour standards of mobile phone manufacturers in India*, Finnwatch, Cividep and SOMO – Centre for Research on Multinational Corporations, Amsterdam.

Frandsen, D. M., J. Rasmussen and M. U. Swart, (2011), *What a waste – how your computer causes health problems in Ghana*, Dan Watch.

Gambetta, D., (2011), *Codes of the underworld: how criminals communicate*, Princeton University Press, Oxford.

Garcia-Bernardo, J., J. Fichtner, F. W. Takes and E. M. Heemskerk, (2017), 'Uncovering offshore financial centers: conduits and sinks in the global corporate ownership network', *Scientific Reports* 7, 6246. DOI:10.1038/s41598-017-06322-9

Gatti, F., (2006), 'I was a slave in Puglia', *L'Espresso*, 1 September, available at http://espresso.repubblica.it/dettaglio/i-was-a-slave-in-puglia/137395 (accessed 22 February 2012).

Gerstenberger, H., (2012), 'The historical constitution of the political forms of capitalism', *Antipode*, 43, 60–86.

Glenny, M., (2008), *McMafia: a journey through the global criminal underworld*, House of Anasi Press, Toronto.

Gregson, N. and M. Crang, (2016), 'Illicit economies: customary illegality, moral economies and circulation', *Transactions of the Institute of British Geographers*. DOI:10.1111/tran.12158

Gregson, N., M. Crang, F. Ahamed, N. Akter, R. Ferdous, R. Hudson and F. Mahmud, (2012), 'Bhatiary, Bangladesh as a secondary processing complex', *Economic Geography*, 88, 37–58.

Guerrero, D. and J.-P. Rodrigue, (2014), 'The waves of containerisation: shifts in global maritime transportation', *Journal of Transport Geography*, 34, 151–164.

Hadjimichalis, C. and D. Vaiou, (1990), 'Whose flexibility? The politics of informalisation in Southern Europe', *Capital and Class*, 42, 79–106.

Hall, T., (2013), 'Geographies of the illicit: the case of organised crime', *Progress in Human Geography*, 37, 366–385.

Hampton, M., (1996), *The offshore interface: tax havens in the global economy*, Macmillan, Basingstoke.

Harvey, D., (1982), *The limits to capital*, Edward Arnold, London.

Harvey, D., (2003), *The new imperialism*, Oxford University Press, Oxford.

Harvey, D., (2014), *Seventeen contradictions and the end of capitalism*, Profile Books, London.

Hill, P., (2005), 'The changing face of the Yakuza', in M. Galeotti (ed.), *Global crime today: the changing face of organised crime*, Routledge, London, 97–116.

Hobbs, D., (1988), *Doing the business: entrepreneurship, the working class and detectives in the East End of London*, Oxford University Press, Oxford.

Hobbs, D., (2013), *Lush life: constructing organized crime in the UK*, Oxford University Press, Oxford.

Hudson, A. C., (1998), 'Placing trust, trusting places: on the social construction of offshore financial centres', *Political Geography*, 17, 915–937.

Hudson, R., (2001), *Producing places*, Guilford Press, New York.

Hudson, R., (2005), *Economic geographies: circuits, flows and spaces*, Sage, London.

Hudson, R., (2010), 'Multiplicant els riscs per a la salut I el benestar: els costos inadmisibles de la globalització/Multiplying risks to health and wellbeing: the unacknowledged costs of Globalisation', *Treballs de la Societat Catalana de Geografia*, 70, 101–127.

Hudson, R., (2013), 'Thinking through the relationships between legal and illegal activities and economies: spaces, flows and pathways', *Journal of Economic Geography*, 14, 775–795.

Hudson, R., (2016), *Approaches to economic geography: towards a geographical political economy*, Routledge, London.

Kiezebrink, V., (2017), *Palming off responsibility – labour rights violations in the Indonesian palm oil sector: case studies of Murini Sam Sam and Aneka Inti Persada*, SOMO, Amsterdam.

Kynge, J., (2009), *China shakes the world: the rise of a hungry nation*, Phoenix, London.

Lan, T., (2014), 'Industrial district and the multiplication of labour: the Chinese apparel industry in Prato, Italy', *Antipode*, 47, 158–178.

Latza Nadeau, B., (2018), 'Roadmap to hell: sex drugs and guns on the Mafia Coast', available at http://www.theguardian.com/news/ (accessed 24 February 2018).

Liberti, S., (2013), *Land grabbing*, Verso, London.

Mackay, S., (2004), 'Zones of regulation: restructuring labor control in privatized export zones', *Politics and Society*, 32, 171–202.

Mingione, E., (1999), 'Introduction: immigration and the informal economy in European cities', *International Journal of Urban and Regional Research*, 23, 209–211.

Murphy, R., (2017), *Dirty secrets: what to do about tax havens*, Verso, London.

Nadiruzzaman, M. D. and H. Shewly, (2017), 'Invisible journeys across India-Bangladesh borders and bubbles of corrupt networks: stories of cross-border rural-urban migration and economic linkages', in F. Chiodelli, T. Hall and R. Hudson (eds), *The illicit and the illegal in regional and urban governance and development*, Routledge, London, 37–53.

National Crime Agency, (2017), *Modern slavery and human trafficking: national referral mechanisms statistics: end of year summary 2016*, available at www.nationalcrimeagency.gov.uk/publications/national-referral-mechanism-statistics/2016-nrm-statistics/788-national-referral-mechanism-end-of-year-summary-2016/file

Nordbrand, S., (2009), *Out of control: e-waste trade flows from the EU to developing countries*, Swedwatch.

Nordbrand, S. and P. Bolme, (2007), *Powering the mobile world: cobalt production for batteries in the DR Congo and Zambia*, Swedwatch.

Nordbrand, S. and E. de Haan, (2009), *Mobile phone production in China – a follow up report on two suppliers in Guangdong*, SOMO and Swedwatch, Amsterdam.

Nordstrom, C., (2007), *Global outlaws: crime, money, and power in the contemporary world*, University of California Press, Berkeley.

Norfield, T., (2017), *The city: London and the global power of finance*, Verso, London.

OECD, (2007), *The economic impact of counterfeiting and piracy*, Part 1, available at http://www.oecd.org/dataoecd/36/36/39543408.pdf-3

O'Neill, S., (2017), 'Chinese crime gangs using Britain as soft gateway for huge trade fraud', *The Times*, 25 April, 6.

Palan, R., (2017), 'Four things the Paradise Papers tell us about global business and political elites', *The Conversation*, 5 November.

Palloix, C., (1977), 'The self-expansion of capital on a world scale', *Review of Radical Political Economics*, 9, 1–28.

Peck, J., (2016), 'Macroeconomic geographies', *Area Development and Policy*, 1, 305–322.

Penna, S. and M. O'Brien, (2017), 'The corruption of politics or the politics of corruption? Reconsidering the role of organised crime in the geo-politics of corruption', in F. Chiodelli, T. Hall and R. Hudson (eds), *The illicit and the illegal in regional and urban governance and development*, Routledge, London, 200–220.

Phillips, T., (2005), *Knockoff: the deadly trade in counterfeit goods*, Kogan Page, London.

Polson, M., (2017), 'Planning for marijuana: development, governance and regional political economy', in F. Chiodelli, T. Hall and R. Hudson (eds), *The illicit and the illegal in regional and urban governance and development*, Routledge, London, 141–163.

Portes, R., M. Castells and L. A. Benton (eds), (1989), *The informal economy: studies in advanced and less developed countries*, John Hopkins University Press, London.

Pöyhönen, P. and E. Simola, (2007), *Connecting components, dividing communities: tin production for consumer electronics in the DR Congo and Indonesia*, FinnWatch and SOMO, Amsterdam.

Pöyhönen, P. and D. Wan, (2011), *Game console and music player production in China*, Finnwatch, SACOM and SOMO, available at www.makeITfair.org (accessed 11 January 2012).

Raineri, L., (2017), 'Drug trafficking in the Sahara Desert: follow the money and find land-grabbing', in F. Chiodelli, T. Hall and R. Hudson (eds), *The illicit and the illegal in regional and urban governance and development*, Routledge, London, 20–36.

Rengert, G. F., (1996), *The geography of illegal drugs*, Westview Press, Boulder, CO.

Ruwanpura, K. N. and N. Wrigley, (2011), 'The costs of compliance? Views of Sri Lankan apparel manufacturers in times of global economic crisis', *Journal of Economic Geography*, 11, 1031–1049.

SACOM, (2011), *iSlave behind the iPhone: Foxconn workers in Central China*, SACOM.

Saviano, R., (2008), *Gomorrah: Italy's other Mafia*, Pan, London.

Scambary, J., (2017), 'Gangsters, guerrillas and messiahs: the rise of a neo-patrimonialist state in East Timor', in F. Chiodelli, T. Hall and R. Hudson (eds), *The illicit and the illegal in regional and urban governance and development*, Routledge, London, 54–73.

Schneider, F. and D. H. Enster, (2000), 'Shadow economies: size, causes and consequences', *Journal of Economic Literature*, 37, 77–78.

Shen, A., A. Antonopoulos and K. Von Lampe, (2009), ''THE DRAGON BREATHES SMOKE': Cigarette counterfeiting in the People's Republic of China', *British Journal of Criminology*. DOI:10.1093/bjc/azp069. Available at http://bjc.oxfordjournals.org (accessed 11 April 2012).

SOMO, (2009), *On the move: the electronics industry in central and eastern Europe*, available at www.makeITfair.org (accessed 10 January 2012).

Springer, S., (2013), 'Violent accumulation: a postanarchist critique of property, dispossession, and the state of exception in neoliberalizing Cambodia', *Annals of the Association of American Geographers*, 103, 608–626.

Stephenson, S., (2015), *Gangs of Russia: from the streets to the corridors of power*, Cornell University Press, Ithaca, NY.

Stephenson, S. and E. Zakharova, (2017), 'Criminal community, youth street organizations and illicit territorial regulation in Moscow and Tbilisi', in F. Chiodelli, T. Hall and R. Hudson (eds), *The illicit and the illegal in regional and urban governance and development*, Routledge, London, 74–92.

Streeck, W., (2017), *How will capitalism end?* Verso, London.

Sum, N.-L. and P. Ngai, (2005) 'Globalization and paradoxes of ethical transnational production: code of conduct in a Chinese workplace', *Competition and Change*, 9, 181–200.

Tokatli, N., O. Kizilgun and J. E. Cho, (2011), 'The clothing industry in Istanbul in an era of globalisation and fast fashion', *Urban Studies*, 48, 1201–1205.

Unger, B. and G. Rawlings, (2008), 'Competing for criminal money', *Global Business and Economics Review*, 10, 331–352.

Zucman, G., (2015), *The hidden wealth of nations: the scourge of tax havens*, University of Chicago Press, Chicago.

3 Faces in the clouds: criminology, epochalism, apophenia and transnational organized crime

Dick Hobbs

Introduction

If as social scientists we cling to the ever-declining parameters of critical scholarship, rather than hanging on to the shirt-tails of law enforcement policy makers, the concept of organized crime emerges as an interesting area of analysis as opposed to an uncontested fact of life. The concept of transnational organized crime (TOC) is of course a construction that has emerged from a very specific set of converging political economic forces, and this convergence, along with its consequences, should constitute the fundamental basis for any form of meta-analysis. Yet TOC is seldom interrogated, with sceptical voices being confined to an echo chamber consisting largely of critical political scientists (see Bigo, 1994, 2000). Criminology, with very few exceptions, has joined law enforcement at the trough. TOC is 'a thing', an identifiable malady to be extinguished by the heroic efforts of administrative criminology, which is not dissimilar to expecting the meteorology community to render rainfall extinct. This chapter will address organized crime, and in particular its transnational variant (TOC), focusing upon Othering, the concept that rests at its centre, and some key aspects of TOCs configuration.

TOC is a political construct of the late twentieth century that is marked by an alarming reading of globalization (Findlay, 2008: 151–152), and normally relates to cross-border activity involving the explicit exclusion of the state (Hobsbawm, 1994). Yet if this notion was operationalized then it would be applied historically to frame the activities of criminal entrepreneurs who have collaborated with overseas trading partners during eras that predate the TOC era (Karraker, 1953). For instance, during the Prohibition era the illegal trade in alcohol was greatly enhanced by the importation of both alcoholic beverages and the precursors for their manufacture (Behr, 1996; Kyvig, 2000), activities that contributed to economic development rather than to societal threat (Haller, 1985). Yet these aspects of Prohibition were never defined as transnational, for it was American crime performed, at least in its most public sense, by Americans. Similarly, some of the iconic names of twentieth-century British crime were, even in the pre-drug era, sometimes engaged in crime that involved international partnerships (Hobbs, 2013: 41–85). Yet Billy Hill, the Kray twins and others never received the transnational tag. For transnational crime was only invoked when crime was defined as being not merely cross-border, but more importantly perpetrated by the Other, and performed during a defined epoch.

This chapter will also suggest that Othering has had an alternative utility within criminal cultures as a positive characteristic, and will refer to a set of conversations that the author carried out with veteran London-based criminals. The chapter suggests that ethnographic rather than administrative concerns should be placed at the forefront of enquiries into illegal trading and the cultures that sustain them, and that criminology has proved to be an inadequate tool with which to carry out critical enquiries into TOC. The chapter proceeds to critique the tendency towards epochalism in the study of organized crime, and suggests that to overplay the notion of organization is a symptom of apophenia, the human tendency to seek patterns in random information. By focusing upon the British experience, it is hoped that a more nuanced view of organized crime might be established. In particular, and despite the geographical specificity of the chapter, some doors might be opened on the sociological back history of criminology and might make it possible to unpick the social construction of the concept of organized crime.

Context: criminology

Up until the late 1980s, criminology in the UK was limited largely to the University of Cambridge Institute of Criminology, which in turn educated many of those who became prominent within both academic and governmental settings (Radzinowicz, 1961, 1988).[1] However, the study of deviance was the domain of sociology, a discipline that benefitted greatly from the expansion of UK higher education during the 1960s. The subsequent organization of the sociology of deviance expressed a growing dissatisfaction with conventional criminology as represented by the Cambridge Institute, and led to the formation of the National Deviancy Conference (NDC) in 1968 (see Cohen, 1971: chapter 1; Radzinowicz, 1972) – made up of, 'Anarchists, CND, Young Communists and International Socialists' (Cohen, 1974: 27), as well as 'interactionists . . . phenomenologists, and Marxists' (Sumner 1994: 262). The most influential text to emerge from the NDC declared that 'deviance is normal' (Taylor et al., 1973), a statement alluding more to Durkheim than to Marx, that stood in stark contrast to the administratively bound scholarship of the Cambridge Institute which was far more at home within faculties of law than the self-consciously neo-Marxist output of the NDC.[2] A small number of notable scholars influenced by the 'New Criminologists' engaged in ethnographic work (Ditton, 1977) and both the Chicago School (Downes, 1966) and interactionism (Matza: 1969; see Atkinson,

---

1 The Institute of Criminology was closely linked to the UK Home Office. From the 1990s onwards prominent Cambridge-trained Home Office-based researchers who had been responsible for some high-profile government policies became highly valued members of newly created departments of criminology.

2 The output of the NDC was rejected by formal Marxists who rejected the notion of a sociological theory of crime, in favour of a strict Marxist, somewhat mid-nineteenth-century rendition of the relationship between the industrial working class and the lumpenproletariat (Hirst, 1975).

1990: 170–174) retained a voice (Rock, 1973), particularly among those scholars embracing subcultural studies (Cohen, 1971: 9–24). The watering down of deviancy amplification theory to an at times embarrassing liberal cult of labelling (Hall, 2012), which was almost exclusively limited to youth studies, occupied a lot of scholarly space, yet, cumulatively, fieldwork-based research seeking out 'the meaning of actions and events to the people we seek to understand' (Spradley, 1979: 5) was promoted as an alternative to the positivism typified by 'mainstream criminology' (Cohen, 1974: 1–40),[3] and ethnographic work in particular, then as now, was presented as a symbol of authenticity.

From the late 1960s, with few exceptions, crime was interrogated from within sociology departments, with undergraduate modules in the sociology of deviance forming the bedrock of a broad area that included policing, penology, criminal justice and in particular the study of deviant youth. The sociology of deviance was taught and researched alongside evolving curricula that featured the sociologies of education, housing, race, gender, etc. Alongside a theoretically informed schooling in methodology, sociological theory lay at the core of both undergraduate and postgraduate study and 'a sense of craft and disciplinary induction was inculcated' (Hobbs, 2013: 262). Importantly, until the early 1990s' expansion of higher education, those tasked with teaching and researching these areas were overwhelmingly identified as sociologists.

The expansion of higher education in the UK was driven by commodification, and it was this process that created criminology degrees, lectureships, departments, journals, conferences, publishers, and the invention of a criminological tradition which has succeeded in ignoring many key fields of transgression, limiting the discipline's methodological toolkit and fetishizing theory (see Hobbs, 2013: 268). Although the bulk of criminology would make a claim on some variation on being 'radical' or 'critical', the rapid rise of criminology as a discipline, which in turn was enabled by the expansion of a heavily marketized higher education system, ensured that students would aspire to the edgy scientism of criminological glamour rather than the tweedy hit-and-hope liberalism of sociology. Increasingly inspired by forensic-based TV fantasies such as *Silent Witness* and the *NCIS* franchise, or by this week's liberal raison d'être, 'criminology became a cash cow for an expanded university sector' (Hobbs, 2013: 262), and along the way abandoned the comparatively wide-open intellectual spaces of sociology (Carrabine, 2015, 2016, 2017). 'The ethnomethodology and phenomenology of crime, deviance and control have apparently been expunged' (Rock, 2005: 3), and as a consequence the construction of crime is now seldom questioned. With reference to organized crime, and to TOC in particular, the expansion of state engagement in various wars on crime further inspired an administrative tendency that marginalized critical writing, reducing theory to a niche (Maruna, 2008), and establishing criminology as '... a practical

---

3 The central contribution of the NDC was to discuss the social parameters within which deviant worlds were created, rather than to analyse those worlds. At the NDC's first 14 symposia consisting of 70 papers, less than ten featured fieldwork-based studies.

pursuit, devoted to helping society deal with those it found troublesome' (Becker, 1964: 1).[4]

Context: organized crime

While there was a small and important academic literature on professional crime,[5] the term failed to make very much of an impact upon curricula, and was even less significant in terms of social policy. However, the 1990s' commencement of criminology's astonishing expansion parallels exactly with the British construction of organized crime, a construction that was linked closely to the concept of transnationality. Until the 1990s organized crime was a problem that was difficult to locate in either political or academic discourse in the UK, and although serious acquisitive crime was occasionally perceived by the British police as a problem experienced in a few cities (Levi, 2005: 825), which resulted in a range of essentially local solutions (Sillitoe, 1955), the term organized crime was seldom invoked. Historically specific forms of vice had triggered a racist pathology that located certain ethnic groups as culpable for the corruption and degradation of British society (Hobbs, 2013; Knepper, 2007), and images of collaborations of foreign criminals were especially alarming (Slater, 2007), as a British version of 'alien conspiracy theory' settled at the foundations of what eventually was to become the UK's policy on organized crime.

A creation of post-Second World War USA (US Senate 1951; Woodiwiss, 1993; Woodiwiss and Hobbs, 2009), alien conspiracy theory, '(an) expression of a moral conspiracy aimed at the vitals of American life' (Block, 1983: 123), was afforded academic respectability by Cressey (1969), but based entirely upon testimony from law enforcement personnel (Moore, 1974). Although subsequently criticized by American scholars (Albini, 1971: 210; Block, 1983; Smith, 1975, 1980), alien conspiracy theory legitimized exclusionary policies at home and violent oppression abroad (Picketing, 2001: 48–49). After President Nixon's declaration of a 'war on drugs' (Elwood, 1994; Woodiwiss, 1988: 221–222), and the Reagan presidencies' pressure on the international community (Woodiwiss and Hobbs, 2009), UK Prime Minister Margaret Thatcher enthusiastically embraced American policies (Woodiwiss, 1988: 222), and by the 1990s organized crime emanating from overseas had become accepted as a reality within British political and media circles (see Hobbs, 2013: 13–40).

With transnationality established as a threat, in 1992 the British created the National Crime Intelligence Service (NCIS) a specialist nationwide law enforcement unit dubbed as a 'British FBI'. The end of the Cold War created security spaces in Europe (Edwards and Gill, 2003: 264), and in 1997 the EU action plan against organized crime was published, followed by a range of legislative tools

---

4 I once worked with a sociologist who at social gatherings would describe himself as a criminologist in the belief that it made him more interesting. It didn't work.

5 For an overview of the literature on professional crime see Hobbs (1995b).

and institutional arrangements (Edwards and Levi, 2008; Sheptycki, 1995). The EU required law enforcement agencies to formalize cooperation across the EU, and the United Nations Convention against TOC repositioned organized crime as a major internal threat to Europe (Harfield, 2008).

The British reading of TOC emphasized the deviant pathology of strangers and new arrivals and is closely allied to 'the universalization of the particular characteristics of an economy embedded in a particular history and social structure, that of the United States' (Bourdieu, 2003: 87). British organized crime policy, particularly in its early stages, was modelled on American-based alien conspiracies, often in conjunction with the United Nations (Bigo, 2000; Mena and Hobbs, 2010) and post-Cold War demonology (Hobbs, 2013: 13–40). The early threats came not from the everyday logic of the political economy (Bell, 1953: 152; see Block and Chambliss, 1981), but from Triads, Yardies, Russians, Colombians, Italians and Turks (NCIS, 1993a, 1993b). The threat of organized crime was clearly transnational. However, after Russia had joined the G8 group in 1998, the Russian organized crime threat had apparently declined, and in 2000 NCIS was able to state that, 'Judging from current intelligence, the UK is not facing an "invasion" by a "red mafiya"' (NCIS, 2000: n.p.). Organized crime is a highly malleable, essentially political device.

Yet British academe, and criminology in particular, paid scant attention to organized crime or its precursors. More importantly, it ignored the secretive, democratically unaccountable institutions that were created to deal with it (Hobbs, 2013: 13–40). The unpublished Home Office pilot study for a 'British Organised Crime Survey' suggested an element of chaos surrounded the very concept of organized crime, and detailed intense hostility to NCIS among the law enforcement community (Dunnighan and Hobbs, 1996; Hobbs and Dunnighan, 1998a, 1998b). In addition, political scientist Frank Gregory produced a critique of the evidence base upon which British organized crime policy relied (Gregory, 2003), and exposed the notion of foreign criminal invasion as a fallacy. Yet there remained little criminological interest in interrogating the alleged transnational threat (see Edwards and Gill, 2003; Hobbs, 1998; Sheptycki, 1995, 1998), which continued to be vigorously promoted by state institutions that were well embedded in law enforcement orthodoxy, and it was some time before British academics critically addressed the development of British organized crime policy (Bowling and Ross, 2006; Elvins, 2003; Harfield, 2008; Hobbs and Hobbs, 2012; Levi, 2005).

Particularly in the era of mass immigration and subsequent cosmopolitanism, the concept of transnational organized crime has laid the foundations for the creation of global crime threats, and the emergence of an enforcement orthodoxy that expunges the ambivalence of the stranger (Marotta, 2002: 42) by insisting, '. . . that righteous citizens are being perverted, intimidated, and forced into vice by alien forces' (Potter, 1994: 10). Subsequently, boundaries between natives and 'foreigners, lower class, ethnic offenders or a combination thereof' (Van Duyne, 2011: 2) distinguish between criminal and non-criminal via the platform of Othering (Agozino,

2000), and by 'stereotyping, humiliating, dehumanizing, stigmatizing identities . . .' (Bauman, 2004: 38).

While the transnational trope identifies aliens as a principal threat to society, this threat pre-dates the creation of the organized crime menace and its subsequent institutionalization. Indeed, at times of crisis various ethnic groups such as Jews, Chinese, and Maltese were subjected to the process of Othering and associated with international crime long before transnationality was used as a vehicle for the formal introduction of organized crime into UK political and law enforcement narratives (Hobbs, 2013). Importantly, these precursors to TOC are vital in informing vernacular understandings of deviant behaviours that are embedded in the fine grain of working-class culture, yet this is a culture increasingly ignored by contemporary academic practice.

Particularly for young scholars labouring under the yoke of criminology, the acceptance of the authority of law enforcement in the construction of TOC has become a signal of academic virtue. For the decline of sociological sensibilities, and the pre-eminence of data 'owned' by specialist law enforcement agencies, along with the subservience of academics within academic/police 'partnerships', has diluted the consequent epistemological products – products that should carry the warning 'the content of this file are the fruits of police activity' (Kitsuse and Cicourel, 1963), a sceptical disclaimer that was integral to the study of crime and control when it was taught and researched from within the sociology of deviance. Yet from within criminal cultures there are other voices which – due to law enforcement's increasing domination of data, the organization of research in higher education, and the theoretical timidity that is integral to the contemporary criminological enterprise – are seldom heard.

A Jock on the firm: some notes on inter-city Otherness

> A lot of firms used to like a Jock on the firm . . . They was heavy, very heavy . . . minding, bit of debt collecting. Very heavy solid reliable geezers. (Bob A)

Before transnationalism emerged to provide a dominant narrative for organized crime in the 1990s, a process of positive Othering can be identified operating within the professional crime community in relation to Scottish criminals.[6] Here we look at the manner in which the criminal community, quite separately from the narratives of police and academics, assigns value to ethnically orientated deviant essences. In this case the value assigned is affirmative, awarding the dehumanized Other favourable status. Particularly with reference to Glaswegians, individual

---

6 In 1994, when the organized crime debate was in its infancy in the UK, the Home Affairs Committee placed its emphasis on 'professional' as opposed to 'organized' criminality, and the Association of Chief Police Officers referred to organized crime as 'serious crimes committed by career criminals who network with each other across the UK, across Europe and internationally' (Home Affairs Committee, 1994: 16–17).

essences (Katz, 1975) are reduced to criminal competency, and Scottish identity is condensed to the ability to perform particular criminal acts, which in turn highlight abilities inherently related to ethnicity. This provides an alternative view to that contained in the dominant narratives of law enforcement agencies, and in particular to those academics hanging on to law enforcement's 'shirt-tails'.

Professional theft and the resultant stolen goods networks were at the very core of criminal culture during the Industrial era, and within major metropolitan centres, particularly those boasting a major port, theft and the trade in stolen goods were normalized, and encompassed a wide swathe of the working-class population, rather than being the exclusive terrain of specialists (Hobbs, 1995a, 2013). As populations became more mobile and illegal/unlicensed markets began to expand, the interchange of goods, services and personnel between cities gained in prominence. For instance, Glasgow was but one supplier of stolen goods to London's voracious marketplace, and with police forces operating as self-contained fiefdoms, if stolen goods could be shifted to markets beyond police boundaries the odds against detection were high (Porter, 1996). Markets in high-value goods such as cigarettes and whiskey were established during the rationing of the Second World War and its immediate aftermath (Smithies, 1982; Thomas, 2003), and in the 1950s Glaswegian thieves built valuable individual reputations for themselves, particularly in the West End of London where both licensed and unlicensed premises cashed in on the post-war consumer boom. Many of these premises were connected to networks of theft and extortion with bases all over working-class London, while the West End represented a 'honey pot' (Hill, 1955: 117; Hobbs, 2013: 65) of opportunity for thieves and violent entrepreneurs. These key connections, established during the war and the immediate post-war years, were to mature along with the status of a number of the key players.

Anonymity as a specialism

> No idea how they got connected. They turned up and went to work. Yeah (there were) rumours about who they were and who they was with up north and what they had done. (Arthur) Thompson came up. To be honest he is the only Jock (villain) I heard of. (Stan)

Springburn's Arthur Thompson proved over the 1950s and 1960s to be an enduring node of criminal connections between Glasgow and London, and his initial contact with the capital was via the post-Second World War stolen goods' network. McKay (2006: 70) explains that Thompson worked in debt collecting, minding and robbery for the Kray twins, the Richardson brothers,[7] and most of the major players in London, as well as freelancing (McKay, 2006: 42–53). The stoic reputations of Scottish couriers and minders were enhanced by their perceived abilities as men of violence, 'The English guys recognize that Scotland produces good heavies and

---

7 McKay goes on to claim that via his friendship with Buster Edwards, Thompson had put himself forward to be recruited for what turned out to be the 1963 Great Train Robbery (McKay, 2006: 72).

that is why they have so many on their firms' (Boyle, 1977: 163). The reliability of Glaswegians associated with networks of theft was matched by the value of their anonymity in London, and a number were employed to collect and transport illegal proceeds from businesses across the capital. As Boyle notes, 'London was a dream as it was so big that one could hit different parts of it each day and so remain anonymous' (Boyle, 1977: 90). Scottish imports were anonymous both to the police, who lacked anything resembling a national database, and to rival London villains who were only familiar with players from their own or adjacent neighbourhoods[8] (Boyle, 1977: 169).

There was a long-standing Scottish community in London's Kings Cross district, adjacent to the rail terminus that linked Glasgow and the capital (Boyle, 1977: 89), and while freelance Scottish villains were not unknown in the capital,[9] by the mid-1950s the Glaswegian criminal in London was regarded as a highly prized, dependably violent alien.[10] The Kray twins were particularly keen on both collaborating with their Glaswegian colleagues (Boyle, 1977: 156), and on using violent Celtic labour (Boyle, 1977: 163): '. . . they liked them to be around them in the clubs and pubs. Bit of show like' (Paulie B). Indeed, the Krays were sufficiently taken with the kudos of having a 'Jock on the Firm' that they employed Glaswegian 'Big' Pat Connelly, in addition to two natives of Edinburgh, 'Scotch' Jack Dickson, '. . . the twins liked the cut of his Scottish jib' (Campbell, 1991: 71) and Ian Barrie, who were employed by the Krays as minders and drivers, apparently on the strength of no more than their ethnicity (Dickson, 1986: 1–15). 'Somebody always owed them dough, so when one of these Scottish geezers turns up outside a car lot or a garage or whatever, when they get out the motor the money would come out, no problem' (Bob A). Until they began consorting with the Krays, these three Scottish imports had no criminal records (save for one conviction for vagrancy): their value was in the assumptions made regarding the violent nature and staunch disposition that constitute the essential essences of Scots.[11] 'Lovely fellas, respectful, good

---

8 On occasions, criminal craftsmen with highly individualistic methods that would make them easily traced by local police were brought into London for specific jobs, where their modus operandi was not recognizable. For instance, Thompson's associate Paddy Meehan, who in the 1960s was the victim of a controversial miscarriage of justice in Scotland, had during the 1960s travelled to London working for a London firm (Kennedy, 1976).

9 Men such as Jack Buggy who had arrived in the UK as a member of the American Forces and settled in Glasgow before travelling to London and becoming involved in all manner of violent crime, in particular extortion. While serving time for a shooting, Buggy had become friendly with train robber Roy James, and on his release from prison set out to recover the robbers' share of the loot, which had been stolen. Buggy's body was recovered from the sea off the south coast in 1967 (Morton, 1993: 270–272).

10 Glaswegian gangster and robber Victor 'Scarface' Russo was a key figure in the Jack Spot vs. Billy Hill conflict in mid-1950s London (Hill, 1955).

11 Apart from acting as the Krays' doorman and bodyguard, Connelly also acted as an emissary between the Krays and Glaswegian villains, and this sometimes led to problems, a fact that was referred to by Reg Kray at his twin's funeral (see https://www.youtube.com/watch?v=2ULoWu9UXVI). Connelly only acquired a criminal record after meeting the Krays, and from 1957–1968 he was convicted of five offences including receiving stolen goods and possession of a firearm (CRO No22062/50 CRIM 1/4900). Barrie's criminal record (CRO 4953/64MEPO2/10922) indicates that his only pre-Kray era conviction was for vagrancy. However, in 1969 he was sentenced to life imprisonment with a recommendation that he serve at least 20 years in prison for his part in the murder of George Cornell. Dickson

company. They used them for debt (collecting)' (Paulie B). The Krays also employed Glaswegians as peripatetic specialists of violence (McKay, 2006: 65–68; Pearson, 1973: 185, 282–298), yet this violent specialism was more of an example of the advantages of distance and anonymity than an indication of pathology.[12]

Safe havens and state visits

Before budget airlines offered a safe haven in Amsterdam, Spain or Thailand, numerous Scottish criminals wanted by the police, or sought after by rivals, were offered sanctuary in London. Of these individuals, Jimmy Boyle is the most well-known, and writes of the way in which good relations between Glaswegian criminals and the Kray twins ensured a safe haven at times of strife. 'They looked after me very well while I was with them. They had plenty of respect in Scotland . . . and I thought highly of them' (Boyle, 1977: 168; see Mason, 1994: 184–187). Of those making the opposite journey, Andy Anderson, who had escaped from Wandsworth Prison in 1965 along with train robber Ronnie Biggs and another man, was spirited up to Edinburgh by Frank Fraser who used his connections to Glasgow's Arthur Thompson to keep Anderson out of harm's way for almost a year (Fraser, 1994: 201–205; McKay, 2006: 72–73). In 1991 Thompson's son 'Fatboy' was murdered and the funeral was attended by many London criminals and ex-criminals including train robber Buster Edwards, and Teddy Dennis a close friend of the Thompson family.[13] The connection between Thompson and Fraser had been made in the 1950s when Thompson had made regular sojourns to the capital, and when Thompson died in 1993 Fraser attended the funeral along with a wreath of 200 red roses (Fraser, 1994: 326–327).

State visits of the kind regularly performed by Fraser and other players of the 1950s and 1960s are referred to in various biographies and true-crime tomes, and are indicative of social as well as purely business motives. 'They (Scots) was Faces. They was known and respected, and they was all over the right places, especially in the West End. Big steady geezers who could look after themselves' (Terry). Birthdays, anniversaries and in particular funerals are well-attended by criminal players who exude a somewhat regal air in delivering bouquets, wreaths and especially elaborate brotherly hugs from 'our friends north or south of the border'. Suffice to say that

---

turned Queen's Evidence against the Krays and was rewarded with a token nine-month sentence (Dickson, 1986: 145–159).

12 Glaswegians with prominent facial scars made guest appearances in a variety of London-based TV crime series throughout the 1970s and 1980s, reinforcing the hardman stereotype. For instance, in the popular Soho-based television series *Budgie* (London Weekend Television, 1971–1972), a key character is a large intimidating Glaswegian named Charlie Endell, a criminal businessman involved in pornography, police corruption and various scams. While the programme was cancelled after 26 episodes due to the ill-health of the eponymous *Budgie*, played by Adam Faith, a short-lived spin-off series was produced by Scottish Television in the late 1970s entitled *Charles Endell Esquire*.

13 Dennis was a highly regarded West London 'Face', who at Ron Kray's 1995 funeral held hands over the coffin with representatives from North, South and East London 'as a symbol of peace'. See also Ferris and McKay (2005: 144).

I for one had never witnessed this latter theatrical device until after *Goodfellas* entered the criminal/thespian consciousness.

Consultancies

Although Glaswegian faces have continued to nurture these relationships, they are often no longer resident in Glasgow, and some of the more consistent illegal trading networks feature ostensibly retired gangsters residing in other parts of the UK or abroad acting as ciphers for hubs of networks. These Glaswegian ex-pats use reputations that were often acquired during the visceral and exceedingly local era of professional crime and lend an aura of trust and relative security to business arrangements that could otherwise be fragile. Collection and delivery of money, money laundering and the distribution of counterfeit currency have all in recent times been enhanced by the networked connections provided by ex-pat Scots operating relatively risk free at arms-length from direct criminal action. They are essentially consultants. As one London-based ex-armed robber explained of a sociable Glaswegian Face: 'He would never get at it himself not any more. But he is always helpful to people with a problem . . . He knows everybody, very dependable, and good company' (Marsh). Thanks in no small part to the prison system, these highly valued men have connections all over the UK, and the deviant ex-pat community has ensured that nodes of illegal commerce and leisure are well established in Europe and beyond. Similarly, these same Faces are able to lend their reputations to legal activities such as security and debt collection, and I found that in the case of the latter they can find themselves competing with other 'retired' Faces whose reputations carry considerable clout – even within some of the more ambiguous alcoves of the corporate world.

Change: another other

> Cities used to be islands in crime terms and few players travelled from one to another. (Ferris and McKay, 2005: 316)

Although London businesses had been voracious customers for stolen goods during an era when Glasgow and London seemed to be on different continents, changes in policing have been significant in dismantling some, but far from all, of the localism that has pervaded detective work from its very inception (Hobbs, 1988). One key change that has affected networks of theft and receiving is of course the creation of national police units and the construction of related databases, which has made the mere crossing of police borders somewhat less of a criminal masterstroke than in previous eras (Porter, 1996).

However, if we are serious about understanding the changing nature of crime, it is vital not to valorize the impact of law enforcement, for the market along with its social context needs to be examined. The decline of Britain's ports and dockside populations, and the obliteration of key interconnected sites of plunder such as ware-houses and lorry parks, coincided with the rise of the private security industry and technological advances that would have seemed akin to science fiction to both cops and robbers of the era of padlocks, barbed wire and nightwatchmen. Cheap imports have also affected the marketplace, making the theft and resale of everyday items such as clothing and alcohol cheaper than the contraband alternative. It is remark-able that criminologists in particular have ignored the joint impact of the decline of the opportunity for theft and the increased availability of legal and therefore risk-free cheap alternatives. While the onward rise of consumer culture (Hayward and Smith, 2017) assures that the allure of 'knock-off' alternatives will never disappear, the trade in illegal drugs has joined the booty of shoplifters and workplace thieves in the ver-nacular markets of back-street entrepreneurialism. However, unlike petty theft the drug trade implicates networks of a glocal as well as local nature, as drugs are traded and moved across continents and between regions and cities.

Scottish criminals remain part of the essential connective tissue of serious crime networks (Ferris and McKay, 2005: 15–18), and even in their active retirement have maintained strong social ties to London (Ferris and McKay, 2005). Several indi-viduals who remain active at some level of the contemporary crime scene were able to affirm that Scottish firms did, on occasion, work with dealers in the south east of England. However, most of these deals were conducted on a relatively ad hoc basis and were dependent purely upon the availability of the particular drug. This would appear to be particularly true in relation to relatively new commodities whose market was first developed outside of Scotland. For instance, in the 1990s a Scottish motorcycle group bypassed Manchester and Liverpool and purchased large amounts of ecstasy for the Scottish market from an overstocked London supplier. The con-nection was initially provided at a price by an ex-criminal with long established links to London and Scottish firms, and once the motorcyclists were established in the Scottish ecstasy market they were able to source supplies closer to home.

Relationships established during previous eras could be highly relevant with regard to new commodities, and this is certainly what occurred with regard to the demand for temazepam. Disparate firms from Manchester provided for the huge demand for the drug in Glasgow and Edinburgh, and when demand outstripped supply the same dealers along with firms from Glasgow and Edinburgh worked with significant players in London to provide the drug. As with ecstasy, relationships established in the 1990s have remained important in relation to a number of commodities, including firearms and cocaine. But with regard to Glasgow, links to Manchester, and to a lesser extent Liverpool (sometimes via other parts of the UK such as Middlesbrough), have proved to be significant.

Inter-city firms?

While the hierarchy of organized deviant ethnicities changes according to politi-cal contingencies and the subsequent campaigns of law enforcement agencies, the post-Industrial era has seen Glaswegian professional criminals overtaken by Liverpudlians in terms of the common perception of their prevalence in contemporary marketplaces (Pearson and Hobbs, 2001). While these perceptions create convenient cameos in the booming, low-budget, straight-to-DVD British crime film market (Pulver, 2015), they fail to reflect the cosmopolitan sensibilities apparent in sociologically influenced studies of indigenous crime networks. These studies (e.g. Silverstone and Savage, 2010) ignore the administrative drive that is central to most academic writings on TOC, and instead echo the unlicensed capitalism that defines so much of contemporary urban life, placing high value upon competent players whose ethnicity suggests strategic market connectivity. As a consequence, everyone now wants, 'a Turk on the firm' (Bovenkerk and Yesilgoz, 2007; Bovenkerk et al., 2003).

In the post-Industrial city market relations are central to the ethos of contemporary cultural communities. Unlike the underworld of professional criminals that was such a focus of Industrial era urban settings (Hobbs, 1995a), entrepreneurship rather than territoriality dominates both legal and illegal markets (Hobbs, 2013). Post-Industrial society has seen the breakdown of the traditional working class and the territories that defined them, and illegal commodities, services and the knowledge that sustains their associated commerce are now sourced widely, while criminal entrepreneurs are unrestrained by the defunct parameters of industrial working-class terrains.

Both affirmative and negative Othering and the creation of deviant stereotypes now need to be understood in the light of increased cosmopolitanism. This should also be seen in the context of the decline of the territorial imperative that generated so many enduring reputations, along with the rise of the entrepreneurial ethic (Hobbs, 1988, 1995a, 2013). Consequently, the significance of Scottish criminals operating in London has declined, and for London's criminal entrepreneurs their Scottish counterparts are no more or less important than players from other parts of the UK, some of whom are of non-British origins.

Conclusion: problematizing criminological categorization

a great deal of social scientists tend to describe the present as the dawn of a new epoch in human history, in one way or another marking a profound break with hitherto existing social structures of modern societies. (Osrecki, 2015: 131)

Apophenia

Organized crime, particularly its transnational variant, is but one of many silos created by coalitions of law enforcement, politicians and the odd grateful academic as part of the vocabulary of the post-Industrial cosmopolitan threat (Hobbs, 2013: 194–222) which now constitutes perils as diverse as the Taliban, Somali pirates and delinquent youth gangs (Cabinet Office Strategy Unit, 2009). These silos enable law enforcement to order and condense a disparate range of illegal entrepreneurial activity (Bauman, 1989: 44, 1991: 15), and in doing so empower a globalized law enforcement culture to structure a meta-order from both localized transgressive networks and chaotic clusters of post-industrial entities. The result is coherent, quantifiable, ordered, rational and predictable (Bauman, 1999: 79), and it is achieved by constructing meaningful patterns from data that is often random or tangential. Apophenia drives so much of our understanding of organized crime, making connections between individuals and groups that valorize what would in non-transgressive circumstances be regarded as insignificant. Apophenia is a vital precursor to the construction of a criminal case, where, while organized crime does not constitute a discrete legal category in its own right, the use of the term licenses state actors to ramp up the seriousness of the offence via the suggestion of identifiable patterns. By attempting to portray the chaotic nature of illegal markets in terms of what Shermer has termed 'patternicity', 'the tendency to find meaning-ful patterns in meaningless noise' (2008: n.p.),[14] law enforcement contrives in the creation of a meta-structure of transnational conspiracy. Further, this marking, framing and mapping (Perec, 1997: 91) of TOC makes the chaotic, fluid concept stable, durable (Latour, 1993) and ultimately politically expedient (Paoli, 2008).

Epochalism

While TOC confirms illegal trade as an external threat, rather than as an increas-ingly routine economic activity that pervades the UK (Marinetto, 2018), normaliza-tion provides the key to understanding the ever-mutating cluster of activities that have been crammed into the TOC silo (see also Hudson, Chapter 2 this volume). Yet while 'we lack political maps of our own backyards' (Cooke, 1988: 489), aca-demics, particularly those of the post-sociology of deviance era, tend to accom-modate the silos of knowledge relating to unlicensed trading within highly rigid criminological epochs. The subsequent academic products, some of which origi-nated in the corridors of government, should not be taken as literal epochalist models (Savage, 2009). For while 'sociological epochalisms can be regarded as a legitimate strategy of raising public awareness for sociological debates' (Osrecki, 2015), they constitute genres of reasoning that lack historical or cultural context and feature an absence of distinctly unambiguous categories. For instance, both industrialism and post-industrialism are processes that not only overlap but co-exist (Soja, 2011). Within post-industrial society mutating industrial cultures are now banished to the hinterlands, and the neighbourhoods from which urban working-class crime collaborations have traditionally emerged are subjected to a range of conflictual and complimentary processes. Consequently, the epochs of professional crime identified with pre-industrial and industrial society, and organ-ized and transnational crime identified with globalized post-industrial society, should be regarded as blurred genres with boundaries that deserve, indeed require, interrogation. That their host communities are housed in territories vulnerable to intrusion (Bauman, 2000: 113), and with mutating boundaries that no longer

---

14 Levi described organized crime as being like the Rorschach blot, whose 'attraction as well as . . . weakness is that one can read almost anything into it' (2002: 887).

benefit from the regulatory rigours of Fordism (Bauman, 2000: 56), settlement and class homogeneity, feels like a dated cliché (Young and Willmott, 1957) as the ebb, flow and churn of 'subaltern insurgent cosmopolitanism' (Harvey, 2009: 283) create new challenges for academics (see Back and Sinha, 2018). The hard facts of work and housing have been more influential upon the lived realities of working people and their subsequent adaptations, of which crime is but one, than the enforced categorizations brought about by political, administrative and academic convenience.

Formulated by academics, and often supported by state institutions, these official categories are seldom acknowledged by proponents of transgression. For the messy realities, shifting identities and fluid economies of the post-industrial city produce deviant forms that tend to fall outside of political or administratively convenient categories that, for anyone genuinely seeking to understand those who operate in and around criminal markets, are as much use as a chocolate teapot. Post-industrial lives are not as conveniently ordered (Winlow and Hall, 2006) as suggested by the transplantation, and then elaboration, of organized crime narratives and law enforcement strategies originating in the USA. But criminology is a predominantly administrative field and as we see from the UK's construction of the organized crime problem, its utility by policy makers, especially at the initial stage of problem construction, often entails crude racial stereotypes and the racialization of criminal activity (Hall et al., 1978; Monrose, 2016). However, as discussed in the section regarding Scottish criminals, if academics could reverse their adherence to official sources it can be seen that criminal cultures have their own way of utilizing Othering, affording pragmatic racial characteristics in a manner that generates and valorizes competent practice.

Although the rapidly changing post-industrial milieu has rendered many criminological categorizations problematic, their dominance in curricula and textbooks can be attributed to the emergence of criminology as a self-contained discipline whose self-imposed parameters are generated by market-led criminological concerns (Hobbs, 2013). However, gentrification, rehousing and a proletarian residue constantly enhanced by a shifting churning cosmopolitan population have created a chaotic contemporary urban milieu that can no longer rely upon the predictability that emanated from settled working-class neighbourhoods imbued with the restraints, certainties and hierarchies of industrial society of which the professional criminal underworld was a product (Hobbs, 1995a). The contemporary amorphous, 'liquid', loose-knit trading milieu blends the post-industrial epoch with elements of its 'solid' predecessor, constituting a wide-based community of practice supplemented by a churning cosmopolitanism, rather than by racially defined criminal hierarchies based upon Othering (Hobbs, 2013).[15]

---

15 The appetite for criminological cliché is voracious. A researcher contacted me recently asking me about the Italian Mafia's influence on London's organized crime scene. I explained that this influence was negligible, but that he should perhaps look at London's financial market, and in particular London's role in laundering dirty money. This was not what he wanted to hear and he demanded documentary proof that the Mafia were not active on London's streets. When organized crime is invisible it is often taken as proof of the success of a clandestine phenomenon (Van Duyne, 1996).

TOC should not negate local actions and interpretations but instead stress the influence of globalization upon the local social order (Hobbs and Hobbs, 2012; Robertson, 1992, 1995). For global forces operationalize local identities and cultures (Bauman, 1998) and shape socio-economic spaces and places that are essentially local readings of global markets (Robins, 1991). As a self-contained category, transnational organized crime and its accompanying epoch attempt to manage the unpredictable forces unleashed by post-industrialism (Bauman, 2000: 3). However, while the term suppresses the chaotic nature of the multiple groups and individuals who are immersed in illegal markets, it succeeds in corralling and systemizing a disparate range of entrepreneurial activity and contributes to the imposition of a universal transgressive social order.

The tendency of much academic discourse to adopt a particularly rigid model of criminological epochs fails to reflect the messy realities of urban life, the constant churn of its population and the ever-mutating nature of the economies that underpin everyday life. Indeed, criminology has been notably remiss in locating deviant behaviour as a mere component of banal urban existence, preferring to focus upon legally defined criminal action rather than the mundane rule infraction that pervades post-industrial society (Hall et al., 2008). For it is the accumulation of these everyday examples of unlicensed capitalism that constitutes the vocabularies of meta-narratives such as transnational organized crime and the epoch in which it sits. By ignoring the inconvenient truths of everyday urban life, and by obsessing upon the leaky umbrella of transnational organized crime, criminology avoids having to deal with seemingly eccentric reactions such as positive Othering. Indeed, any academic discipline that swerves the rich ambiguity of ethnographically derived data is vulnerable to administrative orientated generalized conceits and fictions. Epochs overlap, conflict and compliment, and should be regarded as lazy generalizations contrived as a way of avoiding the dirty details integral to the socio-spatial minutiae of diverse economies (Hudson, 2009; Leyshon et al., 2003).

References

Agozino, B. (2000), 'Theorizing Otherness, the war on drugs and incarceration', *Theoretical Criminology*, 4 (3), 359–376.

Albini, J. (1971), *The American Mafia: Genesis of a Legend*. New York: Appleton-Century-Crofts.

Atkinson, P. (1990), *The Ethnographic Imagination*. London: Routledge.

Back, L. and Sinha, S. (2018), *Migrant City*. London: Routledge.

Bauman, Z. (1989), *Legislators and Interpreters*. Cambridge: Polity.

Bauman, Z (1991), *Modernity and Ambivalence*. Ithaca, NY: Cornell University Press.

Bauman, Z. (1998), *Globalisation: The Human Consequences*. Cambridge: Polity.

Bauman, Z. (1999), *In Search of Politics*. Cambridge: Polity.

Bauman, Z. (2000), *Liquid Modernity*. Cambridge: Polity.

Bauman, Z. (2004), *Identity*. Cambridge: Polity.

Becker, H. (ed.) (1964), *The Other Side*. New York: Macmillan.

Behr, E. (1996), *Prohibition: Thirteen Years that Changed America*. New York: Arcade Publishing.

Bell, D. (1953), 'Crime as an American way of life', *The Antioch Review*, 13, 131–154.

Bigo, B. (1994), 'The European internal security field: stakes and rivalries in a newly developing area of police intervention', in Anderson, M. and den Boer, M. (eds), *Policing Across National Boundaries*. London: Pinter, pp. 161–173.

Bigo, D. (2000), 'When two becomes one: internal and external securitizations in Europe', in Kelstrup, M. and Williams, M. C. (eds), *International Relations Theory and the Politics of European Integration. Power, Security and Community*. London and New York: Routledge, pp. 171–204.

Block, A. (1983), *East Side-West Side: Organizing Crime in New York, 1930–1950*. Newark, NJ: Transaction.

Block, A. and Chambliss, W. (1981), *Organizing Crime*. New York: Elsevier.

Bourdieu, P. (2003), *Firing Back: Against the Tyranny of the Market 2*. London: Verso.

Bovenkerk, F. and Yesilgoz, Y. (2007), *The Turkish Mafia*. Liverpool: Milo.

Bovenkerk, F., Siegel, D. and Zaitch, D. (2003), 'Organised crime and ethnic reputation manipulation', *Crime, Law & Social Change*, 39, 23–38.

Bowling, B. and Ross, J. (2006), 'The Serious Organised Crime Agency: should we be afraid?', *Criminal Law Review*, December, 1019–1034.

Boyle, J. (1977), *A Sense of Freedom*. London: Pan.

Cabinet Office Strategy Unit (2009), *Extending our Reach: A Comprehensive Approach to Tackling Serious Organised Crime*. Norwich: The Stationary Office.

Campbell, D. (1991), *That Was Business, This is Personal: The Changing Faces of Professional Crime*. London: Mandarin.

Carrabine, E. (2015), 'Contemporary criminology and the sociological imagination', in Frauley, J. (ed.), *C. Wright Mills and the Criminological Imagination Prospects for Creative Inquiry*. Farnham: Ashgate Publishing, pp. 73–98.

Carrabine, E. (2016), 'Changing fortunes: criminology and the sociological condition', *Sociology*, 50 (5), 847–862.

Carrabine, E. (2017), *Crime and Social Theory*. London: Palgrave.

Cohen, S. (1971), 'Introduction', in Cohen, S. (ed.), *Images of Deviance*. Harmondsworth: Penguin, pp. 9–24.

Cohen, S. (1974), 'Criminology and the sociology of deviance in Britain', in Rock, P. and McIntosh, M. (eds), *Deviance and Social Control*. London: Tavistock, pp. 1–40.

Cooke, P. (1988), 'Modernity, postmodernity and the city', *Theory Culture and Society*, 5 (2–3), 475–492.

Cressey, D. (1969), *Theft of the Nation: The Structure and Operations of Organized Crime in America*. New York: Harper and Row.

Dickson, J. (1986), *Murder Without Conviction*. London: Sidgwick and Jackson.

Ditton, J. (1977), *Part Time Crime: An Ethnography of Fiddling and Pilferage*. London: Macmillan.

Downes, D. (1966), *The Delinquent Solution: A Study in Subcultural Theory*, London: Routledge and Kegan Paul.

Dunnighan, C. and Hobbs, D. (1996), *A Report on the NCIS Pilot Organised Crime Notification Survey*. London: Home Office. (Unpublished.)

Edwards, A. and Gill. P. (eds) (2003), *Transnational Organised Crime: Perspectives on Global Security*. London: Routledge.

Edwards, A. and Levi, M. (2008), 'Researching the organisation of serious crimes', *Criminology and Criminal Justice*, 8 (4), 363–388.

Elvins, M. (2003), 'Europe's response to transnational organised crime', in Edwards, A. and Elwood, W. (1994), *Rhetoric in the War on Drugs: The Triumphs and Tragedies of Public Relations*. Westport, CT and London: Praeger.

Ferris, P. and McKay. R. (eds), *Vendetta*. Edinburgh: Black and White Publishing.

Findlay, M. (2008), *Governing through Globalised Crime*. Cullhompton: Willan.

Fraser, F. (1994), *Mad Frank*. London: Little Brown.

Gregory, F. (2003), 'Classify, report and measure: the UK Organised Crime Notification Scheme', in Edwards, A. and Gill, P. (eds), *Transnational Organised Crime*. London: Routledge, pp. 78–96.

Hall, S. (2012), *Theorizing Crime and Deviance: A New Perspective*. London: Sage.

Hall, S., Winlow, S. and Ancrum, C. (2008), *Criminal Identities and Consumer Culture: Crime, Exclusion and the New Culture of Narcissism*. London: Willan.

Hall, S., Critcher, C., Jefferson, T., Clarke, J. and Roberts, B. (1978), *Policing the Crisis: Mugging, the State, and Law and Order*. London: Palgrave Macmillan.

Haller, M. (1985), 'Bootleggers as businessmen: from city slums to city builders', in Kyvig, D. (ed.), *Law, Alcohol, and Order: Perspectives on National Prohibition*, Westport, CT: Greenwood, pp. 139–157.

Harfield, C. (2008), 'Paradigms, pathologies, and practicalities – policing organized crime in England and Wales', *Policing*, 2 (1), 63–73.

Harvey, D. (2009), *Cosmopolitanism and the Geographies of Freedom*. New York: Columbia University Press.

Hayward, K. and Smith, O. (2017), 'Crime and consumer culture', in Liebling, A., Maruna, S. and McAra, L. (eds), *The Oxford Handbook of Criminology*. Oxford: Oxford University Press, pp. 306–325.

Hill, B. (1955), *Boss of Britain's Underworld*. London: Naldrett Press.

Hirst, P. (1975), 'Marx and Engels on law, crime and morality', in Taylor, I., Walton, P. and Young, J. (eds), *Critical Criminology*. London: Routledge and Kegan Paul.

Hobbs, D. (1988), *Doing the Business: Entrepreneurship, the Working Class and Detectives in the East End of London*. Oxford: Oxford University Press.

Hobbs, D. (1995a), *Bad Business: Professional Crime in Modern Britain*. Oxford: Oxford University Press.

Hobbs, D. (ed.) (1995b), *Professional Crime*. Dartmouth, MA: International Library of Criminology, Criminal Justice and Penology.

Hobbs, D. (1998), 'Going down the glocal: the local context of organised crime', *The Howard Journal*, Special Issue on Organised Crime, 37 (4), 407–422.

Hobbs, D. (2013), *Lush Life: Constructing Organised Crime in the UK*. Oxford: Oxford University Press.

Hobbs, D. and Dunnighan, C. (1998a), 'Organised crime and the organisation of police intelligence', in Carlen, P. and Morgan, R. (eds), *Crime Unlimited*. London: Routledge, pp. 57–75.

Hobbs, D. and Dunnighan, C. (1998b), 'Glocal organised crime: context and pretext', in Ruggiero, V., South, N. and Taylor, I. (eds), *The New European Criminology*. London: Routledge, pp. 289–303.

Hobbs, D. and Hobbs, S. (2012), 'A bog of conspiracy: the institutional evolution of organised crime in the UK', in Allum, F. and Gilmour, S. (eds), *The Handbook of Transnational Organized Crime*. London: Routledge.

Hobsbawm, E. (1994), *The Age of Extremes*. Harmondsworth: Penguin.

Home Affairs Committee (1994), *Organised Crime: Minutes and Memoranda*. London: Home Office.

Hudson, R. (2009), 'Life on the edge: navigating the competitive tensions between the "social" and the "economic" in the social economy and in its relations to the mainstream', *Journal of Economic Geography*, 9 (4), 493–510.

Karraker, C. (1953), *Piracy was a Business*. Rindge, NH: Richard R. Smith.

Katz, J. (1975), 'Essences as moral identities: on verifiability and responsibility in imputations of deviance and charisma', *American Journal of Sociology*, 80 (May), 1369–1390.

Kennedy, L. (1976), *Presumption of Innocence: The Amazing Case of Patrick Meehan*. London: HarperCollins.

Kitsuse, John. I. and Cicourel, Aaron, V. (1963), 'A note on the uses of official statistics', *Social Problems*, 11, 131–139.

Knepper, P. (2007), 'British Jews and the racialisation of crime in the age of Empire', *British Journal of Criminology*, 47 (1), 61–79.

Kyvig, D. (2000), *Repealing National Prohibition*, 2nd edn. Kent, OH: Kent State University Press.

Latour, B. (1993), *We Have Never Been Modern*. London: Harvester Wheatsheaf.

Levi, M. (2002) 'The organization of serious crimes', in Maguire, M., Morgan, R. and Reiner, R. (eds), *The Oxford Handbook of Criminology*. Oxford: Oxford University Press.

Levi, M. (2005), 'The making of the United Kingdom's organised crime policies', in Fijnaut, C. and Paoli, L. (eds), *Organised Crime in Europe*. Netherlands: Springer, pp. 823–852.

Leyshon, A., Lee, R. and Williams, C. C. (eds) (2003), *Alternative Economic Spaces*. London: Sage.

Marinetto, M. (2018), 'What Britain's organised criminals think of Brexit', *New Statesman*, 12 March.

Marotta, V. (2002), 'Zygmunt Bauman: order, strangerhood and freedom', *Thesis Eleven*, 70 (August), 36–54.

Maruna, S. (2008), 'Review symposium: Merton with energy, Katz with structure, Jock Young with data', *Theoretical Criminology*, 12 (4), 534–539.

Mason, E. (1994), *Inside Story*. London: Pan.

Matza, D. (1969), *Becoming Deviant*. Englewood Cliffs, NJ: Prentice Hall.

McKay, R. (2006), *The Last Godfather: The Life and Crimes of Arthur Thompson*. Edinburgh: Black and White Publishing.

Mena, F. and Hobbs, D. (2010), 'Narcophobia: drugs prohibition and the generation of human rights abuses', *Trends in Organised Crime*, 13 (1), 60–74.

Monrose, K. (2016), 'Struggling, juggling and street corner hustling: the street economy of Newham's Black community', in Antonopoulos, G. (ed.), *Illegal Entrepreneurship, Organized Crime and Social Control Essays in Honor of Professor Dick Hobbs*. Switzerland: Springer, pp. 73–85.

Moore, W. (1974), *Kefauver and the Politics of Crime*. Columbus: University of Missouri Press.

Morton, J. (1993), *Gangland: London's Underworld*. London: Warner Books.

NCIS (1993a), *An Outline Assessment of the Threat and Impact by Organised/Enterprise Crime Upon United Kingdom Interests*. London: NCIS.

NCIS (1993b), *Organised Crime Conference: A Threat Assessment*. London: NCIS.

NCIS (2000), *An Outline Assessment of the Threat and Impact by Organised/Enterprise Crime Upon United Kingdom Interests*. London: NCIS.

Osrecki, F. (2015), 'Constructing epochs: the argumentative structures of sociological epochalisms', *Cultural Sociology*, 9 (2), 131–146.

Paoli, L. (2008), Keynote lecture: 'Organized crime: a new label, new phenomenon or policy expedient?' World Congress of the International Society of Criminology.

Pearson, G. and Hobbs, D. (2001), *Middle Market Drug Distribution*. Home Office Research Study No. 227. London: Home Office.

Pearson, J. (1973), *The Profession of Violence*. London: Granada.

Perec, G. (1997), *Species of Spaces and Other Pieces*. Harmondsworth: Penguin.

Picketing, M. (2001), *Stereotyping and the Politics of Representation*. Houndmills: Macmillan.

Porter, M. (1996), *Tackling Cross Border Crime*. Crime Detection and Prevention Series Paper 79. London: Home Office.

Potter, G. W. (1994), *Criminal Organisations*. Long Grove, IL: Waveland Press.

Pulver, A. (2015), 'Gangsters, geezers and guns: the men behind Britain's booming low-budget crime-flick industry'. *The Guardian*, 2 April.

Radzinowicz, L. (1961), 'The study of criminology in Cambridge', *The Medico-Legal Journal*, 29 (3), 122–133.

Radzinowicz, L. (1972), 'Them and us', *Cambridge Law Journal*, 30, 260–279.

Radzinowicz, L. (1988), *The Cambridge Institute of Criminology: Its Background and Scope*. London: HMSO.

Robertson, R. (1992), 'Globality and modernity', *Theory Culture and Society*, 9 (2), 153–161.

Robertson, R. (1995), 'Glocalisation: time-space and homogeneity-heterogeneity', in Featherstone, M., Lash, S. and Robertson, R. (eds), *Global Modernities*. London: Sage, pp. 25–44.

Robins, K. (1991), 'Tradition and translation: national culture in its global context', in Corner, J. and

Harvey, S. (eds), *Enterprise and Heritage: Crosscurrents of National Culture*. London: Routledge, pp. 21–44.

Rock, P. (1973), *Making People Pay*. London: Routledge and Kegan Paul.

Rock, P. (2005), 'Chronocentrism and British criminology', *British Journal of Sociology*, 56 (3), 473–491.

Savage, S. (2009), 'Against epochalism: an analysis of conceptions of change in British Sociology', *Cultural Sociology*, 3 (2), 217–238.

Sheptycki, J. (1995), 'Transnational policing and the making of a postmodern state', *British Journal of Criminology*, 35 (4), 613–635.

Sheptycki, J. (1998), 'The global cops cometh: reflections on transnationalization', *British Journal of Sociology*, 49 (1), 57–74.

Shermer, M. (2008), 'Patternicity: finding meaningful patterns in meaningless noise: why the brain believes something is real when it is not', *Scientific American*, 299 (5): no page. https://www.scientificamerican.com/article/patternicity-finding-meaningful-patterns/ (accessed 21 May 2018).

Sillitoe, P. (1955), *Cloak Without Dagger*. London: Cassells & Co.

Silverstone, D. and Savage, S. (2010), 'Farmers, factories and funds: organised crime and illicit drugs cultivation within the British Vietnamese community', *Global Crime*, 11 (1), 16–33.

Slater, S. (2007), 'Pimps, police and filles de joie: foreign prostitution in interwar London', *The London Journal*, 32 (1), 53–74.

Smith, D. (1975), *The Mafia Mystique*. New York: Basic Books.

Smith, D. Jr. (1980), 'Paragons, pariahs, and pirates: a spectrum-based theory of enterprise', *Crime and Delinquency*, 26, 358–386.

Smithies, E. (1982), *Crime in Wartime*. Sydney and London: Allen and Unwin.

Soja, E. (2011), *Postmodern Geographies*. London: Verso.

Spradley, J. P. (1979), *The Ethnographic Interview*. New York: Wadsworth Group/Thomas Learning.

Sumner, C. (1994), *The Sociology of Deviance: An Obituary*. Buckingham: Open University Press.

Taylor, I., Walton, P. and Young, J. (1973), *The New Criminology*. London: Routledge and Kegan Paul.

Thomas, D. (2003), *An Underworld at War*. London: John Murray.

US Senate (1951), *Special Committee to Investigate Organized Crime in Interstate Commerce*. New York: Didier.

Van Duyne, P. C. (1996), 'The phantom and threat of organized crime', *Crime, Law and Social Change*, 24 (4), 341–377.

Van Duyne, P. C. (2011), *(Transnational) Organised Crime, Laundering and the Congregation of the Gullible*. Valedictory, 14 March 2011, Tilburg University.

Winlow, S. and Hall, S. (2006), *Violent Night: Urban Leisure and Contemporary Culture*. Oxford: Berg.

Woodiwiss, M. (1988), *Crime, Crusades and Corruption: Prohibitions in the United States, 1900–1987*. London: Pinter.

Woodiwiss, M. (1993), 'Crime's global reach', in Pearce, F. and Woodiwiss, M. (eds), *Global Crime Connections*. London: Macmillan, pp. 1–31.

Woodiwiss, M. and Hobbs, D. (2009), 'Organized evil and the Atlantic alliance: moral panics and the rhetoric of organized crime policing in America and Britain', *British Journal of Criminology*, 49 (1), 106–128.

Young, M. and Wilmott, P. (1957), *Family and Kinship in East London*. London: Routledge and Kegan Paul.

4 War, terrorism and criminal justice

John Lea

Introduction

The present period seems to be one of intensification of international armed conflict. Much of this increase has taken the form of civil wars and a major focus has been the Middle East and sub-Saharan Africa. The period 2011–17 saw a sixfold increase in battle deaths and a recent United Nations study noted that conflicts 'are becoming more intractable and less conducive to traditional political settlements' (von Einsiedel 2017: 4). The same study noted that the death rate of civilian non-combatants was also at an all-time high.

International criminal justice has a precariousness not shared by domestic criminal justice systems. For the latter, however high the crime rate within the territory of a state, criminal justice remains the only agency of legitimate response. Alternatives such as citizens' vigilante organizations are no longer officially tolerated and their activity is itself regarded as criminal, not to say a symptom of social breakdown. International criminal justice is different. Warfare between states remains as not only an alternative to courts and prosecutions but one that has a far longer pedigree and high status. In areas where states have collapsed civil wars involve varieties of powerful 'vigilante' non-state actors. Furthermore, unlike any domestic criminal justice system international criminal justice faces the distinction between war as such and the legitimate conduct of warfare. To criminalize certain modes of conducting war as war crime, or crimes against humanity (jus in bello) is one thing. The attempt to criminalize war as such (jus ad bellum) is entirely another. Against such a background and in the context of current serious armed conflicts, it is pertinent to ask what has happened to international criminal justice.

Nuremberg, the United Nations and the post-war settlement

The period immediately following the Second World War saw major developments aimed at placing armed conflict beyond the law as a method of settling disputes between states and there were major advances in the formulation of human rights delegitimizing armed force. The 1946 Nuremberg (and Tokyo) trials of the leaders of the Axis powers declared aggressive war as the 'supreme international crime' and also that those organizing it could be held individually responsible, as in normal crime.

The UN Charter of 1945 prohibited recourse to international armed force (Article 2(4)) except in self-defence under 'armed attack' (Article 51) and then only while the UN Security Council Military Staff Committee mobilized resources from member states to act as a police force and intervene to stop the conflict. Nuremberg and the Charter provided for a comprehensive ban on warfare as a method of settling disputes between states (see Degenhardt 2015: 144).

The second, parallel element of what can be called the post-war settlement concerned human rights. Nuremberg had made it clear that political leaders could be put on trial by international tribunals for crimes against humanity committed against their own citizens in addition to war against other states. The 1948 UN Universal Declaration of Human Rights was progressively developed in a variety of treaties and agreements. The European Convention on Human Rights backed by the European Court of Human Rights (ECtHR) is a comprehensive statement covering protections against 'inhuman or degrading treatment or punishment' and slavery, the right to life, security, liberty, privacy, freedom of expression and association, to a fair trial. In the same year the UN adopted the1948 Convention on the Prevention and Punishment of the Crime of Genocide.

Of particular importance in the European Convention is the right to life (Article 2) which stipulates that lethal force, e.g. by police, is lawful only as a last resort when other means such as arrest or non-lethal incapacitation are absent. This is quite central for the shifting of war into the sphere of crime. The traditional 'law of war' based on the Geneva Conventions usually known today as 'International Humanitarian Law' (IHL) which applies in situations of military conflict permits deliberate killing provided it is against military targets and is part of a force proportionate to the threat. International Human Rights Law (IHRL) on the other hand sees force only as a last resort and also guarantees a fair trial. To the extent that state armed action is still seen as war then both sets of rights may be applied and may conflict. This conflict has become more important in recent years as we shall see.

Criminal justice requires courts and prosecutions. The Cold War effectively delayed development in this area and it was not until 2002 that the International Criminal Court (ICC), which can be seen as the much-delayed legacy of the Nuremberg tribunal, came into effect, though there have been a number of preceding tribunals for particular conflicts – such as in Yugoslavia and Rwanda – under UN auspices. The ICC will, however, only be able to act on the crime of aggressive war itself, the key Nuremberg inheritance, as from July 2018 following final agreement by the states supporting the court, on an acceptable definition (see Ferencz 2015).

Initial problems for international justice

There were, nevertheless, problems built into the Nuremberg and UN settlements which have become arguably more important in recent decades. The first problem concerns bias in the remit of the Nuremberg tribunal itself. Given the horrendous nature of Nazi crimes this may seem implausible. But the eminent lawyer Hans Kelsen saw Nuremberg as bad legal precedent because it did not function as an impartial court and prosecution system but focused purely on German atrocities, while ignoring those of the Allies (e.g. the bombing of Dresden and the horrors of Hiroshima and Nagasaki). The tribunal thus became, in Kelsen's opinion, in effect a form of 'victor's justice' or the continuation of hostilities by other means. This problem would return later as a criticism, for example, of the International Criminal Tribunal for Former Yugoslavia which from 1993 proceeded to arraign the President of Serbia and various lesser military and political figures for war crimes while ignoring violations by NATO forces. In the opinion of Danilo Zolo 'a dual-standard system of international criminal justice has come about in which a justice "made to measure" for the major world powers and their victorious leaders operates alongside a separate justice for the defeated and downtrodden' (Zolo 2009: 31).

A second problem concerns enforcement, not only of the judgements of international courts and tribunals but also against states that violate the UN prohibition on the use of armed force except in temporary self-defence. The initial idea of a UN Military Staff Committee directing a permanent UN military force rapidly gave way to dependence on the member states to provide military and police resources to enforce UN interventions in conflict zones. In fact, with the changed nature of war – discussed presently – the dependence on member states to provide 'boots on the ground' proved less of a problem. But that presupposes that the UN is actually able to come to a consensus. The fact that some states are more powerful than others was given de facto recognition in the formation of the UN Security Council currently composed of five permanent members: China, France, the Russian Federation, the United Kingdom and the United States, plus ten non-permanent members elected for two-year terms. Each of the permanent members have a veto on Security Council actions and there is much criticism that large states from the global south, India for example, are not members. Zolo's argument is perhaps evidenced in the fact that notwithstanding the UN Charter the major powers rapidly proceeded to use military force in pursuit of their global interests. US action in Korea, Vietnam, Cambodia, Panama and elsewhere and the Soviet invasion of Hungary and Czechoslovakia are major examples which serve to illustrate the weakness of the system (Jacoby 2007; Parmar 2018). But despite these limitations, the criminalization of war was on the agenda and 'by the early 1990s, after the Cold War had ended and the Berlin Wall had been torn down, the liberal Anglo-American vision of a rules-based international system appeared to be becoming a reality, albeit an imperfect one' (Sands 2005: 13).

The foundations of the post-war settlement

Despite all the events since the end of the Cold War, optimists continue to emphasize the potential for further development (Archibugi and Pease 2018). Others have commented on the particular conditions that underpinned the post-war settlement and their exhaustion in the current period.

> For the era of the Cold War and the non-aligned stance of a growing bloc of former colonies and dependencies that lends meaning to the notion of a Third World, were compromises, in which the West recognised the reality and by implication, legitimacy, of the organisation of blocs against it, just as the capitalist class recognised the existence of organised labour. All negotiation through the era of what I call corporate liberalism (roughly from the 1930s and 40s to the 1980s) was premised on the sovereign equality of the other side. It was this recognition that was abandoned in neoliberalism. (van der Pijl 2013)

The idea of a community of states which, whatever their differences and conflicts, recognize one another as legitimate entities whose interests need to be taken seriously and compromised through trade and diplomacy as far as possible, can be seen as the best underpinning for the criminalization of warfare. The Cold War years (1947–91) were a period of anxiety but the West did not seek to deny the USSR the status of legitimate state with interests that had to be recognized. A passing familiarity with the espionage thrillers of John le Carré serves as ample illustration.

Added to this was a widespread expectation that continuous global economic expansion would produce a gradual equalization of levels of economic development between the West (the US and Western Europe) and the rest of the world (Rostow 1962). In particular, the ending of colonial empires and the welcoming of former colonies as new sovereign states led by 'modernising elites' (Deutsch 1966) would displace both wars of imperialist conquest on the one hand and national liberation struggles on the other by a process of accommodation and adjustment in which the US would play a leading part. As already noted, this was more optimistic than the facts warranted.

Furthermore, an important effect of post-war economic expansion, full employment and the growth of consumer society lay in fostering a decline in militarism as a component of national culture and the consolidation of a 'post-military society' (Shaw 1991) in which war was seen as increasingly tangential to the pursuit of national interests through diplomacy and trade. Internal and international developments would hopefully reinforce each other. Recognition, within states, of the legitimacy of different social classes and their interests as occasions for compromise rather than conflict would reinforce the recognition of the legitimacy of other states and the methods of diplomacy and trade rather than armed conflict. Both domestically and internationally, serious crime and serious conflict would be the exception rather than a normal form of social or international relations. In both cases such conflict would be relatively easy to criminalize and act against on the basis of consensus. The public would support the police against criminal deviance while the community of states would support UN action against deviant rogue states and states would have collaborated to effectively marginalize non-state criminal actors such as terrorists and organized crime. Things have turned out rather differently.

New world disorder

The period of sustained economic growth gradually slowed from the mid-1970s. The subsequent period of neoliberalism has been characterized by a general return to emphasis on the free market and the pursuit of national interests by powerful states. It has also been a period of slow growth and economic downturns of which the most recent was the financial crisis of 2008. This has created a contradictory environment both more obstructive to the development of international criminal justice while at the same time creating new situations amenable to crime control rather than warfare. There are several factors at work.

First, the slowing of economic growth and the squeeze on corporate profits (Roberts 2016) has provoked leading industrial states such as the US to become more aggressive on behalf of their corporations to secure resources and market opportunities and at the same time impede the growth of rival states. For a long time this was facilitated by the collapse of the USSR in 1991 which left the US in the position of global hegemon with virtually unchecked power to pursue its interests including through aggressive war. The UN and the institutions of international justice were progressively backgrounded as Afghanistan, Iraq, Libya and latterly Syria have felt the effects of unmediated US military might deployed in the last analysis to guarantee domination over oil resources.

States incurring US displeasure such as Russia, China, Iran and Syria were characterized negatively as 'regimes' by reference to their present leadership, implied as temporary or abnormal. Thus, Syria has become 'the Assad regime' and Russia the 'Putin regime' (see Cohen 2011). In this way the US withdraws effective legitimacy from states not under its direct influence (van der Pijl 2006, 2013). If any state that the US or its allies dislike is pre-emptively criminalized as some variety of 'rogue regime' a suitable candidate for 'regime change', then the whole strategy of criminalization becomes politicized and absorbed by the leading states into their arsenal of coercive measures alongside, rather than as an alternative to, warfare. As we shall note presently, the working of the ICC has faced precisely this problem.

Second, the hoped-for assimilation of the global south to the political and socio-economic structures of the leading industrial states, anticipated during the 1950s and 1960s, has been a process of differentiation. While some states such as China have begun to assimilate, and indeed to challenge US global dominance, others have fallen behind. In the poorest states of the south, in sub-Saharan Africa for example, massive internal inequality and social polarization combined with the diffusion of mass media have created an acute sense of relative deprivation among the population which, combined with anger at the military policies of the powerful states under US leadership, has led to increasing 'revolt from the margins' (Rogers 2010).

The result has been a new world disorder exemplified in the changing nature of warfare. Many of the poorest states are ravaged by poverty, corruption, organized crime and intermittent civil war. These 'new wars' (Kaldor 1999), not between states but resulting from state collapse and frequently oriented to ethnic cleansing and genocide, are fought by mixtures of guerrilla militias, mercenaries, state militaries, drugs and arms traffickers and criminal gangs, with clandestine support from transnational mineral corporations, global cybercriminal networks and other non-state actors. Although Kaldor's (1999) iconic study of new wars was based on the collapse of Yugoslavia following the dissolution of the USSR, the majority of new wars are in the poor states of the global south, Southeast Asia, the Middle East and sub-Saharan Africa.

The term 'new wars' is probably too general to cover the variety of armed conflicts currently underway in these states. There are at least three varieties. First, local insurgent forces fight a central government directly backed by US military. The Taliban in Afghanistan is the main current example. Second, in Syria, for example, the official government military, supported by Russian, Iranian and Lebanese forces, is engaged in armed conflict with several different elements. These involve internationally recruited Islamist Jihadi militias notably 'Islamic State' (IS) and Al-Qaeda aiming to establish an Islamic Caliphate on the territories of Syria and Iraq, Kurdish militia groups aiming to defend and extend territory for a future state of Kurdistan, and US military acting both against the Islamic militias (though uninvited by the Syrian government) and also against the Syrian government itself, though avoiding (so far) direct military contact with government forces and their Russian allies. A third variety can be seen in the various civil wars in sub-Saharan Africa characterized by three-way conflicts between weak government forces and insurgent militias who also fight each other for territory. An important current example is the Democratic Republic of the Congo (Burke 2018) The insurgent militias may be covertly supported by mineral extraction transnational corporations aiming to secure access to diamonds and precious metals. In some African conflicts the US has intervened directly (e.g. in Somalia) assimilating the situation to the Afghanistan model but in others national government forces are supplemented by South African based mercenary and private military organizations with UN peacekeeping operations (see below) attempting to enforce both the cessation of armed hostilities and social re-stabilization.

But new wars are not just characterized by imploding states. They are, particularly in the Middle East variant, associated with a new wave of globally organized terrorism. Contrast the localized nature of the Afghan Taliban, fighting a foreign invader (the US-led coalition), with globally recruited Jihadi groups such as IS and Al-Qaeda that fight governments and their allies in collapsed or weak states across the Middle East and at the same time recruit from global networks of supporters prepared not only to travel to these regions as mercenaries but also to engage in terrorist actions in their European home countries. Radical Jihadi Islam has succeeded in achieving a degree of ideological hegemony over the 'revolt from the margins' and linking disaffected and marginalized youth both in the industrial north and global south with a vision of a global defence of the Muslim world against the US and its local allies in the Middle East (see Githens-Mazer 2008). A key aspect of this global network war (Arquilla et al. 2003) has been terrorism as a form of asymmetric warfare (Mohamedou 2007) utilizing both armed military confrontation in the Middle East and urban outrages in the US and Europe using the panic of populations caused by bombs and killings as a tool to fight their governments. As such it is both an easily identifiable war crime and in the domestic context a clear case of conspiracy to murder. The question is, which of these two perspectives comes to predominate. In many respects, as we shall see, terrorism is the 'Achilles heel' of change not only within international criminal justice but substantial aspects of domestic criminal justice as well.

Varieties of intervention

The new world disorder has set up contradictory pressures which both impede and facilitate the development of international criminal justice. On the one hand, global inequality both within and between states has made it easier for powerful states such as the US to assert their interests globally by the deployment of military power at the expense of the criminalization of war. On the other hand, the fragmentation and collapse of some states into new wars has provided new opportunities for the UN and the ICC to criminalize the use of armed force. This is clear if we survey the various current strategies of intervention in armed conflict, including measures to combat terrorism.

UN peacekeeping

New wars and civil wars in the global south can frequently only be halted by external intervention. None of the various factions competing for state power internally are sufficiently powerful to bring the conflict to a halt. A UN-brokered ceasefire followed by a peacekeeping mission externally resourced by the UN is one, albeit temporary, solution. Although not envisaged in the original UN Charter these missions, under the umbrella of 'humanitarian intervention', have become the main form of armed intervention by the UN. The UN Charter focused on warfare between states. Peacekeeping operations following conflicts in which the state has collapsed do not face the problem of criminalizing the actions of states. The distinction between warfare and criminality has already collapsed into 'armed conflict'. UN intervention is analogous to situations within states in which armed police action attempts to suppress or at least enforce a truce between armed mafias or drugs cartels. Mexico comes immediately to mind. Those who survive such armed encounters and are arrested by police will face normal criminal justice processes, hopefully within the framework of human rights. Police may conform to human rights law by using violence only as a last resort but, realistically, the last resort becomes the norm as police seek to suppress armed violence in order to protect citizens.

UN interventions in new wars are similar, though they may be more comprehensive and may involve mixtures of soldiers, police and civil administrators, all aimed at the restoration of stability and the rule of law. IHRL will predominate over IHL precisely because in such operations:

> use of force was normally restricted to response to actual or imminent threat. As a result, the operational legal focus tended more towards issues related to interacting with and treatment of the local civilian population than with the application of combat power in a manner analogous to such application during armed conflict. (Corn 2010: 59)

IHL of course prohibits lethal force against non-combatants, and in situations where large numbers of civilians are caught in the crossfire this is important. In 2017 there were 14 UN peacekeeping operations in existence, attempting to stabilize regions afflicted by civil war. They are becoming increasingly complex and indeed for some considerable time complaints of underfunding, lack of equipment and too few personnel have been frequent (Aguirre and Abrisketa 2009). Thus, in the current UN deployment in the Democratic Republic of the Congo, currently the largest UN deployment and where fighting between armed factions is ongoing, the vulnerability of the UN forces is illustrated by the 93 deaths of military, police and civilian personnel since the mission was established in 2010 (Burke 2018).

Criminal prosecution

A crucial aspect of effective criminalization is of course the prosecution of crimes which have already taken place – including on the part of intervening forces. Again, the character of new wars creates a terrain on which the ICC has been able to function, albeit with a very limited success. Issues surrounding the court's inability to prosecute the crime of aggressive war as such (until 2017) are less important under conditions of state collapse and where the character of war, frequently involving attempts at genocide and ethnic cleansing, is virtually coterminous with war crime and crimes against humanity and where the option of prosecution by domestic courts is unlikely to be exercised.

Delivery to the ICC is a problem if the indicted is currently head of a viable state, as in the case of Sudanese President Omar al-Bashir – accused of crimes against humanity and war crimes in Darfur during the fighting there since 2003. Other state signatories to the ICC, including South Africa and Jordan, failed to arrest Bashir when they had an opportunity to do so. In the case of former heads of state, or regional warlords from conflicts now ceased, court delivery is easier, as are convictions. It is arguably inevitable in terms of the ease of court delivery and effective prosecution, not to mention political pressure and threats by the major states to withdraw support for the ICC or reduce funding, that the work of the ICC has a bias towards conflict zones in the global south, sub-Saharan Africa in particular, and has avoided attention to the activities of the major states. This is due to some extent to the role of the ICC as a court of last resort, for when domestic criminal justice systems have been unable or unwilling to prosecute. The number of actual convictions has been few. Since its activation in 2002, 39 individuals have been indicted by the ICC with a total of nine convictions. A number of African states, including South Africa, have recently withdrawn or contemplated withdrawal from the court.

The focus on prosecutions arising out of new wars in the global south combines with the failure of the court and its predecessor institutions to indict any members of the states that intervene in conflicts. There were, for example, no indictments of the NATO bombing of civilians in Belgrade during the Yugoslav wars, and none for the bombing of Libya in 2011. This of course repeats the 'victor's justice' problem first identified in relation to the Nuremberg tribunal (Zolo 2009). Nevertheless, the ICC is currently (2018) attempting to widen the remit of its indictments to include, for example, the actions of CIA agents and US troops in Afghanistan (Gallagher 2018). But given that the US currently refuses to recognize the ICC the chances of any successful prosecution of its agents in Afghanistan are slender, and perhaps rather than indicate any 'coming of age' on the part of the ICC the issue may serve to illustrate precisely the formidable obstacles on the road to criminalization of war and armed conflict.

Invasion and 'regime change'

This brings us to the issue of the freedom of the powerful states to use their military might in the new world disorder, unchecked by the relatively weak institutions of the UN and the ICC. Currently, the major focus of such military power is Afghanistan, Iraq and Syria as part of the armed conflict in the Middle East. We may consider three illustrations of the effective marginalization of criminalization concerns in armed conflict involving the military forces of the major powers.

First, continuing with the theme of the problems facing the ICC, in the Middle East the conflict between the criminalization and warfare paradigms, and the greater power of the latter, are most graphically illustrated. For example, in 2014 Russia and China vetoed a UN Security Council resolution to refer the conflict in Syria to the ICC. Critics of the resolution argued that ICC intervention with indictments and prosecutions would obstruct possible strategies of politically negotiated compromise (Cronin-Furman 2013, 2014). Indeed, such a position had previously been argued by the US itself (Kersten 2016).

The deployment of human rights violations as a rationalization for invasion or military action such as bombing is a second element in the overriding of international criminal justice by warfare. The US and its allies invaded Afghanistan in 2001, Iraq in 2003, bombed Libya in 2011, and intervened in Syria from 2014 and, indirectly, in Yemen. In each case referral of issues to the ICC was nowhere to be seen. Instead the US coalition saw its actions as a proactive version of UN peacekeeping, conforming to principles of Nuremberg and human rights by means of 'humanitarian intervention' aiming at the removal of regimes that had violated human rights. The right of external intervention was indeed established at Nuremberg but only with the authority of the UN.

The debate concerning the legality of the US-UK invasion of Iraq in 2003 has been well aired and need not be considered in detail here (see Nasr 2016). The UK in particular felt it necessary to claim some legitimacy in relation to the UN Charter and three arguments were deployed. Initially the claim was self-defence under Article 51 in response to the 'revelation' that Iraq possessed weapons of mass destruction which threatened the US, the UK and other states. Later, this was shown to be fabrication and the justification shifted to crimes committed against Iraqi civilians by its governing regime and the legality of humanitarian intervention. The third element was a legal argument about whether the UN Security Council had explicitly authorized the US and the UK to engage in military action.

The uneasy coexistence between the right of external intervention under UN authority to enforce human rights and the outlawing of war against sovereign states has been known and much debated by international law scholars since Nuremberg, and has been resolved to the extent that state sovereignty has been redefined over the years to include a duty to respect, or 'responsibility to protect' human rights (see Negeri 2011). Nevertheless, the problem surrounding actual intervention has not been resolved (see Engdahl 2015) and indeed resurfaced in April 2018 when, in response to the Syrian government's alleged deployment of internationally prohibited chemical weapons against its own citizens, the UK government joined with the US and France in the aerial bombardment of Syrian targets.

The UK government justified its actions by reference to humanitarian intervention to prevent the suffering caused by the use of chemical weapons. However, leaving aside the issue of whether it was the government – rather than Jihadi opposition groups – that used the weapons or, indeed, whether any had actually been used, some international lawyers questioned the legality of the bombing, firstly on the grounds that it lacked the authorization of the UN Security Council, yet alone the ICC. That is to say, it is not up to individual states to decide whether or not humanitarian intervention is justified (see Akande 2018). Such a position amounts to armed vigilantism. In the 2003 invasion of Iraq, the UK government at least claimed that it had UN authority.

A second objection was that following the chemical incident, and with the agreement of the Syrian government, inspectors from the Organisation for the Prevention of Chemical Weapons (a UN agency) arrived to gather evidence. But the US, the UK and France did not even wait for this work to begin before launching their action. Both the Russian representative to the UN Security Council and the Russian Foreign Minister Sergei Lavrov referred to the mad Queen in Lewis Carroll's *Alice in Wonderland*, who famously demanded 'sentence first – verdict afterwards' (Sackur 2018).

Fighting insurgencies

The invasions of Afghanistan (2001) and Iraq (2003) by US-led coalitions resulted in sustained insurgencies by well-organized militias with both local and global recruitment networks. The response to organized insurgency directed at the invading military forces (leaving aside the dubious justification for the invasions themselves) put the US-led coaliton in a different position to UN forces attempting to enforce truce between armed factions – though in both situations close interaction of military with civilians, refugees and civilian aid organizations is an important feature. In addition, the insurgents, deploying tactics of irregular asymmetric warfare frequently hid within civilian populations.

UK courts and the ECtHR have been enforcing the applicability of IHRL in situations where their troops are involved, either as part of UN or other national deployments (Lea 2017). But the advance of IHRL into the governance of ongoing armed conflicts – rather than peace enforcement – has met with resistance from the invading militaries and their political supporters. IHL prohibits both disproportionate force in military encounters and the deployment of force against civilians but allows both lethal force as a first, rather than last, resort and allows detention and internment for reasons of security. IHRL, by contrast, emphasizes that lethal force should be a last resort and detention must be followed promptly by police investigation and due process. For critics this has the potential to place military forces in danger. The requirement that IHRL govern the conduct of UK and other EU forces operating in theatres such as Afghanistan and Iraq has been condemned as amounting to the expectation that military forces 'operate in violent combat conditions according to a system more suited to the regulation of police powers on a Saturday night in the West End of London' (Ekins et al. 2015: 8; see also Tugendhat and Croft 2013). However, many of the IHRL violations claimed, for example by Iraqi civilians engaging in legal action against British military forces for torture and degrading treatment in detention arising from the Iraq invasion of 2003, did not concern detention as such but rather the conditions under which it was exercised. The reaction of the British government included the stated intention to derogate from the jurisdiction of the ECtHR in future military actions overseas (see Lea 2017).

Such problems are arguably symptomatic of the steady advance of human rights concerns into armed conflict situations and may, at least in theory, be resolved by a more careful and versatile mix of police and military aspects of operations and versatility in deployment (Friesendorf 2012). But even if this occurs it remains very much within the framework of the criminalization of certain aspects of armed conflict rather than of the recourse to armed conflict as such. The return of a multi-polar world in which the US and its allies are less free to pursue national interests by military means may arguably re-emphasize the role of military stand-off between rival powers followed by political compromise. This might be one conclusion from the current conflict in Syria where Russian and Iranian regional power has prevented the US from actually invading Syria to remove the 'Assad regime' no doubt as a form of 'humanitarian intervention'. Such a 'balance of power' scenario does not in any obvious way enhance the prospects of a criminal justice approach to armed conflict.

The domestic analogy is that of police and prosecutors watching powerless from the sidelines as powerful mafia groups organize their own truce and compromise without any reference to criminal justice. The police are only able to act as peace-keepers when the contending mafias have exhausted themselves and tacitly agreed that certain of their less important members may be offered up for trial to give the impression that justice has been done. If this scenario is what faces domestic criminal justice systems in some parts of the world it is a certainly a general char-acteristic of international criminal justice. However, there is one key area in which the direction of change is reversed with the chaotic state of international criminal justice infecting domestic systems: terrorism.

The new war on terror

As noted, Islamic Jihadi groups such as IS and Al-Qaeda engage in a combination of armed conflict in the Middle East – mainly Syria and Iraq but spreading to the northern sub-Saharan Africa (the Sahel) – and criminal terrorist outrages in the urban centres of the global north (mainly Europe). From the standpoint of the criminalization of armed conflict, in theory both theatres of operation should be amenable to strategies of arrest and prosecution through the ICC in the Middle East while urban terrorism meanwhile can be dealt with by police and security services through IHRL-compliant arrest and prosecution in domestic courts for murder or conspiracy to murder. Similarly, the global mode of operation and recruitment of terrorist groups could be dealt with through the normal channels of inter-state cooperation. An assumed consensus between states, characteristic of the post-war settlement, would maximize collaboration between police forces regarding data exchange, arrest and extradition of fugitives.

However, the ICC faces severe problems in acting against terrrorist networks in the Middle East. In 2015 the ICC chief prosecutor said that despite 'crimes of unspeakable cruelty' in Syria and Iraq committed by IS the ICC cannot proceed because neither Iraq, Syria nor Libya are signatories to the Court and the UN Security Council has not authorized proceedings (Associated Press 2015). In theory IS operatives captured by these forces could, if the UN Security Council wished, be regarded as arrested criminal suspects and be prosecuted in the same way as war-lords from conflicts in sub-Saharan Africa (see Kenny 2017). However, none of the major military forces in the area has oriented to obtaining arrests for prosecution before the ICC. Given the interests of the major powers, specifically the defence or removal of the current Syrian government, warfare and politics associated with those aims remain predominant.

This neutralization of a criminal justice approach has been strongly reinforced since the terrorist outrage of 9/11 in 2001 by the US so-called 'war on terror' inaugurated by the Bush administration and which went beyond both warfare, governed by IHL, and criminal justice, governed by IHRL. At the notorious Guantánamo Bay interrogation centre, located (in US held territory) in Cuba, terrorist suspects were unilaterally allocated an entirely new legal status of 'unlawful enemy combatants' entitled neither to the protections of IHL under the Geneva Conventions nor to domestic criminal justice and IHRL. The status of detainees has been the subject of a long legal campaign by lawyers and civil rights activists. This unilateral violation of the law of both war and human rights by the US at Guantánamo and other more secret US 'prisons beyond the law' (Margulies 2017) was accompanied by outsourcing of suspects to 'black sites' located in states prepared to violate human rights and enable the US to attempt information extraction by 'torture at a distance' (Bigo 2018). Finally, the process of 'rendition' of terrorist suspects to Guantánamo and other sites of US custody from locations around the world violated normal processes of extradition which would have required the US to demonstrate probable cause or reasonable suspicion in the courts of another state. Instead, suspects were simply kidnapped, either by clandestine US agents or local groups acting for money, with the result that many individuals with no connection to terrorism found themselves in Guantánamo. In Afghanistan for example 'scores of . . . innocent farmers, rug sellers, cooks, and taxi drivers [were] rounded up' by the US and its allies or, 'sold to the Americans by opportunistic warlords in return for thousands of dollars' (Blake et al. 2011). The US saw its global hegemonic power as enabling it to act in this way and take a very pragmatic view of the sovereignty of other states (Lee 2015). In order to justify this the US developed the doctrine that it was entitled to act where other states were 'unable or unwilling' (Edwards 2017: 7). It is of course a non sequitur that the inability of other (chaotic) states to render terrorist suspects to the US justifies the incarceration of the latter in Guantánamo in violation of human rights and due process.

But a key aspect of the approach was that of acting against individuals on the basis of flexible notions of risk or likelihood of being involved in terrorism rather than any notion of reasonable suspicion or probable cause as required for legitimate police action. This methodology has been carried over into the latest phase of US action against terrorists located in weak states in the Middle East. Rather than rendition to Guantánamo the aim seems to be the pre-emptive killing of individuals either suspected of terrorist behaviour or at risk of engaging in it in the future. A strategy of pre-emptive killing of individuals perceived as risks and threats, that is to say not necessarily in the process of either waging war or organizing criminal conspiracy for violence but likely to be contemplating either, involves a fundamental departure from both normal military action governed by IHL and a criminal justice approach governed by IHRL. In the case of IHL there is an insufficient attempt to identify the targets as actual combatants as opposed to simply civilians or otherwise hors de combat, e.g. wishing to surrender (Boyle 2015; Lee 2015). In addition, there is the legal problem of armed action on the territory of states with which the US is not at war – but which the US has judged as 'unable or unwilling' basically to act as an agent of US action. Meanwhile from the standpoint of IHRL there is no use of force as a last resort after other attempts (e.g. arrest) have been exhausted. Furthermore, it is alleged that the target lists are assembled by the CIA in the US case and based on 'intelligence'. Even if such action were legally and morally justifiable the latitude for mistakes is obvious, and this is amplified 'by the US practice of "signature strikes" approved even if the personal identity of the target is unknown. These are authorised on the basis of evidence such as "pattern of life" and documented suspicious or hostile behaviour of potential targets' (Barela 2015: 262).

Drone killings illustrate not simply resistance to criminalization of war but rather the emergence of a new paradigm that goes beyond both warfare and criminalization: a paradigm of armed security based on the management of risk. It is, as we shall see, an orientation in which aspects of both armed conflict and domestic criminal justice have been steadily merging. This is clear in the handling of terrorism by domestic criminal justice. For reasons of space we shall focus on the situation in the UK.

Returning Jihadis

In Syria, IS has suffered major military defeats at the hands of the Syrian military alliance. In the UK this resulted in a focus on the issue of UK citizens who illegally joined IS in Iraq and Syria now returning to the UK as potential urban terrorists. Normally, once such individuals have returned to the UK a criminal justice perspective would be expected to predominate, with risk assessment conducted by police and security services seeking to determine which individuals should be under surveillance, served with various preventative orders under existing anti-terrorist legislation or prosecuted for terrorist conspiracy in the UK. In short, they would expect to be treated in the same way as domestic terrorists, the vast majority of whom are dealt with by normal criminal justice processes.

However, the question of the role of killing of former IS fighters by armed drones became controversial towards the end of 2017 when senior UK government ministers voiced the opinion that the appropriate response to British citizens who had fought with Jihadi groups and were now seeking to return to the UK where they would constitute a terrorist threat, was to kill them, in the words of Rory Stewart, Minister for Courts and Justice, 'in almost every case' (McCann 2017). In fact, actions of this type had been underway for a considerable time. In 2015 the British Jihadi Mohammed Emwazi, known as 'Jihadi John', was allegedly killed in a US drone strike over Syria. Around the same time, Reyaad Khan and two other alleged British IS fighters were killed by RAF drones. Emwazi was allegedly responsible for the earlier murder of journalists and aid workers (Phipps et al. 2015). Those killings took place while armed conflict with IS was ongoing and thus could be seen as military actions though with the problems for IHL noted above. Jeremy Corbyn, British Labour Party leader, responded to the killing of Emwazi by noting his 'callous and brutal crimes' but adding that 'it would have been far better for us all if he had been held to account in a court of law' (Phipps et al. 2015). The logic of course is that of referral to the ICC for war crimes.

However, the issue of returning IS fighters who are UK citizens, as it emerged in 2017, hung very much on the question of whether these could still be seen as actions against military enemies. If the fighters intending to return to the UK were engaged in armed combat then, even if not actually fighting, it would be legitimate under IHL to kill them (with the qualifications already noted above) on the basis of their status as enemy combatants. But if armed combat as such had ceased – in December 2017 the Iraqi government declared victory against IS – then killing them was assassination and a fundamental contravention of IHRL, in particular the right to life and the right to due process and fair trial. They should rather have been arrested and charged on return to the UK. They could be tried by UK courts or referred to the ICC.

The UK Attorney General, Jeremy Wright QC, produced an argument that these people were enemy combatants in that they placed the UK under imminent threat with the result that killing them was legitimate self-defence under Article 51 of the UN Charter. Wright argued:

> In a world where a small number of committed plotters may be seeking to inspire, enable and direct attacks around the world, and indeed have a proven track record of doing so, we will not always know where and when an attack will take place, or the precise nature of the attack. But where the evidence supports an assessment that an attack is imminent it cannot be right that a state is prevented from meeting its first duty of protecting its citizens without nailing down the specific target and timing of an attack. (Wright 2017: 17)

In other words, as with US drone killings, the 'balance of risk' is the core of the argument. The intentions of returning Jihadis are being inferred from who they *are* and from this is derived a risk that they have intentions to wage war on the streets of the UK. Even within this war paradigm they may of course be *hors de combat*, wanting to surrender, depressed and seeking social reintegration. But the 'balance of risk' is considered too great to wait for them to apply for psychiatric counselling and rehabilitation. It is legitimate to kill them for who they are. Risk is the key driver for a fusion of warfare and criminal justice into a new anti-terrorist armed security paradigm.

This type of argument has been around for some time in the domestic criminal justice context. In 2005 the then head of the security service MI5, Eliza Manningham-Buller, described the dilemma facing police and security services in countering domestic terrorist threats while remaining within the traditions of due process and human rights. Evidence of impending terrorist action is 'patchy and fragmentary and uncertain' and 'all too often . . . falls short of evidence to support criminal charges to bring an individual before the courts, the best solution if achievable'. This gives rise to the 'central dilemma, how to protect our citizens within the rule of law when intelligence does not amount to clear cut evidence and when it is fragile' (Manningham-Buller 2005). This problem lies behind the watering down of standards of proof as the basis for pre-emptive action to restrict the liberties of those suspected of involvement in terrorist activities (through 'control orders' introduced in 2005 and succeeded in 2011 by revised 'terrorism prevention and investigation measures') and wide definitions of what constitutes preparation for, or incitement to, terrorist activity (Walker 2018).

It is also echoed in other areas of domestic criminal justice in the growth of 'pre-emptive criminalisation' (Fitzgibbon 2007; Hallsworth and Lea 2011; Lea 2015) or 'pre-crime' (Zedner 2007; McCulloch and Wilson 2015) in which various behaviours – ranging from 'anti-social behaviour' to possession of unexplained wealth – are targeted not as criminal conduct per se but for the risk that they lead to, or may be indicators of, such. Pre-emptive action shifts the emphasis from actual conduct, as would be established by a criminal conviction, to status characteristics such as lifestyle, contacts and associations, travel and internet communication habits. This approaches the military paradigm of legitimate action against individuals based on their status as enemy combatants rather than their actual conduct. In both cases action is justified in terms of the elimination of risk (Lee 2015). Thus, the risk presented by returning Jihadi fighters is inferred from their having participated in armed conflict, featured in web videos, etc., and the same criteria can be used to justify either a drone strike or pre-emptive restriction, the first if they are yet to reach the UK and the second if they have already arrived. Which action is taken depends therefore on their location.

It is a reasonable assumption that the public would not countenance drone strikes within the UK. But the possibility of alternatives is illustrated in the controversy over alleged police 'shoot to kill' actions in which deadly force is used as a first resort, for example in the interdiction of suspects, rather than as a last resort as when a terrorist incident is in progress. In the fatal shooting by police in Stockwell (London) in 2005 of Jean Charles de Menezes, a Brazilian electrician mistakenly identified as a terrorist suspect, Punch (2011) identified the adoption of a 'military paradigm' in the use by police of deadly force. Menezes was identified as a target on the basis of a risk profile – he had exited from a building under observation, fitted the stature of the suspect, etc. Most important, the police seem to have abandoned minimum force as a last resort. 'With Stockwell there can be no shadow of doubt that a fundamental shift in policy on police use of firearms in Britain had taken place' (Punch 2011: 160; see also Squires and Kennison 2010). As yet there have been no further shootings of terrorist suspects (as opposed to terrorists in action) similar to the Menezes case. But if the shift identified by Punch and others has taken root then the return of former Jihadi fighters – known to have received training in armed combat and bomb-making and thus further weighting the bal-ance of risk in favour of pre-emptive action – may create a situation in which such incidents are more likely.

Conclusion

We have attempted to trace, very briefly and in bare outline, the process whereby the original optimism regarding the criminalization of war and actions within war has run into the sand. The success or failure of policies is very dependent on the environment in which they are conceived and then carried into action. The origins of modern attempts at such criminalization lay in the post-war settlement, the optimism for a new world order which was the context of Nuremberg, the UN Charter and the Declaration of Human Rights. That optimism, we have argued, presupposed a stable world order of mutually respectful nation states.

Criminalization has had some successes as evidenced in the work of the ICC and UN peacekeeping, despite their weakness and confinement to relatively peripheral conflict areas. The enforcement of human rights globally has made some progress. Paradoxically, this success has been dependent on the fragmentation of the post-war settlement and is rooted in the profound inequalities of the 'new world disorder'.

But warfare, largely in the form of armed conflict involving major states and non-state actors, has been resurgent and powerful states like the US and its allies, Russia and Iran, (with China as a sleeping giant yet to flex its military might), have become key actors. Decisive action by the UN is obstructed by the fact that conflicts between the major states are reflected in the UN itself, and criminalization – except as political polemic – has been displaced almost entirely in the Middle East, currently the major theatre of armed conflict, by warfare and political manoeuvre. Finally, the impact of terrorism as an aspect of that conflict that crosses the boundaries between warfare and criminality has been to lay the foundation for a new paradigm that amalgamates elements of both warfare and crime control, in a pragmatic focus on risk and security. In this new amalgam the progress of human rights remains as precarious as ever.

References

Akande, D. (2018) 'The legality of the UK's air strikes on the Assad government in Syria. Opinion of Professor Dapo Akande, Professor of Public International Law University of Oxford. Oxford Institute for Ethics, Law & Armed Conflict, University of Oxford'. Available at: https://d3n8a8pro7vhmx.cloud front.net/campaigncountdown/pages/2243/attachments/original/1523875290/Akande_Opinion_UK_Government%27s_Legal_Position_on_Syria_Strike_April_2018.pdf? (accessed 2 May 2018).

Aguirre, M. and Abrisketa, J. (2009) 'Pressing issues for UN Peacekeeping Operations. Transnational Institute'. Available at: https://www.tni.org/en/article/pressing-issues-for-un-peacekeeping-operations (accessed 12 April 2018).

Archibugi, D. and Pease, A. (2018) *Crime and Global Justice: The Dynamics of International Punishment.* Malden, MA: Polity Press.

Arquilla, J., Ronfeldt, D. and Zanini, M. (2003) 'Networks, netwar and information-age terrorism', in Lesser, I. and Hoffman, B. (eds) *Countering the New Terrorism.* Washington, DC: Rand Corporation, pp. 39–84.

Associated Press (2015) 'ICC has no jurisdiction to prosecute Isis despite "crimes of unspeakable cruelty"', *The Guardian,* 8 April.

Barela, S. (2015) *Legitimacy and Drones: Investigating the Legality, Morality and Efficacy of UCAVs.* 1st edition. Farnham: Routledge.

Bigo, D. (2018) 'Dramaturgy of suspicion and the emergence of a transnational guild of extraction of information by "torture at a distance"', in Guild, E., Bigo, D. and Gibney, M. (eds) *Extraordinary Rendition: Addressing the Challenges of Accountability*. Abingdon: Routledge, pp. 30–52.

Blake, H., Ross, T. and Harper, C. Q. (2011) 'WikiLeaks: children among the innocent captured and sent to Guantanamo', *The Telegraph*, 26 April.

Boyle, M. J. (2015) 'The legal and ethical implications of drone warfare', *The International Journal of Human Rights*, 19 (2): 105–126.

Burke, J. (2018) 'The wars will never stop' – millions flee bloodshed as Congo falls apart', *The Guardian*, 3 April.

Cohen, S. (2011) *Soviet Fates and Lost Alternatives*. New York: Columbia University Press.

Corn, G. (2010) 'Mixing apples and hand grenades: the logical limit of applying human rights norms to armed conflict', *Journal of International Humanitarian Legal Studies*, 1 (1): 52–94.

Cronin-Furman, K. (2013) 'Managing expectations: international criminal trials and the prospects for deterrence of mass atrocity', *International Journal of Transitional Justice*, 7 (3): 434–454.

Cronin-Furman, K. (2014) 'Would an ICC referral have helped Syria?', *Washington Post*, 25 May.

Degenhardt, T. (2015) 'Crime, justice and the legitimacy of military power in the international sphere', *Punishment & Society*, 17 (2): 139–162.

Deutsch, K. W. (1966) *Nationalism and Social Communication: Inquiry into the Foundations of Nationality*. Cambridge, MA: The MIT Press.

Edwards, H. (2017) 'Does international law apply to the Islamic State? Towards a more comprehensive legal response to international terrorism'. GCSP Strategic Security Analysis. Available at: http://www.gcsp.ch/News-Knowledge/Publications/Does-International-Law-Apply-to-the-Islamic-State (accessed 25 March 2018).

Ekins, R., Morgan, J. and Tugendhat, T. (2015) *Clearing the Fog of Law: Saving our Armed Forces from Defeat by Judicial Diktat*. London: Policy Exchange.

Engdahl, O. (2015) 'Protection of human rights and the maintenance of international peace and security: necessary precondition or a clash of interests?', in Bailliet, C. M. and Larsen, K. M. (eds) *Promoting Peace Through International Law*. Oxford: Oxford University Press, pp. 109–131.

Ferencz, D. (2015) *The Nuremberg Legacy and the Crime of Aggression: A Promise Betrayed or Merely Delayed?* Oxford Centre for Criminology Blog. Available at: https://www.law.ox.ac.uk/centres-insti tutes/centre-criminology/blog/2015/02/nuremberg-legacy-and-crime-aggression-promise (accessed 20 March 2018).

Fitzgibbon, D. (2007) 'Institutional racism, pre-emptive criminalisation and risk analysis', *Howard Journal of Criminal Justice*, 46: 128–144.

Friesendorf, C. (2012) *International Intervention and the Use of Force: Military and Police Roles*. Geneva: Geneva Centre for the Democratic Control of Armed Forces.

Gallagher, K. (2018) 'The ICC must hold the US accountable for crimes in Afghanistan', *The Guardian*, 16 February.

Githens-Mazer, J. (2008) 'Causes of jihadi terrorism: beyond paintballing and social exclusion', *Criminal Justice Matters*, 73 (1): 26–28.

Hallsworth, S. and Lea, J. (2011) 'Reconstructing Leviathan: emerging contours of the security state', *Theoretical Criminology*, 15 (2): 141–157.

Jacoby, T. (2007) 'Hegemony, modernisation and post-war reconstruction', *Global Society*, 21 (4): 521–537.

Kaldor, M. (1999) *New and Old Wars: Organized Violence in a Global Era*. Cambridge: Polity.

Kenny, C. (2017) 'Prosecuting crimes of international concern: Islamic State at the ICC?' *Utrecht Journal of International and European Law*, 33: 120–145.

Kersten, M. (2016) Prosecuting war crimes in Syria: many tribulations, but no trials (yet)', in *Justice in Conflict*. Available at: https://justiceinconflict.org/2016/09/30/prosecuting-war-crimes-in-syria-many-tribulations-but-no-trials/ (accessed 4 June 2018).

Lea, J. (2015) 'From the criminalisation of war to the militarisation of crime control', in Walklate, S. and McGarry, R. (eds) *Criminology and War: Transgressing the Borders*. Abingdon: Routledge, pp. 198–207.

Lea, J. (2017) 'War, crime and human rights', *British Society of Criminology Newsletter*, 80: 37–41.

Lee, S. (2015) 'Human rights and drone "warfare"', *Peace Review*, 27 (4): 432–439.

Manningham-Buller, E. (2005) 'The international terrorist threat and the dilemmas in countering it', Security Service MI5. Available at: https://www.mi5.gov.uk/news/the-international-terrorist-threat-and-the-dilemmas-in-countering-it (accessed 21 March 2018).

Margulies, J. (2007) *Guantanamo and the Abuse of Presidential Power*. New York: Simon & Schuster.

McCann, K. (2017) '"The only way" of dealing with British Islamic State fighters is to kill them in almost every case, minister says', *The Telegraph*, 22 October.

McCulloch, J. and Wilson, D. (2015) *Pre-crime: Pre-emption, Precaution and the Future*. London and New York: Routledge.

Mohamedou, M. (2007) *Understanding Al Qaeda: The Transformation of War*. London: Pluto.

Nasr, L. (2016) 'The doctrine of humanitarian intervention: lessons from the Chilcot Report', in *LSE Human Rights*. Available at: http://blogs.lse.ac.uk/humanrights/2016/08/22/the-doctrine-of-human itarian-intervention-lessons-from-the-chilcot-report-2/ (accessed 21 March 2018).

Negeri, L. (2011) *The Tension Between State Sovereignty and Humanitarian Intervention in International Law*. Master's Thesis in Public International Law. University of Oslo, Oslo.

Parmar, I. (2018) 'The US-led liberal order: imperialism by another name?', *International Affairs*, 94 (1): 151–172.

Phipps, C., Wintour, P. and McCurry, J. (2015) '"High degree of certainty" that US strike killed Mohammed Emwazi', *The Guardian*, 13 November.

Punch, M. (2011) *Shoot to Kill: Police Accountability, Firearms and Fatal Force*. Bristol: Policy Press.

Roberts, M. (2016) *The Long Depression*. Chicago, IL: Haymarket Books.

Rogers, P. (2010) *Losing Control: Global Security in the 21st Century*. London: Pluto.

Rostow, W. (1962) *The Stages of Economic Growth: A Non-communist Manifesto*. Cambridge: Cambridge University Press.

Sackur, S. (2018) BBC interview of Russian Foreign Minister Sergey Lavrov, *BBC World Service 'Hard Talk'*, 18 April. Available at: https://www.bbc.co.uk/programmes/w3cswjds (accessed 20 March 2018).

Sands, P. (2005) *Lawless World: America and the Making and Breaking of Global Rules*. London: Allen Lane.

Shaw, M. (1991) *Post-military Society: Militarism, Demilitarization and War at the End of the Twentieth Century*. Cambridge: Polity.

Squires, P. and Kennison, P. (2010) *Shooting to Kill?: Policing, Firearms and Armed Response*, 1st edition. Chichester and Malden, MA: Wiley-Blackwell.

Tugendhat, T. and Croft, L. (2013) *The Fog of Law: An Introduction to the Legal Erosion of British Fighting Power*. London: Policy Exchange.

van der Pijl, K. (2006) *Global Rivalries From the Cold War to Iraq*. London: Pluto.

van der Pijl, K. (2013) *The Financial Crisis and the War for Global Governance*. Available at: http://anti capitalists.org/2013/05/26/financial-crisis-and-war-for-global-governance (accessed 2 April 2015).

von Einsiedel, S. (2017) *Civil War Trends and the Changing Nature of Armed Conflict*. United Nations University Centre for Policy Research, Occasional Paper 10. Tokyo: United Nations University.

Walker, P. (2018) 'Anti-terrorism plans "will make thoughtcrime a reality"', *The Guardian*, 6 June.

Wright, J. (2017) 'The modern law of self-defence': Attorney General's speech at International Institute for Strategic Studies. UK Government (GOV.UK). Available at: https://assets.publishing.service.gov. uk/government/uploads/system/uploads/attachment_data/file/583171/170111_Imminence_Speech _.pdf (accessed 12 March 2019).

Zedner, L. (2007) 'Pre-crime and post-criminology?' *Theoretical Criminology*, 11: 261–281.

Zolo, D. (2009) *Victors' Justice: From Nuremberg to Baghdad*. London and New York: Verso.

5 War crimes, genocide and the value of a social harm approach in a post-accountability world

Daniel Mitchell

Introduction

This chapter examines the role of the state in the commission of war crimes and acts of genocide and the ways in which pre-existing notions of legitimacy are exploited to deny accountability for the harms that result from such actions. Governments have always been capable of distancing themselves from their direct role in the consequences of war and mass killing, seeking to individualize responsibility. Modern warfare, characterized by remote assassination via drone technology and special ops commando raids (Burke, 2011; Scahill 2013, 2017), extraordinary rendition and black site torture (DiMento and Geis, 2006; Gregory, 2011), and the use of private military contractors (Scahill, 2007; War on Want, 2016) signifies the evolution of the state's potential to deny complicity in criminal acts that destroy lives and destabilize local and global communities. This layering of agents and responsibility, creating a buffer between the state and harmful acts committed to further its interests, permits the state to deny responsibility (Cohen, 2001) for a variety of harms ranging from genocide and war crimes to environmental destruction (see Altopiedi, Chapter 6 this volume).

The history of cases before the International Criminal Court, which have mainly focused on African states, is a demonstration of the fact that it is unlikely that any powerful democratic nation, particularly a Western one, will ever be answerable to a global institution when it comes to the potential commission of war crimes or aiding/ignoring acts of genocide. The contention of this chapter is that as far as crimes against humanity go, where Western nations are concerned, we inhabit a post-accountability world (see also Lea, Chapter 4 this volume).

By examining the importance of the state to a discussion of war crimes and genocide, addressing the concept of legitimacy in particular, the intention of this chapter is to highlight the value of a social harm approach to the discussion of accountability beyond the restrictions and deliberate obfuscations of official state discourse. Social harm is not only useful as a perspective on war crime and genocide, for drawing out the socially destabilizing quality of such acts, as they are perpetrated and sanctioned by states, it can also play a significant role in challenging the resort to war by states in the first place (Swanson, 2011).

The criminal state, war and social disruption

> The most important type of criminality organized by the state consists of acts defined by law as criminal and committed by state officials in pursuit of their job as representatives of the state. (Chambliss, 1989: 347)

Chambliss, in his brief assessment of state-organized crimes such as drug and arms smuggling, state sponsored assassination and piracy, takes the view that the most identifiable forms of state criminality, rather than harm, are those that directly contravene the laws state representatives are meant to support and uphold. Chambliss argues that the law 'is a fundamental cornerstone in creating legitimacy and an illusion (at least) of social order' (1989: 354); this is due to the symbolism of the law as possessing universal qualities and an impartial applicability.

Chambliss' recognition of the need for states to emphasize the universality of law, with its implied legitimacy, echoes Bourdieu's work on law as a juridical field (Hagan and Levi, 2005). As a field, law develops in accordance with the demands of a rational and systematic process that ensures standardization, which can be read as fairness, a core quality of justice. The problem that arises in the creation and application of law from this perspective is that it reflects the need for legitimacy on the part of privileged and powerful actors, acting as representatives of their respective countries in the case of war crimes tribunals, while excluding the needs of less powerful individuals and groups (Pain, 2009), a process that is facilitated by the requirement to be rational and systematic. Law, as a field, is simultaneously a guarantor of legitimacy and a protection against accusations of selectivity and unequal treatment.

State crime, all of which could be described as organized, not only in the sense that McIntosh (1975) uses the term meaning that all crime is organized, but also that the state is an organization (Douglas, 1986) no matter how we may choose to configure its organizing principles theoretically, is invariably defined as action committed by those in official positions, agents of the state, which either infract domestic or international law and/or victimize the powerless (Green and Ward, 2004; Ward, 2004; Jamieson and McEvoy, 2005; Stanley, 2005). War crimes very often involve powerless victims caught up in wars initiated by official states but there are also contingents of unofficial actors, civilians who stand by, watch and do not act (Cohen, 2001), militias operating at the behest of state representatives/ leaders while resisting formal categorization (Ramet, 2002) and civilians who conspire with occupying forces to bring about the slaughter of particular ethnic/racial/ social groups (Burleigh, 2000).

The complicity of non-state actors in the commission of state crime makes the harms involved harder to detect and regulate by blurring the distinction between the state and the civilian population. Civilian accountability for complicity in state crime signifies a blurring of boundaries between different types of agency and objective (Ginsberg, 2013). State operatives seeking to consolidate power encourage violence on the part of civilian actors who utilize this violence to reinforce a sense of threatened national identity, for instance (see Stephenson, Chapter 9 this volume). State crime of this nature presents a formidable problem when it comes to the provision of justice; when so many state and civilian agents are involved the purpose of accountability becomes unclear as it is problematic to argue to whom or what it should apply when all of the parties involved regard themselves as justified in their actions. By making civilians participants in state crime, state actors are able to fashion an alternative route to legitimacy, as civilian actors are unlikely to want to incriminate themselves (Robertson, 2000).

A number of authors (Green and Ward, 2004; Ward, 2004; Jamieson and McEvoy, 2005; Stanley, 2005) have characterized state crime as the victimization of the powerless by the powerful. Accountability for such victimization is automatically concealed by the nature of the role the state plays in the definition and adjudication of what constitutes crime/criminality (Schoultz, 2014). The state, in state crime discourse, is represented by official/governmental institutions including the police, the military and the intelligence services (Jessop, 2008); collusion with business corporations may also be a factor (Green and Ward, 2004; Chouliaris, 2010; Ruggiero, 2010). State crime is ostensibly characterized by the infraction of laws these representatives are meant to uphold to further their own power interests (Chambliss, 1989).

The discourse on the criminality of the state is often concerned with the criminalization of power (Box, 1983; Cohen, 1988; Morrison, 2006) but power, as a quality, in the context of war can develop in sites once bereft of power and emanate from individuals and groups that were powerless. Progressive theorization in this area (Box, 1983; Slapper and Tombs, 1999; Wells, 2001; Pemberton, 2004; Tombs and Whyte, 2007) expanded the conceptualization of agency through recognition of the role that lower-level employees play in the commission of white-collar and corporate offences. This follows Foucault's (1975) exposition of power as a quality that is not the sole property of the state, channelled only through official institutions – the prison, the asylum, the army barracks – but that power can be developed by the individual through resistance and reinterpretation of social reality. An expansive conception of power is significant to an understanding of the diverse quality of agency and responsibility in war where powerless individuals acquire 'control' in chaotic situations through the instrumental use of violence. Thus, the fluctuation of power that war generates results in a correlative alternation of responsibility and agency.

When undertaking research relating to war crimes and genocide, theoretical approaches have to be developed in a manner that is mindful of the tendency to criminalize and punish those individuals/groups immediately connected to acts perceived as breaches of the laws of war or instances of mass atrocity. This is the structural tendency, mediated through state institutions such as the International Criminal Court, locally and globally, to individualize agency and accountability. Accepting this limited process, ceding power exclusively to the state, means that the wider structural issues remain unacknowledged by the general public, which allows many of the social divisions that enabled conflict to develop in the first place. A social harm perspective, responsive to the social disruption state activities perpetuate, cannot be restricted to purely legal formulations of criminality.

Social division, war and genocide

The state, as a concept, is of great theoretical importance to criminology. This structured gathering and enfolding of power becomes the predominant definer of that which is, technically, perceived as 'criminal'. This concentration of power, administered through state institutions and agencies, draws its legitimacy from society, or at least an idea of society, distilling and codifying common concerns and reproducing them in the form of law and its enforcement. In essence, the state exists as a systematic mechanism for the mediation of legal prescriptions. In a democracy these laws are meant to represent the consensus values of a society, a conception of order derived from the 'collective conscious' (Durkheim, 1984: 47–48). In principle, the state achieves legitimacy through the equitable and just implementation of law.

Durkheim (1984: 33) observed the law as the 'visible symbol' of 'social solidarity', a consensus value. Law, for Durkheim, is the 'most stable and precise element' (1984: 34) of an organized society. To extend this interpretation in relation to the changing structure of the state preceding and during conflict, where 'social life' is less stable, due to unremitting threats of violence, it follows that the position of the law will also become less stable, but this does not mean that the law vanishes – rather, it becomes more 'pliable'.

In one way the state retains a classical interpretation of its role; from a Weberian perspective it rests the strength of its legitimacy on the 'monopoly . . . of physical force' (Weber, 1968: 77). However, Weber would have contested the legitimacy of a state that extends this monopoly of force beyond the 'given territory' (1968: 77) of its historically delineated borders (Anderson, 1991). To reach beyond this domain is to enter into a relationship with an external (international) community, which, it must be noted, did not play a part in the formation of the intervening state and, therefore, is not certain to possess the same 'shared' values; in the aftermath of conflict when trials such as the 1946 International Military Tribunal at Nuremberg are convened the extension of specific state values are evident. It follows that interactions with the international community usually involve 'force', or the threat of force, as a language rather than the 'dialogue' customarily linked to the development of a bond between those who govern and those who are governed. To hold onto its legitimacy the state acts as the embodiment of a legal ethos and in a post-modernistic sense by assuming this guise it is assured that the power it has is transferable in a real and physical way.

> If a country is 'at war' . . . psychologically and politically, if not behaviourally . . . then
> the state is given a virtually unrestricted discretion that includes an array of emergency
> powers to enable it to carry out its role of offering protection against the internal and
> external enemies. (Falk, 1991: 105)

The process of enemy construction and the deadening of public resistance to the
mentality it fosters can be seen in the ways in which new 'suspect communities'
come to be framed (Pantazis and Pemberton, 2009; Allen, 2010). This perpetuates
the notion that the 'enemy' is always present and always a danger and that the
vulnerable public may not always know who the enemy is, but the state, with its
intelligence and surveillance networks, can identify and engage the threat. Allowing
this approach to the 'problem of terrorism' on the part of the state, unimpeded by
any concerted critical challenge, is how we end up with extraordinary rendition,
black sites and torture being used as acceptable measures in the fight against terror.

The ceaseless 'war on terror': stepping away from accountability

The use of extraordinary rendition, 'ghosting', black sites and torture not only
challenges the feasibility of the laws of war and 'human rights' in the 'war on terror'
but also places US and British military and intelligence (CIA, MI6) agencies in a
position where they do not have to account for their actions nor take responsibility
for the harm they are inflicting. The concept of harm seems the most appropriate
here since it is technically difficult to apply a 'criminal' label to activities transpiring
in a place that is impervious to the restraint of law. As Rolston (1991) and Conroy
(2000) have shown, using internment and interrogation in Northern Ireland during
the 1970s and 1980s as a case study, torture serves no purpose other than to inflict
pain; it certainly will not produce reliable information. The individual subjected to
torture will eventually say anything, confess to any harm or crime, to 'stop the pain'.
From the standpoint of the state operative this is a confession nonetheless (Rose,
1996).

State legitimacy is not limited to a given population within national borders; it
also has global implications. When governments perceive themselves as completely
justified in waging war they are conveying the message that what they are doing is
right – morally and legally. Adjustment of the focus from the means of war to the
war itself results in a limited degree of critical reflection being directed at the use
of torture. The desire to place objectives above means leads 'legitimate' Western
nations down a path where they set a bad example for the rest of the world. If they
are the figureheads of justice and fairness, then it can be argued there is nothing
questionable about other nations perpetuating the same harms.

Another criticism of this approach to 'terrorism' is that, as far as proportionality
is concerned (Tonry, 1994), it is counter-productive to the achievement of the
'greater good'. As Burke (2005) has argued, in his extensive critical study of the
'Al-Qaeda' mythos, a failure to be more circumspect when it comes to the aetiology

of 'terrorism' and the adoption of a reactionary stance instead ensures future waves of 'hijackers' and 'suicide bombers': 'They will be "freelance" operators who have no obvious connection to any existing group. They will, often, have no previous involvement with terrorism' (Burke, 2005: 276).

The aggressive 'counter-terrorist' doctrine favoured by Britain and the US, Burke believes, only leads to greater resentment towards the West. Governments which nurture such strategies not only oppress and harm their own populations through questionable legislation and reinterpretations of legal parameters, they are also encouraging a higher probability of attacks by militants who wish to pass on the damage to which they themselves have been subjected (Weiss and Hassan, 2015; Wood, 2017). It is in this way that the state will experience the renaissance of its victimhood, following numerous momentous acts of organized violence, after teetering on the brink of 'criminality', in the eyes of its population and the rest of the world. 'The fact that the legal system has been distorted beyond recognition is easily forgotten in the blaze of rhetoric. "Criminalisation" has been a success in propaganda terms' (Rolston, 1991: 161).

Governments act as the defining influence behind the ways in which the 'war on terror' is perceived, and, ironically, the way in which 'terrorists' are perceived. The 'war on terror' is not only about a 'clash of civilizations', 'us' and 'them', it is an amalgamation of the past and the future; a conventional neo-classical view of the state anchored to the tenets of law and due process interspersed with a state in flux as it corresponds its actions with those of the enemy. In fact, the state is always the forerunner when it comes to inflicting the most terror. Whether proportionality is perceived from the vantage point of 'justice' or as a pragmatically utilitarian objective, the decisive act that provides no room for response and thus ends the 'war', the state is always the more disproportionately violent of the two forces. The degree of 'criminality' it projects onto others through its policies and the media (Hall et al., 1978; Herman and Chomsky, 1989) combined with its 'innate legitimacy' as a democracy, 'elected by the people for the people', precludes the application of the criminal sanction to its own actions: 'Political democracy has come to exempt the national security choices of the state from any normative accountability' (Falk, 1991: 108).

The adversarial state excludes any critical debate on its actions and motivations through the perpetuation of fear among a populace. Deliberately encouraging a culture of fear (Furedi, 2002; Burke, 2005), and subsequently hatred (Kaldor, 2006) relating to 'terror', referring to the indelible images of destruction, such as those associated with the 9/11 attacks, it calls upon the possibility that these things could happen again, but they will be much worse, making the inconceivable, as abstract as it is, a very 'real' threat; it is in such a milieu that people are easily able to identify themselves as potential victims even if the risk of victimization is minute (Wilkins, 1991: 140). Attacks against public targets in Paris in 2016 and London in 2017 by groups/individuals professing allegiance to IS have, in some ways, given credibility to reactionary tendencies and subsequent exercises in fear-mongering (Carnagey and Anderson, 2007) since, statistically speaking, the threat of victimization from such attacks remains very low in Western states.

Between 1989 and 2014 the threat of a terrorist attack was 60 per cent higher in countries not experiencing civil conflict before 11 September 2001 than it was following that event (Smith and Ziegler, 2017: 4). This means that Western nations, which have instigated and engaged in external conflicts, are less likely to experience terrorist incidents. What is often neglected in relation to studies of civilian victimization through terrorist attacks and fear of terrorism (Pain, 2009) is the fact that the probability of an attack has been greatly increased for countries besieged by civil war, where terrorism is a feature of those conflicts (Smith and Ziegler, 2017). When it comes to public fear about terrorism and the reality of such attacks it is the exaggerated fear of privileged and heavily protected communities that often supersedes the real and constant dangers faced by more vulnerable populations (Pain, 2009). Exposing the manner in which fear is amplified for political purposes is central to any research approach which espouses a social harm objective, as it allows for a clearer insight into the victimization of hidden groups that are often legally 'othered' (Jamieson and McEvoy, 2005; Wolfendale, 2007) by Western states in their global prosecution of the 'war on terror' (Gregory, 2011).

Human rights, crime and social harm

War crimes often elude convenient identification because they signify a deviation within a deviation, an excessive or cruel application of force in an environment characterized by the necessity of force and violence (Hedges, 2002, 2012), but within limits prescribed by the laws of war. A war crime is often deemed to be such as a consequence of observation and comparison, a relative critique of different forms of violence. Violence which is judged to operate at an accepted level, achieving an objective, delivered with calculated efficiency, is less likely to be deemed a war crime. In this sense a war crime is judged ex post facto as the quality of the act itself rather than the complexion of the motive behind it since civilians were never the intended targets. However, we could argue that it is war in itself which is problematic here, as war has a distinct nature, it is destructive, and yet its character is unknowable, which leads to fear (Herr, 1978; Burke, 2005; Walsh, 2014) and the escalation of violence, and it also means that it is a challenge to the soldier on the ground or in the air, or both in the case of drone operators, to effectively judge what is acceptable and what is transgressive, morally and legally, when it comes to the instrumental and supposedly dispassionate use of violence.

Taking a criminological approach to war crimes filtered through the prism of human rights requires a universal acknowledgement of humanity, which in itself entails the recognition of the progenitors and executors of war crimes and genocide as human beings. In war, individuals often carry the dual status of victim/offender. Victimhood may be derived from brutality at the hands of the enemy during war or it may come as part of a carefully managed programme by the state, that institution which developed to control people, to protect them from themselves and from their unchecked 'natures', setting them within a historical context of repeated victimization. Examples of this are evident in the destruction of the European Jews and the conflicts in the Balkans. Grievances, the assault on 'rights' as they are perceived by a certain collective, a community, a nation, are used to consolidate abstract notions of unity and solidarity, bringing together separate and distinct human beings, deindividuating them, so as to communalize their suffering, even if it is imagined. Victims become aggressors as a means of reclaiming power. The problem such a position has for a criminological understanding of the agency behind war crimes and atrocities is that those who commit these abuses may often fall back on their victim status, rather than acknowledging their significance as a perpetrator, meaning that their actions are in some way another matter, apart from them, and it is merely their methodology in redressing the imbalance of power that is questionable. Human rights are the province of victims and to accept them without adequate critical scrutiny leaves us with fallacious accounts of the role of power, responsibility and agency. It is impossible, even for a critical criminology, not to take sides.

The corporate absorption of rights does not signify a corresponding acknowledgement of responsibility on the part of governmental institutions/agencies for harms they commit (Pain, 2009). Rights, wielded by official actors, may represent a barrier to openness and accountability as they reinterpret such rights as a right to use forceful intervention (Robertson, 2000; Hersh, 2005) or unlawful detention (Green and Ward, 2004; Jamieson and McEvoy, 2005; Scahill, 2013) – turning rights into actions. Through these situations and events, the original meaning and intention of human rights is lost, certainly the general appeal to equality, and a differently conceived version is transmitted through action; rights are particularized, limited and assimilated into official discourse and the contested territory of rights returns to the subject of ownership. This contest takes place between governments and populations; it is a power struggle for legitimacy.

The 'war metaphor' (McEvoy, 2003; Steinert, 2003) of state action, a traditional focus of criminology, is apt in this instance for this distance between the powerful and the powerless is a conflict between the state and the people. This theoretical model illustrates the process by which states turn social problems, drug addiction and violence into political/cultural phenomenon – the 'drug problem' for instance – and in creating this new community provide a suitable target on which to launch a major assault: the 'war' on drugs, the 'war' on crime' (McEvoy, 2003: 320). In this development of strategy and rhetoric there is an enemy to be fought and conquered and the emotive use of the term war means that any methodology is acceptable, in this war/emergency situation, and that the campaign will go on indefinitely. The core value to extrapolate, the one most beneficial to the state, is that the war metaphor simplifies matters; it nurtures a 'them' and 'us' mentality (Ruggiero, 2003).

Conclusion

A criminological concern with war and genocide shares intellectual space with critical agendas focused on white-collar and corporate criminality, sexual violence or broader formulations of state crime. Its value is derived from the powerful challenge it brings to the relationship between responsibility, criminality and justice. In the context of armed conflict and mass atrocities the core concepts of criminological thinking are amplified and continuously *resignified*, the theories developing out of an engagement with the evolving nature of this environment mean that we have another way of thinking about those concepts, and this knowledge can be applied to other areas of criminological investigation.

Criminological theory expands and burgeons through the study, analysis and discourse on war; this includes the rhetorical power of war as a metaphor (McEvoy, 2003) and the conceptualization of crime as a dispute (Chambliss, 1975; Christie, 1977, 1981, 1994, 2004; Hulsman, 1986). The study of war and genocide possesses its own specialized concerns but it also has a great deal to offer a wider criminological field of study with respect to conceptions of the individual, the multidimensional configuration and appreciation of responsibility, the significance of punishment, perceptions of justice, the power of the criminal label and censure, the role of human rights, and the central importance of conflict and dispute. We should be drawn to its ambiguity and find intellectual validation in its forceful evasion of oversimplifying paradigms and expeditious categorizations. The important point to make, which encapsulates the overriding incentive for criminologists to study war, is that we do not have to define war in a particular way or make its caprices theoretically manageable, but instead find inspiration in the challenge it presents.

Harms are difficult to evaluate effectively because they are often those acts that states are able to deny because of their legitimacy, a legitimacy derived from a common consciousness that, it could be argued, is limited as a result of the selective apportioning of information, the pervasion of fear throughout the public and private domains and the demands of the market society. If we accept the Durkheimian foundation for criminality, the assault on the collective conscience, we may discover that the collective conscience is besieged by 'moral indifference' rather than indignation: 'With the exception of critical criminology, the discipline of criminology has largely ignored the question of moral indifference to harm' (Pemberton, 2004: 68).

Pemberton's observation echoes Sim's (2004) lament that criminology is ignoring not harm per se but the problems of evaluating harm. The fine line criminologists walk in this respect places them between an actuarial measurable type of harm, which is more aligned to the administrative model of crime, and facilitating a discussion of harm that does not become, as stated above, too abstract. Criminology, Pemberton avers, needs to be more aware of the different forms that society, like the state, assumes.

Confronting harm may have more to do with offering a basis for resistance rather than the provision of fresh conceptions of criminality. For this to occur harm has to be instilled with the power of the criminal label without capitulating to the administrative demands of criminalization. The identification and description of harm, as a preferable alternative to measurement, must serve to emancipate notions of abuse, pain and suffering from constrictive legalistic definitions. By undertaking this discussion of harm we must still be able to address issues of responsibility, transparency and accountability.

Social harm is important in a world of conflict where the search for accountability seems to be little more than an intellectual exercise. Legal parameters limit conceptions of accountability to relatively powerless actors, be they the leaders of rogue states or soldiers on the ground. But the technology of warfare (the use of drones and remote killing), its increasingly global character (facilitating extraordinary rendition and black site torture), and the blatant refusal to accept that powerful democratic states can commit war crimes and abet acts of genocide has also rendered official accountability an ineffective channel to reducing the harms of social conflict (see Lea, Chapter 4 this volume). When researching state crime, in the form of war, war crime and genocide, a social harm perspective is vital because it reaches past legal prescriptions and prohibitions to address the fundamentally destabilizing nature of war as it is utilized by states and it frames accountability in terms of structural inequalities and divisiveness – it is socially empowering in a post-accountability political environment.

References

Allen, C. (2010), *Islmaophobia*, London: Routledge.

Anderson, B. (1991), *Imagined Communities: Reflections on the Origin and Spread of Nationalism*, London: Verso.

Box, S. (1983), *Power, Crime and Mystification*, London: Routledge.

Burke, J. (2005), *Al-Qaeda: The True Story of Radical Islam*, London: Penguin.

Burke, J. (2011), *The 9/11 Wars*, London: Allen Lane.

Burleigh, M. (2000), *The Third Reich: A New History*, London: Macmillan.

Carnagey, N. L. and Anderson, C. A. (2007), 'Changes in attitudes towards war and violence after September 11, 2001', *Aggressive Behavior*, 33 (2), 118–129.

Chambliss, W. J. (1975), 'Toward a political economy of crime', *Theory and Society*, 2 (2), 149–170.

Chambliss, W. J. (1989), 'State-organized crime', in Henry, S. and Einstadter, W. (eds), *The Criminology Theory Reader*, New York: New York University Press.

Chouliaris, A. (2010), 'The reason of state: theoretical inquiries and consequences for the criminology of state crime', in Chambliss, W. J., Michalowski, R. and Kramer, R. C. (eds), *State Crime in the Global Age*, Oregon: Willan Publishing.

Christie, N. (1977), 'Conflicts as property', *British Journal of Criminology*, 17 (1), 1–15.

Christie, N. (1981), *Limits to Pain*, Eugene: Wipf & Stock Publishers.

Christie, N. (1994), *Crime Control as Industry*, London: Routledge.

Christie, N. (2004), *A Suitable Amount of Crime*, London: Routledge.

Cohen, S. (1988), *Against Criminology*, London: Transaction Publishers.

Cohen, S. (2001), *States of Denial*, London: Polity.

Conroy, J. (2000), *Unspeakable Acts, Ordinary People: The Dynamics of Torture*, California: University of California Press.

DiMento, J. F. C. and Geis, G. (2006), 'The extraordinary condition of extraordinary rendition: the C.I.A. the D.E.A, kidnapping, torture, and the law', *War Crimes, Genocide and Crimes against Humanity*, 2, 35–64.

Douglas, M. (1986), *How Institutions Think*, London: Routledge and Kegan Paul.

Durkheim, E. (1984), *Durkheim and the Law*, Oxford: Basil Blackwell.

Falk, R. (1991), 'The terrorist foundation of recent US foreign policy', in George, A. (ed.), *Western State Terrorism*, Cambridge: Polity Press.

Foucault, M. (1975), *Discipline and Punish: The Birth of The Prison*, London: Penguin.

Furedi, F. (2002), *Culture of Fear*, London: Continuum.

Ginsberg, B. (2013), *The Value of Violence*, New York: Prometheus Books.

Green, P. and Ward, T. (2004), *State Crime: Governments, Violence and Corruption*, London: Pluto Press.

Gregory, D. (2011), 'The everywhere war', *The Geographical Journal*, 177 (5), 238–250.

Hagan, J. and Levi, R. (2005), 'Crimes of war and the force of law', *Social Forces*, 83 (4), 1499–1534.

Hall, S., Critcher, C., Jefferson, T., Clarke, J. and Roberts, B. (1978), *Policing the Crisis: Mugging, the State and Law and Order*, London: Macmillan.

Hedges, C. (2002), *War is a Force that Gives Us Meaning*, Oxford: Public Affairs Limited.

Hedges, C. (2012), *The World as it is: Dispatches on the Myth of Human Progress*, Oxford: Nation Books.

Herman, E. S. and Chomsky, N. (1989), *Manufacturing Consent: The Political Economy of the Mass Media*, London: Vintage.

Herr, M. (1978), *Dispatches*, London: Picador.

Hersh, S. M. (2005), *Chain of Command*, London: Penguin.

Hulsman, L. H. C. (1986), 'Critical criminology and the concept of crime', *Contemporary Crisis*, 10 (1), 63–80.

Hulsman, L. H. C. (1996), 'Critical criminology and the concept of crime', in Muncie, J., McLaughlin, E. and Langan, M. (eds), *Criminological Perspectives: A Reader*, London: Sage.

Jamieson, J. and McEvoy, K. (2005), 'State crime by proxy and juridical othering', *British Journal of Criminology*, 45 (4), 504–527.

Jessop, B. (2008), *State Power*, Cambridge: Polity Press.

Kaldor, M. (2006), *New and Old Wars: Organized Violence in a Global Era*, Cambridge: Polity Press.

McEvoy, K. (2003), 'Beyond the metaphor: political violence, human rights and "new" peacemaking criminology', *Theoretical Criminology*, 7 (4), 319–346.

McIntosh, M. (1975) *The Organisation of Crime*, London: Macmillan.

Morrison, W. (2006), *Criminology, Civilisation and the New World Order*, Abingdon: Routledge/ Cavendish.

Pain, R. (2009), 'Globalized fear? Towards an emotional geopolitics', *Progress in Human Geography*, 33 (4), 466–486.

Pantazis, C. and Pemberton, S. (2009), 'From the "old" to the "new" suspect community: examining the impacts of recent UK counter-terrorist legislation', *British Journal of Criminology*, 49 (5), 646–666.

Pemberton, S. (2004), 'A theory of moral indifference: understanding the production of harm by capitalist society', in Hillyard, P., Pantazis, C., Tombs, S. and Gordon, D. (eds), *Beyond Criminology: Taking Harm Seriously*, London: Pluto Press.

Ramet, S. P. (2002), *Balkan Babel: The Disintegration of Yugoslavia from the Death of Tito to the Fall of Milosevic* (fourth edition), Oxford: Westview Press.

Robertson, G. (2000), *Crimes Against Humanity*, London: Penguin.

Rolston, B. (1991), 'Containment and its failure: the British state and the control of conflict in Northern Ireland', in George, A. (ed.), *Western State Terrorism*, Cambridge: Polity Press.

Rose, D. (1996), *In the Name of the Law*, London: Jonathan Cape.

Ruggiero, V. (2003) 'Criminalizing war: criminology as ceasefire', *Social and Legal Studies*, 14 (2), 239–257.

Ruggiero, V. (2010), 'War as corporate crime', in Chambliss, W. J., Michalowski, R. and Kramer, R. C. (eds), *State Crime in the Global Age*, Oregon: Willan Publishing.

Scahill, J. (2007), *Blackwater: The Rise of the World's Most Powerful Army*, London: Serpent's Tail.

Scahill, J. (2013), *Dirty Wars: The World is a Battlefield*, London: Serpent's Tail.

Scahill, J. and the staff of The Intercept (2017), *The Assassination Complex: Inside the Government's Secret Warfare Program*, New York: Simon and Schuster.

Schoultz, I. (2014), 'European Court of Human Rights: accountability to whom?', in Rothe, D. L. and Kauzlarich, D. (eds), *Towards a Victimology of State Crime*, London: Routledge.

Sim, J. (2004), 'The victimised state and the mystification of social harm', in Hillyard, P., Pantazis, C., Tombs, S. and Gordon, D. (eds), *Beyond Criminology: Taking Harm Seriously*, London: Pluto Press.

Slapper, G. and Tombs, S. (1999), *Corporate Crime*, London: Harlow.

Smith, M. and Zeigler, S. M. (2017), 'Terrorism before and after 9/11 – a more dangerous world?', *Research and Politics*, 4 (4), 1–8.

Stanley, E. (2005), 'Truth commissions and the recognition of state crime', *British Journal of Criminology*, 45 (4), 582–597.

Steinert, H. (2003), 'The indispensable metaphor of war', *Theoretical Criminology*, 7 (3), 265–291.

Swanson, D. (2011), *War is a Lie*, London: Biteback Publishing Ltd.

Tombs, S. and Whyte, D. (2007), *Safety Crimes*, Cullompton: Willan.

Tonry, M. (1994), 'Proportionality, parsimony and interchangeability of punishments', in Duff, A. and Garland, D. (eds), *A Reader on Punishment*, Oxford: Oxford University Press.

Walsh, C. (2014), *Cowardice: A Brief History*, Princeton, NJ: Princeton University Press.

War on Want (2016), 'Mercenaries unleashed: the brave new world of private military and security companies', accessed 10 February 2017 at https://waronwant,org/Mercenaries-Unleashed.

Ward, T. (2004), 'State harms', in Hillyard, P., Pantazis, C., Tombs, S. and Gordon, D. (eds), *Beyond Criminology: Taking Harm Seriously*, London: Pluto Press, pp. 84–100.

Weber, M. (1968), *Economy and Society, Vol. 3*, New York: Bedminster Press.

Weiss, M. and Hassan, H. (2015), *Isis: Inside the Army of Terror*, New York: Regan Arts.

Wells, C. (2001), *Corporations and Criminal Responsibility* (second edition), Oxford: Oxford University Press.

Wilkins, L. (1991), *Punishment, Crime and Market Forces*, London: Dartmouth Publishing Co. Ltd.

Wolfendale, J. (2007). 'Terrorism, security, and the threat of counterterrorism', *Studies in Conflict and Terrorism*, 30 (1), 75–92.

Wood, G. (2017), *The Way of the Strangers: Encounters with Islamic State*, London: Penguin/Random House.

6   Environmental crimes: controversies and perspectives

Rosalba Altopiedi

Introduction

Dealing with environmental crimes means also facing some extremely intricate, even controversial, issues: the problem of definition, the multiple dimensions causing different manifestations of environmental harm and the complex estimate of its extent, the actors involved and the necessary activities to control and hinder it. The attention of criminology to this field is not new, actually we can date it back to the pioneering contribution of Sutherland (1949) and his exhortation to go beyond the legal definition of crime and include all the behaviours producing social harm. His call was heeded by a generation of scholars with different theoretical and methodological backgrounds. The environment, though not as a specific topic of study, has found its place in the contributions dealing with powerful crime in various ways (Pearce, 1976). However, since the end of the 1990s an increasing number of scholars have been highlighting a range of questions that reflects a new interest in environmental issues and, more generally, a green perspective in criminology (Ruggiero and South, 2013a). Nigel South has been one of the first scholars asking key questions in this field: 'Why a green criminology? What kinds of existing work might this build upon? What theoretical issues are opened up? And finally, what directions might a green criminology pursue?' (1998: 211–212). These questions started a renewed social thinking on the environment and the challenges represented by biophysical and socio-economic consequences of the several sources of environmental harm (pollution, damage to resources, loss of biodiversity, climate change, and so on), a thought which develops under the conceptual umbrella of green criminology (Ruggiero and South, 2010: 247). In this chapter, we will analyse the most important theoretical perspectives that draw upon South's insight; in particular we will focus on how environmental harm is conceptualized in different theoretical and empirical perspectives. Furthermore, we will focus on environmental victimization including how to define who, or indeed what, an environmental victim is (Williams, 1996, 1998; White, 2011) and the different victims' responses.

Environmental/green crimes: what are we talking about?

Now green criminology represents a well-established field of study with attendant bodies of empirical research, which, however, does not seem to be a 'theory', but rather a set of theoretical and methodological approaches, an emerging perspective (South, 1998: 212–213; White, 2008; Ruggiero and South, 2013b) open to contributions coming from other disciplines, a theoretical laboratory to consider environmental issues in the broadest sense (South et al., 2013).

While it has been developing within the mainstream of critical criminology (South, 2014; Sollund, 2015), green criminology is characterized by a very peculiar perspective that allows going beyond the boundaries of this specific criminological tradition and including knowledge from other disciplines (natural science, medical science, and so on). The rationale of most criminologists' work is detectable, on the one hand, in the attention paid to the analysis of power relations shaping environmental issues, and, on the other hand, in thinking up new strategies able to transform the current social order. Walters (2010: 320) wrote: 'The promotion of new critical narratives in green criminology provides voices of resistance against state and corporate activities that harm humans, non-humans and the natural environment. This calls for interdisciplinary work as well as a politics of engagement with diverse sources of collective concern, power and governance.' South's call (1998) to expand the criminological imagination into this field represented a theoretical and methodological challenge as it invited a rethink about green issues, starting from the vocabulary through which environmental harm is interpreted and determined. Scientific and technical reductionism should be avoided, since it hides the relevant dimensions of power/dominance. The primacy of official knowledge in the definition of such harm and its extent downgrades the worth and legitimacy of lay knowledge carried by the subjects affected by the consequences of such damage. We will come back to this discussion in the following paragraphs.

What do we know?

Echoing South's pioneering essay, 'A green field for criminology? A proposal for a perspective' (1998), we will try to define and delimit more precisely the field of study to be taken into account. Green criminology can be defined as a perspective in the form of a set of theoretical, methodological and political proposals aimed at the study of the degradation of the natural environment, different species (human and non-human) and the planet (Ruggiero and South, 2013b: 360). Consequently, green criminologists analyse not only those behaviours that the law treats as illegal (from a penal, civil or administrative point of view), but all those actions able to cause social harm. The explicit reference here is to zemiology (Hillyard and Tombs, 2004) and, more generally, to all those theoretical positions which see it as necessary to 'question' the law as an instrument of reproduction of the asymmetrical power relations and inequalities present in our society. This tension is well illustrated by Brisman (2008: 731), who distinguishes two approaches to the study of environmental crimes: the legal-procedural approach and the socio-legal approach. If the former is adopted, environmental crime is nothing more than a behaviour punished by existing law; but if the latter is adopted, the analysis will include also all those practices that, despite being legitimate, are destructive from the environmental point of view: 'lawful but awful' (Passas, 2005: 771–786). Several expressions have been used to define this criminological field.

Starting from the classical, Sutherland's research on crimes of the powerful has dealt with different topics. Examples include: corporate criminality and its impacts on the environment; health and safety in the workplace; industry case studies of corporate crimes (the asbestos and pharmaceutical industries, for example) and the illegal disposal of toxic waste, among others. Only between around 1990 and the end of that decade did a number of scholars around the world begin research on the environment, broadly defined, with what could be identified as an emerging 'green criminology' (Ruggiero and South, 2013b: 359). Here we will try to outline some lines of reasoning beginning with traditional research along the path opened by Sutherland's work on white-collar crimes and then analysing the contributions that focused on the environment as their research topic.

In his now classic contribution, Pearce (1976) coined the term 'crime of the powerful' to include white-collar crime, corporate crime and state-corporate crime. His proposal challenges the traditional idea according to which social 'real' problems take place only in the lower strata of society. On the contrary, it gives importance to political economy in the analysis of criminal behaviours. Pearce's is only the first of a series of contributions which, by including and/or by changing the initial label, examine the ordinary business practices adopted by corporations in order to maximize profits, much to the detriment of the environment, the workers or the citizens (among others) (Pearce and Tombs, 1998; Tombs and Whyte, 2007). On the basis of this existing knowledge, Ruggiero (2013: 262–263) highlights and looks into some crucial overlaps in environmental crime, power crime, white-collar crime and economic crime. Ruggiero claims that environmental harm cannot be reduced to a legal/illegal binary concept, but rather it must be included in the licit/illicit continuum. Along this continuum a new category of crime is detectable: the 'foundational power crime' (2013: 263). This deals with behaviours taking place in that 'grey area' where conducts are waiting for the outcomes of the confrontational process of criminalization/decriminalization. Actually, they might become the subject of regulations which prohibit them or turn to unstigmatized routine. A decisive role in avoiding criminalization is assumed by the same economic logics which support the development model of capitalist economies.

A reference to the role of political economy in the comprehension of the complex phenomena that are the source of environmental harm is included also in Greife and Stretesky's contribution (2013). They refer to the assumptions of the treadmill of production theory (Gould et al., 2008) to provide a political and economic explanation for ecological disorganization, or rather the consequences of the capitalist mode of production which threaten the natural environment, humans and non-human beings. According to Greife and Stretesky (2013: 152), the link between the constant increase of production and ecological disorganization tends to be concealed for three reasons: firstly, green technology makes current production seem to be less harmful for the environment than in the past (green washing); secondly, the relocation of production to developing countries hides pollution from Western eyes; finally, environmental regulations only apparently punish the culprits in environmental degradation. The study by Greife and Stretesky on the US oil industry supports the hypothesis that economic interests play a decisive role not only in the shape of environmental regulations but also in their proper enforcement. For the two scholars, the treadmill of production theory is fully consistent with the assumptions of green criminology in determining the role of economic interests connected to particular modes of production in the process of establishing legislation.

The same perspective is taken by White (2013), who underlines the need to analyse the harms, crimes, injustices and corruption practices within the context of an explicit theoretical understanding of the state or economic relations. In his proposal of an eco-global criminology, White analyses transnational environmental crime as the effect of the exploitation of resources imposed by the capitalist mode of production (White, 2010, 2011, 2013). This system underpins a series of intertwined social processes that are gravely undermining global ecology: resource depletion, problems connected with waste disposal (or rather the waste generated in the processes of production, distribution and consumption), colonization of nature by corporations and, finally, a decrease in the number of species and habitat destruction. To combat this long-term trend, it is necessary to intervene in the system of inequality behind this mode of production and innovate it. In White's perspective, the nature of national states as 'places' or facilitators for environmental harm and crime is the preferential subject of study of green criminology: 'There is a need to move from concern about a state of crime, to concern about crimes of the state, which whether by omission or enablement allow the harms to occur' (2013: 258). The above-mentioned aspects should include the risks associated with the globalization of production and trade in foodstuffs, which deserve specific criminological attention. Hazel Croall (2013: 167–182) explores the modes by which 'food crimes' are associated with harmful activities for individuals and the environment. Through the analysis of several behaviours (including food fraud and adulteration, exploitation and new slavery in the production of foodstuffs, cruelty to animals and false labelling), Croall highlights how often these are 'not really or quasi criminal' activities, specified but rarely prosecuted. This is the case with certain practices adopted by several industries that are within the letter of the law and yet have multiple harmful social consequences: 'The practices of many industries, in other words, are lawful but awful both for underprivileged people or countries and for global capitalism itself' (Passas, 2005: 773). The fine line between legal/illegal and between lawful and unlawful is questioned by economic geography too. Gregson and Crang

(2017), with examples drawn from the food sector, argue that the illicit is embedded within the mainstream economy and illicit economies represent more than transnational organized criminal organizations.

The issue of food safety is the core of Reece Walters' considerations in his book *Eco Crime and Genetically Modified Food* (2011). A crucial aspect discussed in the text is the need to 'politicize' the discourse about the risks, damages and potential benefits of genetically modified organisms (GMO), calling into question the hegemony of the biotechnological discourse on these subjects. The aim is to read such an issue with the analytic instruments of political economy also in the light of the criminological notions of 'state', 'corporate' and 'transnational' crime. On this basis, the British scholar suggests adopting the concept of 'eco crime' to catch the complexity of the issue and provide criminology with suitable lenses to observe the worlds of crime. So, criminology will be able to include global environmental harm in its discourse and take an active part also in political and social areas (Kramer et al., 2010; Loader and Sparks, 2010). Further, a recent contribution by Gaarder (2013: 272–281) focuses on the need for green criminology to assume an active role in the process of transformation of the current social and political orders, as well as in the promotion of collective actions. By combining the notions of state-corporate harm and the social construction of the crime, Gaarder underlines how environmental harm affecting most marginalized groups is actually the expression of asymmetrical power differences, which also hinder a correct determination of the causes. The victimization of the disadvantaged groups and the use of effective strategies of denial (Cohen, 2001) enable most powerful subjects to avoid the criminalization of their behaviours and evade their responsibilities.

An interesting perspective is the one proposed by Sollund (2013, 2015), who explores the potentials of an eco-feminist approach to cast a harsh light on the structures of domination in society. In this perspective, the exploitation of the planet and non-human species is deep-seated in the patriarchal structure of domination and in androcentricity, an ideology that puts the masculine point of view at the centre of the world. For the Norwegian scholar, 'studying one form of abuse sheds light on how to understand another, and those oppressed by such "isms" have the same right to concern, and in being recognized as victims, whether women who are victims of violence and abuse . . . human environmental victims . . . or animal victims' (2015: 6). Similar perspectives are taken in Pellow's contribution (2013: 331–345), who, starting from eco-feminist positions, analyses the differences and the common roots of the environmental justice movement and the animal rights movement. He identifies in the 'total liberation movement' (2013: 336), a common space to challenge all institutional and social forms of domination and oppression, of racism and speciesism. The challenge is to hold together the recognition of exiting inequalities, power struggles and forms of racism in the relation between both human and non-human beings and within the human community. Reporting the contributions of radical criminology (especially in the perspective of state-corporate crimes) to combine them with the acquisitions of green studies will make it possible to connect environmental justice with ecological justice.[1]

The analysis of climate change, one of the most critical phenomena of our time and the subject of consideration in many green contributions (White, 2012), is the focus of the essay written by Kramer and Michalowski (2012: 71–88). They employ the concept of 'state-corporate crime' to analyse the severe social and environmental harms produced by climate change, interpreted as disastrous consequences of the common action of economic and political actors. It has been widely argued within the green criminology literature that criminologists cannot simply conduct academic research, but that they should join scientific research and ethical-political instances (public criminology) together, in tune with Burawoy's call (2007: 85): 'Rather than simply be observers cataloguing state-corporate crimes, criminologists concerned with climate change need to engage as public intellectuals, that is, as overt activists for new visions of how humans can live on this planet and how economic and political institutions can be remade in pursuit of those new visions.'

The role of political and economic actors in (de)constructing climate change as a crime is the key consideration of another important contribution. Avi Brisman in 'The cultural silence of climate change contrarianism' (2012: 41–70) analyses the mass media dispute involving politicians, experts and scientists in an attempt to prove or deny the reality of climate change. Brisman puts the focus on the denial campaigns which produce a 'cultural silence' on the issue, also with contradictory messages that impede the recognition of the phenomenon as a social and environmental problem. This approach considers the dynamics related to the media representation or construction of environmental issues and the ways in which public understanding is shaped by the media. One of the tasks of criminology should be to analyse the social construction of the deception, which denies the criminal dimension of behaviours and underestimates their harmful consequences. Brisman asks: 'What environmental crimes, harms, and risks are being reported? What environmental crimes, harms, and risks are not being reported? What causes and consequences (if any) are being reported?' (2012: 64). Not far from Kramer and Michalowski's conclusions, Brisman believes that, in order to counterbalance denial operations, green criminologists should play a vital role in the construction of climate change as a crime. To this end, it is extremely important to highlight the elements of social construction (connected to the power of political and economic actors) of those positions that promote a sort of 'cultural silence' on this issue, a position that is reflected often in the media, and propose a critical interpretation revealing the criminal component of such behaviours. In this field, it will be

---

1 As highlighted by White (2008: 14-23), the analytical distinction between environmental and ecological justice refers to theoretical approaches that outline how scholars see the nature of environmental issues. Environmental justice refers to the different distribution, in terms of access, use and different impacts of particular social practices and environmental risks on human beings. Ecological justice refers to the relationship of human beings in general with the rest of the natural world. The specific interest is towards the planetary environment (which is often seen to possess its own intrinsic value) and to the rights of other species.

possible to imagine new modes of critically analysing the intersection of culture, crime, justice and environment.

The subject matter of the various perspectives that we can gather under the conceptual umbrella of green criminology is environmental harm (not only crime) and the modes through which such behaviours can be regulated, combated and prosecuted (Ruggiero and South, 2013b: 360). We have seen that green criminology is a constitutively inter- and multidisciplinary field. Therefore, only by drawing on comprehensive knowledge will it be possible to get a wider conceptual and observational picture of criminology. As stated by Ruggiero and South:

> Despite (or more likely strengthened by) openness to other disciplines, a 'green' criminology shares the classic characteristics by which Sutherland defined the criminological task, addressing several simple but clear questions—why and how are laws made? Why and how are they broken? What should be done in response? . . . if we are to understand harmful behaviour, we have to be prepared to transcend statutory designations of crime. (2013b: 361)

One of the manners through which it will be possible to widen the conceptual boundaries of criminology is to adopt the point of view of the subjects who are experimenting with the harmful consequences of such actions, analysing the processes of victimization in the environmental fields. The next section will deal with this analysis.

Victims of environmental crimes: a radical perspective

In a recent contribution, Lynch (2013: 45–48) compares the different levels of victimization produced by environmental crimes and by 'street crimes' in the US. Lynch examines several contexts of victimization: air and water pollution, toxic waste poisoning, and so on. Not unlike what happens for white-collar and corporate crimes, it appears that a large number of victims eludes traditional criminological and victimological approaches, which do not take into account environmental crimes and their severe consequences.

The first call for the development of what was then termed environmental victimology came as early as 1996 in an article by Christopher Williams. His considerations are based on some requests for justice formulated by the victims of the Bhopal disaster[2] to the Permanent Court of Arbitration for Industrial and Environmental Risks and Human Rights. Firstly, they deny the passive conditions of victims and

---

2 Bhopal Union Carbide of India, a subsidiary of Union Carbide Corporation, used the highly toxic chemical methyl isocyanate (MIC) to produce carbamate pesticides. On the night of Sunday, 2 December 1984, more than 40 tons of methyl isocyanate gas leaked from a pesticide plant causing the world's worst industrial disaster. There still remains confusion as to how many people died or have been permanently injured. There is an informal consensus among researchers that at least 5,000 died in the disaster's immediate aftermath and at least 200,000 people were exposed to

ask for a guarantee in order to avoid additional victimization; secondly, they claim the right to receive every possible assistance by the government, the corporations and the communities in case of victimization; finally, they make the request not to be victimized again by the state, the enterprises and the courts. As Williams underlines (1996: 16), the formulation of these requests expresses the urgent need to recognize the importance of the demands for justice which are strictly related to environmental victimization, not only for the most striking forms of disasters like the one that occurred in Bhopal in 1984, but also for less tragic, yet still relevant, phenomena, such as pollution. According to Williams' definition, 'environmental victims' are 'those of past, present, or future generations who are injured as a consequence of change to the chemical, physical, microbiological, or psychosocial environment, brought about by deliberate or reckless, individual or collective, human act or act of omission' (1996: 8).

Environmental victimology, which is included within the theoretical framework of 'critical victimology' (Mawby and Walklate, 1994), adopts a perspective able to catch the structural determinants that make individuals more or less vulnerable to environmental victimization. Although some environmental problems concern everybody (e.g. global warming) others affect larger or smaller groups of the population. The different impacts of environmental problems are well illustrated by urban geography too (Hall and Barrett, 2018): 'The environmental problems in cities tend to impact most severely on the poorest and hence most vulnerable groups in urban society and upon the places in the city that they tend to occupy' (2018: 307). Besides the economic factors, there are other elements that can facilitate exposure to differential levels of risk: age, gender, health status, and so on. Actually, as White (2011) underlines, the process of 'becoming a victim' is not neutral, it is the expression of the system of inequalities that characterizes the society: 'Largely these consist of relations of power, domination and exploitation' (2011: 111). The most dangerous industrial activities are installed in (or moved to) the poorest areas; facilities for the treatment of hazardous waste are located in the suburbs, and so on. The extension of victimization (which often regards entire communities), the distance in time and space between criminal actions and harmful consequences, make these victims virtually invisible and, sometimes, unaware of their victimization.

As with environmental crimes, the status of the victim also cannot be taken for granted. Facing these issues is a crucial theoretical challenge with relevant consequences also for the social construction of environmental crimes: who has (or does not have) the power to determine whether a certain behaviour is a crime and, likewise, whether the people who suffer its consequences are victims? The question is further complicated by the fact that there are different types of environmental victimization (White, 2011: 116–117). Skinnider (2011: 31–42), for example, postulates that environmental victims can be classified by a number of different typologies: (1) the nature of wrongful acts; (2) the nature of the harm to victims; (3) the

---

the toxic gases, of whom more than 60,000 were seriously affected and over 20,000 of these have been permanently injured (Pearce and Tombs, 1989: 117).

extent of damages suffered; (4) the scale of crime; and (5) perpetrator identifiability/ relationship with victim.

The central questions are the following: 'Who has the power to apply the label of victims?' and 'What factors are significant in determining whether or not to bestow it? What is the role of the cultural and economic context?' (Altopiedi, 2015: 355). This can be direct or indirect, immediate or long term, be due to soil/air/water pollution by toxic agents or to industry 'routine processing' (as is the case, for example, with the exposure to asbestos for workers in factories and/or citizens who work/ live next to mines), but also it can be connected with specific events (for example, the release of dioxin or other extremely toxic substances following an accident). Environmental victimization can entail alternative victim coping strategies: from unawareness to coordinated fights to obtain justice; from individual requests for compensation to collective action. As highlighted by White, it is necessary to analyse environmental victimization as an 'active social process involving relations of power, domination and resistance' (2011: 106) and deal with the central questions: 'who defines the issues, who fights for or against on the issues, who owns the struggle and how the struggle is shaped and carried out in regards to local and international participants' (2011: 117). These questions reflect another crucial issue: what knowledge contributes (either exclusively or in combination) to define the terms (not only scientific) of the issue considered?

Environmental victims in the public arena

Becoming a victim is a social process which starts with a criminal offence but also requires a cognitive decision by the person(s) against whom it is directed to see themselves as, and assume the status of, victims as part of their strategy for coping with it (Dignan 2005: 13–40). The different forms that environmental victims' responses can assume, from passive acceptance to direct confrontation, from legal disputes to cooperation activities, are connected to the individual's interpretation of the situation and the different strategies to cope with it. Consequently, the following questions are fundamental for the study of environmental crimes and subsequent damages: Which type of knowledge will be legitimized? Which evidence will be considered valid? Which voices will be given proper space in the public and political arena? As White underlines (2011: 117): 'It is rare that scientific evidence is uncontested and that proof of environmental harm is simply a matter of "let the facts decide".' At the core of the issue there will be interests and discourses participating in the definition of the crime and its subsequent harm. The modes through which pollution and other forms of attacks on the environment and on the human being are interpreted, defined and then evaluated, produce an effect on the possibility that victims could gain awareness of their role. As claimed by Natali (2015: 108) 'no defining process is (politically and ethically) neutral'. White again (2011: 119) makes clear that it is necessary to explore the different narratives around the 'risk' or 'harm' coming from the different stakeholders. In this respect, it is possible to identify several 'discourses': legal discourses, that is, the way the law defines the issues; regulatory discourses; expert and lay knowledge; discourses related to legal disputes (for example, the claims for damages by environmental victims or for reputational and production damages by the industry) and mass-media discourses (such as investigative journalism).

Clearly these discourses reveal opposing, often contrasting, interests. Some of them will find a place in the political arena, some others will be kept out. Starting from these considerations, in an environmental/green criminology perspective it is fundamental to explore the conflicting nature of victimization and victims' forms of activism (or lack of it). In previous contributions (Altopiedi, 2011, 2015), we examined the importance of participating in associations and collective movements to transform one's (private) sorrow into a public experience of participation. 'The acquisition of a role as a victim takes place through collective experiences of direct participation and new citizenry, by establishing relations with others who have comparable experiences' (Altopiedi, 2015: 356). In this regard, the issue of human agency and victims' ability to build coalitions with other significant actors is central. In this process, advocates for community members and the community members themselves who have become victims, and label themselves as victims, can voice their concerns and share their stories. In doing so, they contribute to defining the situation in a different way and enhance democratic participation in that process. The identification of the illegal, unjust, criminal nature of what happened is at the centre of the process to acquire new knowledge, that is to say, to develop a different awareness of what was considered normal and now is defined as oppressive. The social construction of their victimization generated a mirror that led to a process of criminalization. Looking at it from a theoretical point of view represents an interesting challenge as it makes it possible to address victimization as a process, by following the path laid out by a constructionist perspective on the criminaliza-tion of environmental/green crimes. To understand victimization as a process it is necessary to identify the key steps of a 'victimization' career: from an initial phase where the individual processes the damage, identifying it as a non-accidental event, then the identification of causes, and lastly the recognition of responsibility towards one's self, to finally ascribe culpability to the authors of the crime. To understand the learning process of the victims it is necessary to focus on two separate moments: the first phase is when the social actors who suffered the damage do not display any social or public reaction, do not develop a moral career, nor do they redefine themselves and their identities. This is followed by a second phase during which social actors undertake a moral 'career' or follow a moral path redefining their iden-tities, retracing the reasons underlying what happened and making sense of events. Making sense implies changing attitudes towards one's self and one's social roles, reorganizing one's identity around the events which led to victimization.

A research agenda

From a general point of view, a first task that green criminologists (and others) should keep fulfilling is incisive criticisms of the structural factors contributing to the production of environmental harm. Yet, on the basis of a pragmatic approach, this has to be done also through direct inclusion in the design of proposals for a substantial social, political, legal and economic reorganization (Loader and Sparks, 2010; Kramer et al., 2010). Ruggiero (2011: 94) identifies exactly in political activism a distinctive characteristic of green criminology, a proximity that specialists are not willing to admit, a commitment that still has to be anchored to empirical research in some relevant areas (Heckenberg and White, 2013: 96–98). Privileged research subjects should be the specific modes through which environmental crimes and the resulting harms are built.

In this regard, the main subject of empirical research should be the several discourses that take shape in (or are excluded from) the public and political arenas. The analysis will cover the legal discourses, or rather the modes with which the law crystallizes crime and liabilities; the scientific discourses, both those that find space in public regulations (and justify them) and those that are competing; and the discourse of victims, that is the knowledge learning by experience (lay knowledge) during their daily life, when they face the reality of an environmental crime that intersects with the socio-natural contexts in which they live. But, as Sollund underlines (2015: 2–5), the role of critical criminology, or radical criminology (Lynch and Stretesky, 2014), is not only to describe and analyse the crimes and harms committed by the powerful, be they states, corporations or more generally the capitalist system (Stretesky et al., 2013). The aim is to transform the existing system and its unequal distribution of power and wealth by rejecting the criminalization of the most disadvantaged strata of society in favour of a fairer distribution of powers or rights.

References

Altopiedi, Rosalba, (2011), *Un Caso di Criminalità d'Impresa: l'Eternit di Casale Monferrato*, Torino: L'Harmattan Italia.

Altopiedi, Rosalba, (2015), 'The Italian Eternit case', in Judith van Erp, Wim Huisman and Gudrun Vande Walle (eds), *The Routledge Handbook of White-Collar and Corporate Crime in Europe*, London and New York: Routledge, pp. 346–360.

Brisman, Avi, (2008), 'Crime-environment relationships and environmental justice', *Seattle Journal for Social Justice*, 6 (2), 727–817.

Brisman, Avi, (2012), 'The cultural silence of climate change contrarianism', in Rob White (ed.), *Climate Change from a Criminological Perspective*, New York: Springer, pp. 41–70.

Burawoy, Michael, (2007), 'For public sociology', in Dan Clawson, Robert Zussman, Joya Misra, Naomi Gerstel, Randall Stokes, Douglas Anderton and Michael Burawoy (eds), *Public Sociology: Fifteen Eminent Sociologists Debate Politics and the Profession in the Twenty-First Century*, Berkeley: University of California Press, pp. 23–64.

Cohen, Stanley, (2001), *States of Denial: Knowing About Atrocities and Suffering*, Cambridge: Blackwell Publishers.

Croall, Hazel, (2013), 'Food crime: a green criminology perspective', in Nigel South and Avi Brisman (eds), *Routledge International Handbook of Green Criminology*, London and New York: Routledge, pp. 167–183.

Dignan, James, (2005), *Understanding Victims and Restorative Justice*, Maidenhead: Open University Press.

Gaarder, Emily, (2013), 'Evading responsibility for green harm: state-corporate exploitation of race, class, and gender inequality', in Nigel South and Avi Brisman (eds), *Routledge International Handbook of Green Criminology*, London and New York: Routledge, pp. 272–281.

Gould, Kenneth A., Pellow, David N. and Schnaiberg, Allan, (2008), *The Treadmill of Production: Injustice and Unsustainability in the Global Economy*, Boulder, CO: Paradigm Publishers.

Gregson, Nicky and Crang, Mike, (2017), 'Illicit economies: customary illegality, moral economies and circulation', *Transactions of the Institute of British Geographers*, 42 (2), 206–219.

Greife, Matthew B. and Stretesky, Paul B., (2013), 'Crude laws: treadmill of production and state variations in civil and criminal liability for oil discharges in navigable waters', in Nigel South and Avi Brisman (eds), *Routledge International Handbook of Green Criminology*, London and New York: Routledge, pp. 150–166.

Hall, Tim and Barrett, Heather, (2018), *Urban Geography*, fifth edition, Abingdon: Routledge.

Heckenberg, Diane and White, Rob, (2013), 'Innovative approaches to researching environmental crime', in Nigel South and Avi Brisman (eds), *Routledge International Handbook of Green Criminology*, London and New York: Routledge. pp. 85–105.

Hillyard, Paddy and Tombs, Steve, (2004), 'Beyond criminology?', in Paddy Hillyard, Christina Pantazis, Steve Tombs and Dave Gordon (eds), *Beyond Criminology: Taking Harm Seriously*, London: Pluto Press, pp. 10–29.

Kramer, Ronald C. and Michalowsk, Raymond J., (2012), 'Is global warming a state-corporate crime?', in Rob White (ed.), *Climate Change from a Criminological Perspective*, New York: Springer, pp. 71–88.

Kramer, Ronald C., Michalowski, Raymond J. and Chambliss, William J., (2010), 'Epilogue: toward a public criminology of state crime', in William J. Chambliss, Ronald C. Kramer and Raymond J. Michalowski (eds), *State Crime in the Global Age*, Cullompton, Devon: Willan Publishing, pp. 247–261.

Loader, Ian and Sparks, Richard, (2010), *Public Criminology?*, London: Routledge.

Lynch, Michael J., (2013), 'Reflections on green criminology and its boundaries: comparing environmental and criminal victimization and considering crime from an eco-city perspective', in Nigel South and Avi Brisman (eds), *Routledge International Handbook of Green Criminology*, London and New York: Routledge. pp. 43–57.

Lynch, Michael J. and Stretesky, Paul B., (2014), *Exploring Green Criminology: Toward a Green Criminological Revolution*, Farnham and Burlington: Ashgate.

Mawby, Rod I. and Walklate, Sandra, (1994), *Critical Victimology: International Perspectives*, London: Sage.

Natali, Lorenzo, (2015), *Green Criminology: Prospettive Emergenti Sui Crimini Ambientali*, Torino: Giappichelli editore.

Passas, Nikos, (2005), 'Lawful but awful: "legal corporate crimes"', *The Journal of Socio-Economics*, 34, (6), 771–786.

Pearce, Frank, (1976), *Crimes of the Powerful: Marxism, Crime and Deviance*, London: Pluto.

Pearce, Frank and Tombs, Steve, (1989), 'Bhopal: Union Carbide and the hubris of the capitalist technocracy', *Social Justice*, 16 (2), 116–145.

Pearce, Frank and Tombs Steve, (1998), *Toxic Capitalism: Corporate Crime in the Chemical Industry*, Aldershot: Ashgate.

Pellow, David N., (2013), 'Environmental justice, animal rights, and total liberation: from conflict and distance to points of common focus', in Nigel South and Avi Brisman (eds), *Routledge International Handbook of Green Criminology*, London and New York: Routledge. pp. 331–347.

Ruggiero, Vincenzo, (2011), 'Book review: green criminology as political activism?' (Rob White (ed.) (2010), *Global Environmental Harm: Criminological Perspectives*, Cullompton: Willan), *Crime, Law and Social Change*, 56, (1), 91–94.

Ruggiero, Vincenzo, (2013), 'The environment and the crimes of the economy', in Nigel South and Avi Brisman (eds), *Routledge International Handbook of Green Criminology*, London and New York: Routledge, pp. 261–270.

Ruggiero, Vincenzo and South, Nigel, (2010), 'Critical criminology and crimes against the environment', *Critical Criminology*, 18 (4), 245–250.

Ruggiero, Vincenzo and South, Nigel, (2013a), 'Toxic state-corporate crimes, neo-liberalism and green criminology: the hazards and legacies of the oil, chemical and mineral industries', *International Journal for Crime, Justice and Social Democracy*, 2 (2), 12–26.

Ruggiero, Vincenzo and South, Nigel, (2013b), 'Green criminology and crimes of the economy: theory, research and praxis', *Critical Criminology*, 21 (3), 359–373.

Skinnider, Eileen, (2011), *Victims of Environmental Crime – Mapping the Issues*, Vancouver: The International Centre for Criminal Law Reform and Criminal Justice Policy.

Sollund, Ragnhild A., (2013), 'The victimization of women, children and non-human species through trafficking and trade', in Nigel South and Avi Brisman (eds), *Routledge International Handbook of Green Criminology*, London and New York: Routledge, pp. 317–330.

Sollund, Ragnhild A., (ed.) (2015), *Green Harms and Crimes Critical Criminology in a Changing World*, London: Palgrave Macmillan.

South, Nigel, (1998), 'A green field for criminology? A proposal for a perspective', *Theoretical Criminology*, 2 (2), 211–233.

South, Nigel, (2014), 'Green criminology: reflections, connections, horizons', *International Journal for Crime, Justice and Social Democracy*, 3 (2), 6–21.

South, Nigel, Brisman, Avi and Beirne, Piers, (2013), 'A guide to a green criminology', in Nigel South and Avi Brisman (eds), *Routledge International Handbook of Green Criminology*, London and New York: Routledge, pp. 27–42.

Stretesky, Paul B., Long, Michael A. and Lynch, Michael J., (2013), *The Treadmill of Crime: Political Economy and Green Criminology*, Abingdon: Routledge.

Sutherland, Edwin. H., (1949), *White Collar Crime*, New York: Holt, Rinehart & Winston.

Tombs, Steve and Whyte, David, (2007), *Safety Crime*, Portland, OR: Willan Publishing.

Walters, Reece, (2010), 'Toxic atmospheres: air pollution, trade and the politics of regulation', *Critical Criminology*, 18 (4), 307–323.

Walters, Reece, (2011), *Eco Crime and Genetically Modified Food*, New York: Routledge.

White, Rob, (2008), *Crimes Against Nature: Environmental Criminology and Ecological Justice*, London: Willan.

White, Rob, (2010), 'Globalisation and environmental harm', in Rob White (ed.), *Global Environmental Harm: Criminological Perspectives*, Cullompton: Willan Publishing, pp. 3–19.

White, Rob, (2011), *Transnational Environmental Crime: Toward an Eco-global Criminology*, London and New York: Routledge.

White, Rob, (2012), 'The criminology of climate change', in Rob White (ed.), *Climate Change from a Criminological Perspective*, New York: Springer, pp. 1–11.

White, Rob, (2013), 'Eco-global criminology and the political economy of environmental harm', in Nigel South and Avi Brisman (eds), *Routledge International Handbook of Green Criminology*, London and New York: Routledge, pp. 243–260.

Williams, Christopher, (1996), 'An environmental victimology', *Social Justice*, 23 (4), 16–40.

Williams, Christopher, (ed.) (1998), *Environmental Victims: New Risks, New Injustice*, London: Earthscan.

7 Transnational governance and cybercrime control: dilemmas, developments and emerging research agendas

Majid Yar

Introduction

The processes of globalization and transnationalization lie at the heart of debates about the development of cyber-society, and figure centrally in how the challenges associated with cybercrime are often understood. Two salient areas of criminological literature – one related to globalization, the other addressing cybercrimes – often converge upon a shared assumption, namely that global integration via electronic communication networks has transformed the contours of criminal activity, unleashing a flow of crime problems that transcends borders and overwhelms attempts to establish control. Such assessment of our present state of affairs is commonplace not only in criminological discourse but also in wider popular and political consciousness. This chapter takes stock of the current contours of global cybercrime and seeks to critically assess (and perhaps challenge) the claim that the processes underpinning it either go unchallenged or are irreversible. In a turbulent period where reactions against globalization are gaining political and popular traction, it is necessary to consider how reassertions of national sovereignty on the economic, political and legal planes might impact upon global flows of illegal and illicit communication, and in turn may reshape efforts to criminalize and control a range of online practices.

The Internet and globalization: cause and effect

Disputes and disagreements notwithstanding, we can suggest that social sciences have converged upon a broad common understanding of globalization as a transformative process that is configured around the attenuation of spatial-temporal barriers to action, interaction and movement. In speaking of 'time-space compression' (Harvey, 1991) or 'time-space distanciation' (Giddens, 1990), we confront the ongoing process, central to the configuration of modernity as a social formation, that extends the spatial scale of human actions and their effects. This spatial reconfiguration has made itself evident across numerous social spheres or systems: manufacturing, finance, work, culture and leisure, to name but a few (Held et al., 2000; Williams et al., 2013; Cohen et al., 2015). These and numerous other phenomena are associated with the reconfiguration of experience under the impact of globalization.

At one level, the communication processes and practices associated with the Internet and related technologies can be seen as just one further instance of the kinds of developments already mentioned. However, it can be argued that the rise of the Internet and computer-mediated communication (CMC) are more than just further *manifestations* of globalization; rather, they are in a crucial sense the *preconditions* or *drivers* that have enabled globalization to advance and develop into its current configurations. This argument is most forcefully and influentially made by Manuel Castells in his monumental three-volume work on 'the network society' (Castells, 1996, 1997, 1998). Here Castells argues that a wholesale revolution across all domains of life (including community, identity, politics and culture, as well as labor) has been enabled not just by the development of information and communication technologies (ICTs) per se, but also their connection into globe-spanning networks of interconnectivity (the Internet comprising the most obvious and significant instance). Not only do these technologies enable a new information-based economy to emerge, but they also enable the radical reconfiguration of human interrelations and institutions, which now transcend locality and place, existing instead in a global 'space of flows.' Increasingly, Castells argues, it is ICT-based interaction that permits the formation of network-based social collectives, communities and social movements, comprising a web-like nexus of manifold individuals brought together via near-instantaneous electronic connectivity. State power, based as it is upon sovereign control over a clearly delimited territorial domain, is incrementally eroded by flows of activity and association that blithely transcend all borders (a pivotal issue for criminology, to which we shall return shortly). The network, based upon digital ICTs, is for Castells nothing less than a new morphology of social life, the organizing force behind a dynamic new global order. This process of globalization may be summarized as the social, economic, political and cultural processes in which local and national spatial limits on interaction are overcome, and come to span the globe.

The preceding line of argument implies that any adequate understanding of global social change, the challenges it generates, and the responses it elicits, needs to accord central importance to the role of digital communications technologies such as the Internet. Moreover, as Aas (2007) argues, the manifestations of globalization include among their number the production, multiplication and distribution of various harms and that serve to exacerbate the problems of human suffering. We need think only of the most pressing political and social problems of the day, including human-induced global climate change, the flows of refugees fleeing war and poverty, and the upsurge of terrorist violence to recognize some of the most troubling and challenging elements of the globalized order. It is in this frame, of course, that the concerns of criminology converge with those of globalization studies. In addition to the aforementioned problems of war and terrorism (see chapters by Lea and Mitchell, Chapters 4 and 5 this volume), globalization is imbricated with numerous other criminologically-relevant problems, including human trafficking and modern slavery, fraud and corruption, land and resource theft, and the trade in everything from prohibited narcotics and counterfeit goods to endangered species and looted antiquities (on counterfeit goods and drugs, see Chapters 8 and 11 in this volume by Large and Martin respectively). As we shall explore below, not only does the Internet generate its own unique global crime problems, but it also plays a pivotal role in facilitating many of the offline illicit and illegal activities just mentioned.

Globalization and cybercrime

Internet crimes, or cybercrimes as they have come to be commonly known, can be defined and classified in a number of ways. In the most straightforward terms, the term cybercrime denotes those legally prohibited activities whose preparation and commission relies centrally upon using the electronic communication networks associated with the Internet. We might wish to classify cybercrimes according to a well-trodden criminological distinction between crimes perpetrated by force and those committed through fraud (Gottfredson and Hirschi, 1990). However, criminologists focusing upon the Internet have found it useful to distinguish between 'computer integrity crimes,' 'computer assisted crimes' and 'computer content crimes' (see in particular Wall, 2001, 2007). Each of these forms of offending depend upon exploiting different facets of the Internet's information and communication infrastructure. As we overview these kind of cybercrimes below, it is important to remember, in the context of the present discussion, that they all routinely transcend the spatial delimitations of locality, region and nation, partaking of a truly global digital 'space of flows.'

Firstly, computer integrity crimes are those aimed at the network of electronic communications itself, targeting variously its computer hardware and the software that enables it to function. These crimes include hacking (unauthorized access, intrusion and potentially interference with a computer system); the distribution of 'malware' (malicious software, such as viruses, worms and Trojans) that can affect the operation of the devices targeted; and 'denial of service' attacks that take web-based services offline, often by flooding them with an unmanageable number of communication requests. It has been reported, for example, that the Russian military now routinely recruits computer specialists and programmers to staff its cyber-warfare efforts, aimed at using such computer intrusion and manipulation techniques against foreign states (Kramer, 2016).

The second kind of offences, computer-assisted crimes, represents, in contrast, a reworking of established forms of offending in the new informational environment. They include various forms of theft and fraud – they may target goods and services, money and finance, or information itself (such as confidential data, personal details, private communications or, as is extremely common, the various forms of legally-protected intellectual properties that are bought and sold online). They also include a variety of forms of interpersonal victimization, such as sexual harassment, virtual abuse and stalking. These are all offences that predate the existence of modern ICTs. However, while they may not be qualitatively unprecedented, their transposition to the medium of digital communication does transform them in significant ways that must be criminologically recognized. For example, fraudsters are now enabled to make their 'pitches' electronically to millions of potential victims worldwide through spam emailing, and can do so simultaneously and at virtually no cost. The increasing use of ICTs for financial transaction (ranging from e-shopping, through e-banking, to cashless payment using mobile devices) renders users vulnerable to appropriation of sensitive information, including details of credit cards and bank accounts. Through communication channels such as email, instant messaging and social media, individuals are made vulnerable to abuse, bullying and threats. The ability to reproduce and virtually distribute digitized content creates seemingly ungovernable levels of unauthorized copying and sharing of musical recordings, motion pictures and computer software. Moreover, all of these offences can be committed at a distance, and with varying degrees of anonymity, which means that the offender can communicate without having his or her identity available to others. These characteristics generate major challenges for policing and securing the information society, especially at the transnational level.

The third type of offences centers on the content of computerized communication itself. Of particular note are those communications that breach legally defined limits on speech, where for example certain types of communication and representation are considered harmful to society and its various social constituencies. These include high-profile and widely debated practices such as the circulation of obscene and violent images, sexualized images of children, expressions that incite political violence (such as terrorism), and messages that express and incite hatred against ethnic, religious, sexual and other minorities. Again, these forms of communicative content have long existed, but take on a new lease of life in the online environment. Networked communications enable such content to be globally disseminated, enable the bypassing of restrictions imposed on established media channels, allow the exploitation of legal differences around restricted speech in different countries, and also afford those responsible a degree of anonymity that makes them difficult to identify and act against. This capacity for extended communication is not, of course, entirely negative, as it can also enable a variety of social actors to bypass state censorship and ensure the circulations of truths and opinions that authorities may otherwise be able to silence.

Global governance and cybercrime control: an emerging architecture

In addition to mapping and explaining cybercrimes, there is a major task facing criminological research in terms of understanding the distinctive challenges such offences present in terms of policing, crime control and crime prevention, and assessing the kinds of responses they incite from both state and non-state actors.

Some of the crime control challenges are readily apparent, such as the aforementioned issue of online anonymity. The ability of individuals to disguise their identity and location, in whole or part, presents serious barriers for victims reporting offences and for criminal justice agencies investigating and prosecuting them. There now exist various widely-available privacy enhancing technologies, such as Virtual Private Networks (VPNs), that enable Internet users to evade straightforward identification (Savchenko and Gatsenko, 2015). While there are legitimate reasons for using such tools when online (for example so as to protect one's privacy and minimize the chances of intrusive state or corporate surveillance), they nevertheless amplify the challenges faced when responding to cybercrimes. Moreover, recent years have seen the rise of hidden electronic networks – so-called 'darknets' or the 'dark web' – which have become associated with 'cryptomarkets' dealing in a wide range of illegal goods including narcotics, weapons and child sexual abuse images, as well the coordination of terrorist-related activity (Omand, 2015; Maddox et al., 2016; Weimann, 2016).

It is noteworthy that a significant proportion of such trade and exchange is international in character (Broséus et al., 2017), part and parcel of the greater global flow of goods, services and cultural communication facilitated by ICTs. Whether taking place in the conventional World Wide Web or its 'dark' counterparts, cybercrimes partake of a de-spatializing logic that defies traditional criminological notions of the crime event (especially the notion that a crime requires a convergence in space and time between an offender on the one hand and a target or victim on the other) (Yar, 2005). Occurring in the 'space of flows' rather than the 'space of place,' cybercrimes present particular problems for the apparatus of policing and crime control that has historically been configured around territorial organization at the levels of locality and nation states. A further complicating factor when confronting cybercrimes relates to the sometimes significant legal differences between sovereign territories, with the selfsame behavior being prohibited in one country but permitted in another (see Hudson, Chapter 2 this volume). This variance in the codification of criminal law is most readily apparent in the case of cyber-based content crimes. For example, certain forms of political, religious and sexual expression/representation may be the subject of criminal sanctions in authoritarian and/or socially conservative countries, but entirely within the bounds of normalized (and indeed legally protected) free speech in others. When such communications routinely flow across and between countries with such potentially different constructions of criminal behavior, there arise inevitable difficulties and conflicts over whether and how they are to be controlled. It is in light of these and other related problems that the Internet has become subject to an emerging architecture of transnational governance.

The emergence of governance as a multi-disciplinary concept in the critical social sciences owes much of its initial impetus to an engagement with Foucault's theorization of power and its rejection of the state-centric, top-down understanding of social ordering proposed by Marxism. From this standpoint, social control emanates not from a single locus of power, but is transversally dispersed across the social fabric, a 'micro-physics' that produces and reproduces conformity through a multitude of practices located in a bewildering array of spaces and sites (Foucault, 1991, 2000). In the field of criminology, this influence made itself felt in a range of interventions including theorizations of the changing character of policing and criminal justice (see for example Feeley and Simon, 1994) as well as wide-ranging socio-historical analyses charting the shifting dynamics of social control across the span of modernity (see in particular Cohen, 1985).

However, during the same period, a much more pragmatic, policy-oriented explor-ation of governance was starting to emerge not in sociology or social theory, but in the fields of public administration and organizational studies. Here, the concept of governance was tied to the idea of multi-party policy networks (spanning public, private and voluntary sectors) which came together in order to effect functions of social coordination or 'steering' (Rhodes, 2007). Governance here refers to 'changed conditions of ordered rule' (Rhodes 1996: 652–3) such that outcomes previously effected through centralized government actions are now achieved through dif-ferent processes occurring outside the institutions of the nation state. Building on this kind of understanding, 'global governance' has been coined and mobilized over recent decades to denote the ways in which state-centric control of society, incrementally frayed by the impact of globalization processes, requires and incites the emergence of new modes of transnational coordination that transcend the bounded territoriality of the nation. Thus, global governance denotes 'any purpose-ful activity intended to "control" or influence someone else that either occurs in the arena occupied by nations or, occurring at other levels, projects influence into that arena' (Finkelstein, 1995: 368). The agents of such governance activity can include states acting in concert or through mutual agreement, but also crucially include numerous non-national state actors such as NGOs (e.g. pressure groups, char-ities) corporations, transnational institutions such as the International Criminal Court and the European Court of Human Rights, and transnational or supra-state organizations such as the United Nations, OECD, IMF, WTO and the World Bank. The 'object' over which these actors seek to exercise control or influence is precisely the span of human activity that ruptures, crosses or overflows national borders. On this understanding, global governance amounts to 'governing, without sover-eign authority, relationships that transcend national frontiers. Global governance is doing internationally what governments do at home' (Finkelstein, 1995: 369). A not insignificant part of this apparatus of governance deals with transnational crime problems. To offer just one example: agencies such as Europol, Interpol and UNODC (the United National Office on Drugs and Crime) respond to the global trade in illicit narcotics, corruption and terrorism through a span of activities that include research, intelligence sharing, training, forensic services, coordination of enforcement operations and assistance with the ratification and implementation of treaties and agreements (Interpol, 2016; UNODC, 2016).

The global governance of the Internet can be seen as a prime and pivotally impor-tant instance of the effort to exercise control over actions, interactions and 'flows' that exceed the territorial boundedness of national spaces. After all, the very nature of the Internet as a globally dispersed network of communication means that the practices it enables routinely transcend such borders. As Cairncross (2000: 177) puts it: 'Government jurisdictions are geographic. The Internet knows few boundaries. The clash between the two will reduce what individual countries can do. Government sovereignty, already eroded by forces such as trade liberalisation, will diminish further.' If nation states cannot effect control over Internet-enabled activities, then an alternative, transnational or global apparatus of governance is cultivated by those in power so as to bring uniformity and order to cyberspace.

At the most basic level, the Internet requires such governance activity so as to establish and enforce the basic rules and operating procedures (such as common technical standards) that enable computers anywhere in the network to connect to, and successfully exchange information with, all other such devices wherever they may be located. It is precisely for this purpose that the first building block for Internet governance was set in place in 1998 in the form of ICANN (Internet Corporation for Assigned Names and Numbers). A non-profit private corporation, created at the behest of the US Clinton administration, ICANN was assigned responsibility for policy around IP addresses, domain names and Internet protocols (Mueller, 1999). Its structure typified the hybridized, pluralistic and multilateral character of global governance, including among its members representatives of 'supporting organizations,' a Governmental Advisory Committee comprising representatives from more than 130 states, as well as observers from a huge range of international and transnational organizations (ranging from space agencies and telecommunications bodies to Interpol, UNESCO and the WHO) (ICANN, 2013). Its structure and operations have not been without controversy, with questions being raised about its authority, accountability and historically-configured proximity to the United States government (Weinberg, 2000; Mueller and Kuerbis, 2014). These controversies notwithstanding, it is important to note that the scope of ICANN's remit deals only with the structures and standards by which the Internet operates, and does not impinge upon any matters related to content or the kinds of activities in which users might engage. In other words, by design and intent, it holds no sway in terms of exercising control over how the Internet is used, including crucial issues about the legality and illegality of online behaviors. For attempts to exercise control over such matters, we need to look elsewhere.

The control or regulation of online behavior (what people *do* with the Internet once commonly agreed standards ensure its smooth running) spans numerous substantive issues, including the kinds of cybercrime problems we have already noted (e.g. malware and hacking, hate speech, stalking, harassment, sexual abuse, terrorist activity, theft and fraud) but also related issues around spam, privacy, consumer protection, financial and business transactions, and management of trademarks and other kinds of intellectual property (IP) (Mueller et al., 2007: 245). Such controls can be sought through a variety of instruments, including laws (criminal and civil), regulatory standards, codes of practice, as well as a range of technical measures or 'fixes' (e.g. digital rights management (DRM) tools to prevent unauthorized copying of protected media content such as movies and software, or user authentication tools to control and limit access to secure systems like those for online banking). There are, we can suggest, two main aspects of these efforts to institute global Internet governance, namely those associated with the *creation* of laws, regulations and standards, and those associated with their *implementation* or *enforcement*. These will be considered below in turn, with the primary focus falling upon crime-related issues.

With respect to the first area of activity, we have already noted that divergences between national legal frameworks present a major obstacle to the creation of a coherent global regime of cybercrime control – after all, if there is no agreement between/across actors as to what is or is not to be deemed a criminal offense, what hope is there of achieving meaningful action so as to generate effective behavioral constraints? In response, one of the primary channels for pursuing common rules and standards for permissible online conduct has been through the forging of transnational and multilateral treaties and conventions to which participating nation states commit themselves. For example, in the area of online IP protection and the corresponding efforts to confront media 'piracy,' we have seen measures under the auspices of the WTO's TRIPS agreement (Agreement on Trade-Related Aspects of Intellectual Property Rights) requiring signatory states (all 162 WTO members) to institute criminal law prohibitions and sanctions for large-scale violations of IP rights, such as copyrights and trademarks. While these efforts predate the Internet and were initially directed at the manufacture and sale of counterfeit goods, they only gained significant momentum as the growth of the Internet elevated the issue of IP protection to one of economic urgency for the advanced industrial economies (Williams, 2010: 477–8). In addition to these 'piecemeal' responses aimed at discrete cybercrime problems, more ambitious efforts in the domain of international law have sought to craft a much more systematic and broad-based framework for crime control as regards the Internet and ICTs. In particular, we can note the Council of Europe's Cybercrime Convention (the so-called Budapest Convention), which requires all ratifying states (presently 56 in number, including 23 non-European states) to criminalize activities related to hacking, the use of computers to commit crimes such as fraud, child sex abuse imagery and IP violations (Clough, 2014; COE, 2017). In addition to such binding obligations set out in international law, we see also activities on the part of various intergovernmental organizations (IGOs) who seek to persuade member states to enact measures to curb or control cybercrimes. For example, the OECD seeks to shape public governance in member countries, including measures to tackle Internet-related problems such as IP violations, Internet-enabled frauds, and trading in illicit goods.

Outside of the intergovernmental sphere we see the creation of self-regulatory regimes by, and among, online service providers intended to set boundaries on permitted behavior. For example, the social networking platform Facebook makes as a precondition of use the adherence to predefined 'community standards' covering issues such as graphic violence, nudity and sexualized imagery, threats and bullying, and the procurement and sale of prohibited goods and sexual services (Facebook, 2017). Similarly, Twitter's 'user agreement' prohibits behavior including

IP violations, posting 'abusive and hateful content,' unauthorized sharing of someone else's private information or 'intimate media' (e.g. nude images, 'sex tapes,' etc.), and distribution of spam and malware (Twitter, 2017). Other popular social media platforms, such as Instagram and Snapchat, also institute comparable constraints upon users. The parameters of such rules – which act as boundary-markers for delineating the acceptable from the harmful, dangerous or illicit – typically enact formal legal sanctions and prohibitions, but can also exceed them by drawing upon broader social and cultural norms about acceptable and unacceptable content and behavior (as, for example, with Facebook's rules against graphic nudity and sexualized content, which are oriented not by laws around obscenity but by user and community concerns that minors and other vulnerable persons not be exposed to content deemed 'inappropriate' or unwelcome). Other non-state actors (such as NGOs, charities, pressure groups and campaigning organizations) may also play a decisive role in negotiating and shaping such rules and sanctions. A notable example is provided by the case of child protection charities that seek to advise and influence service- and content-providers so as to prevent sharing of sexualized images of minors and inappropriate contact between adult users and children. In sum, what we see here is a dynamic 'system' of rule-making that involves numerous state and non-state actors in setting the parameters and rules for the social control of online behavior. We shall return shortly to consider the effectiveness and limitations of these rules at the level of their implementation.

The enforcement of social control measures related to cybercrime can likewise be identified through a range of transnational, multilateral and 'mixed' (state, quasi-state, IGO, NGO, public and private) governance configurations. Part of the day-to-day business of 'policing the Internet' remains with traditional law-enforcement actors located at both state (national, federal) and sub-state (local, regional, state) levels. Taking the example of England and Wales, all 43 of its territorially-based police forces have some kind of specialist provision for tackling computer-related and Internet-based offences, albeit organized in varying configurations; at the national level, the National Crime Agency now incorporates what was previously the Police Central e-crime Unit (PCeU), and takes a lead role in tackling cybercrime alongside related crime problems such as organized crime and economic crime. However, the transnational character of cybercrime problems has led to a significant role for supra-state criminal justice actors, such as the aforementioned Interpol and Europol, as well as IGOs such as UNODC. Interpol, for example, involves itself in research, intelligence gathering, training and enforcement coordination related to various types of cybercrime (such as frauds, thefts, hacking, ransomware attacks), as well as developing analytical tools to help tackle emerging threats such as crime on 'darknets' facilitated by the use of virtual currencies like Bitcoin. In keeping with the hybrid and pluralized character of cybercrime control, some of these activities involve public-private partnerships bringing together organizations like Interpol and commercial entities in areas such as banking and mobile communications (Interpol, 2016: 5–8). Likewise, Europol's European Cybercrime Centre (EC3), established in 2013, participates in enforcement by providing operational support and forensic capacity, as well as engaging in a broader range of activities related to strategy, outreach, training and public awareness and preventive measures (Europol, 2017). Such transnational efforts comprise an important part of the public and quasi-public effort to establish governance over ICT-mediated behaviors.

We can now consider the importance of private (non-state and non-IGO) actors in social control and law-enforcement activities online. It is frequently noted by cybercrime researchers that the capacities of public law enforcement are out-stripped by the scale and complexity of the online environment and there is conse-quently a significant deficit when it comes to the ability of criminal justice systems to respond to cybercriminal conduct (Wall, 2007). Consequently, any account of cyber-governance as regards criminal and transgressive behavior needs to pay proper attention to the pivotal role played by non-state actors in exercising social control. Various forms of informal social control can be exercised by Internet users, as for example when individuals who engage in rule-breaking behavior are socially shamed, criticized or chastised by others (Leukfeldt and de Pauw, 2012). In such instances, Internet users act as 'netizens' who forge and activate shared norms that regulate conduct (Williams, 2006). At a more organized and systematic level, we have already noted the role of service-providers like social networking platforms in creating rules of conduct upon which continued access to media channels is con-tingent. Tied to these behavioral strictures we find ongoing enforcement efforts. Thus, user content and behavior on such platforms are routinely assessed by teams of paid moderators (Facebook currently employs some 7,500 full-time staff in this capacity – Kuchler, 2017) and breach of the rules will result in content removal and even expulsion of offenders from the platform. The effectiveness of such online social control measures has been subject to questioning, with the likes of Facebook being accused of both glaring failures to check harmful and illegal content, and of being heavy-handed by unnecessarily blocking content that is benign and/or socially important. In an instance of the former, lawyers in the United States and Israel have sued Facebook on behalf of 20,000 complainants who allege that the platform has failed to remove content that incites violence against Jews (Jewish News Online, 2015). In a recent instance of the latter, the platform has been accused of banning content that highlights the systematic 'ethnic cleansing' being perpetrated by the Myanmar state against the Rohingya Muslim minority (Wong et al., 2017). The failure to act against content and behavior that is illegal and/or in breach of 'com-munity standards' draws attention to the reality that, just as the sheer volume of online interactions exceeds the reactive capacity of criminal justice agencies, so they may also outstrip the personnel and resources that service-providers are able or willing to commit. For example, in 2013 Facebook alone saw 350 million photos being uploaded by users every day (Smith, 2013), any of which may potentially be in breach of legal or other prohibitions. On the other hand, controversies about the unwelcome removal of content exemplify the dilemmatic character of online social control, where those exercising it must negotiate potentially hotly-contested issues as well as cross-national variations in what is or is not deemed legally permissible. In the aforementioned censoring of content related to the plight of the Rohingya, for example, international human rights activists have decried the decision as an attack on free speech; however, it has been welcomed by the Myanmar authorities as they claim that much of the content is being posted by Arsa, a Rohingya insurgent group that they have outlawed as a 'terrorist organisation' (Wong et al., 2017).

Rethinking global governance and social control of the Internet

The discussion thus far has mapped a research agenda in which criminological analysis of the Internet converges with, and borrows from, the perspective of globalization studies. Consequently, this approach places particular emphasis upon the displacement of nation states in favor of transnational networks of extra- and supra-state actors when it comes to creating and enforcing rules over online behavior. In this final section, we consider a more skeptical standpoint that challenges assumptions about a unilinear and progressive move away from state-centric power where it comes to crime control. This alternative stance has significant implications for how criminologists understand the dynamics that are at play in Internet governance and how they might evolve in the near future.

A first important criticism of the global governance narrative concerns the real extent to which state actors have in fact been disempowered by globalization processes. It is undoubtedly true that with respect to the Internet, as with other domains of the social, recent decades have seen a proliferation of non- and supra-state actors that are involved in rule-setting and rule-enforcement. However, what is less clear-cut is the extent to which globalization processes have 'forced the hand' of state actors and pushed them into increasingly more marginal and limited roles. Drezner (2004) argues that, firstly, while states may delegate or externalize governance functions to other actors (IGOs, NGOs, businesses, and so on) they retain control over the parameters within which those other actors can legitimately function. They set the frameworks and 'rules of the game' within which non-state actors operate, and retain the ability to renegotiate those rules should they deem them to have become disadvantageous to state actors' interests and preferences. In essence, non-state actors such as ICANN are licensed to undertake regulatory functions related to the Internet because states (especially the most politically and economically powerful of them) converge upon and approve the destination to which the regulation leads. State actors will also engage in 'forum shopping' to select and allocate governance functions to those entities they deem 'optimal . . . to advance their preferences' (Drezner, 2004: 485), thereby once again retaining a significant degree of control from 'behind the scenes' (for further discussion of 'forum shopping' in the context of global governance, see Murphy and Kellow, 2013). Moreover, state coercion always waits in the wings if those other actors are deemed to have failed to meet the responsibilities with which they have been allocated. For example, we have already noted the self-regulatory regimes for removing illegal content that have been set up by social networking platforms. However, of late such providers (especially the likes of Facebook) have come under concerted criticism for failure to act sufficiently speedily and thoroughly to remove prohibited content, especially that which relates to the sexualization of children and hateful/

extremist ideology (Elgot, 2017). Consequently, the UK Parliament's influential Home Affairs Select Committee of MPs has raised the possibility both of (a) legal changes which would make failure to remove illegal content itself a crime, and (b) a system of substantial financial penalties for those who 'fail to remove illegal content within a strict timeframe' (Annicelli, 2017; House of Commons Home Affairs Committee, 2017). These developments suggest that research into online crime control needs to pay more attention to the role and influence of state actors, rather than assuming that the delegation of regulatory functions automatically means that states are somehow denuded of power.

A second element of this alternative standpoint, and its implications for criminological research, relates to what happens when states diverge or disagree about their preferred outcomes. Drezner suggests that in such cases the rules agreed under the auspices of treaties and agreements are more a matter of appearance than substance, allowing states to continue pursuit of their own interests, even as they conflict with those of other states. These amount to 'sham standards': 'Governments agree to a notional set of standards with weak or non-existent monitoring or enforcement schemes. Sham standards permit governments to claim the de jure existence of global regulatory coordination, even in the absence of effective enforcement' (Drezner, 2004: 484; see also discussion in Rioux and Fontaine-Skronski, 2015). A prime example of such a scenario is provided by the case of online IP regulation and efforts to curb digital 'piracy.' It was noted earlier that under the auspices of the WTO's TRIPS agreement, all of its 162 member states are required to incorporate into domestic laws and law-enforcement measures (including criminal sanctions) to protect the interests of IP-rights holders. However, while such regulation is clearly in the interests of advanced economies whose businesses own the greatest parts of commercially-exploitable IP rights, it is far less advantageous to less developed nations for whom access to, and exploitation of, protected ideas provides crucial economic opportunities, and access to resources that its citizens could otherwise ill afford. As a consequence, we see that TRIPs has done little or nothing to curtail the levels of online IP rights violations, and that many countries outside the advanced (post-) industrial world appear to tolerate widespread violations by not acting against those who distribute and consume web-based content illegally (MUSO, 2017).

A third important regulatory outcome – again at odds with the idea of increasing global governance – is that, in cases of disagreement, states 'agree to disagree' and insist upon creating and enforcing their own national rules and standards. A clear example of such dissonance, even among Western liberal democracies, is provided by the case of regulating 'hate speech.' Many European nations have enacted criminal law sanctions against speech that incites hatred against minority groups on the basis of characteristics such as race, ethnicity, religion, sexual orientation and disability. However, the maximal constitutionally-afforded protections around freedom of expression in the United States mean that such communications amount to 'protected speech' and thus cannot be outlawed. The only exceptions arise in instances where the communication raises an *imminent* threat of harm to *specific, identifiable* individuals; otherwise, hateful representations directed to social groups as a whole are not only permitted but legally protected (Timofeeva, 2003; Banks, 2010). In extremis, states will consolidate and enforce nationally-based control over online behavior by creating a closed Internet environment that censors access to prohibited content from outside the national territory. In Saudi Arabia, for example, all Internet traffic flows through state-run servers where 'filters' are applied, thereby blocking access to any content emanating from outside the country that is deemed unacceptable on moral, religious, sexual or political grounds. Similar patterns of nationally-based controls are evident in countries such as China, Myanmar, Vietnam and Iran (Kalathil and Boas, 2010; Warf, 2011).

As a final reflection, such assertion (or re-assertion) of state sovereignty over the social control of the Internet may not just be restricted to authoritarian regimes. Rather, we might hypothesize that the recent resurgence of isolationist nationalism, nativism and economic protectionism (such as American President Donald Trump's 'America First' and the UK's 'Brexit' or imminent departure from the European Union) mark an important reaction against the institutions and practices of global governance. In addition to proposals around reducing the authority of IGOs (such as the UN), withdrawal from transnational treaties facilitating free trade (such as NAFTA and the EU's Single Market and Customs Union), we may also now be seeing the first impacts of these orientations on how the Internet is regulated and controlled. We can consider here, tentatively, two areas that might come to exemplify this shift (tentatively because they are very much emerging developments, and we have no certainty as yet about how they will play out). Firstly, the governance of the Internet's rules and operating protocols under the auspices of ICANN has been built around a key principle of 'net neutrality.' This denotes the rule that all providers of access to the Internet cannot discriminate or give preferential treatment (e.g. in terms of access speeds) to some content over others. Net neutrality enshrines a principle of equal access to the means of electronic communication for all users, one that has furnished an international consensus about how the Internet should be ordered. However, in November 2017, the US Trump administration directed the Federal Communications Commission (FCC) to repeal rules on net neutrality, opening the way for ISPs to give preferential treatment to the data of some users over others – specifically, to those with the deepest pockets and the greatest ability to pay (Manjoo, 2017). In essence, if successful, this shift would denote a very significant fracturing of globally-negotiated common standards of governance in favor of nationally-based ones driven by partisan political and economic ideology. A second emerging instance, with a very direct impact upon online crime control, arises in relation to the UK's planned 'Brexit.' Leaving the institutions of the EU will also entail either wholesale withdrawal from numerous arrangements for cooperation in law enforcement (such as the European Arrest Warrant and arrangements for mutual recognition of judicial judgements), or a significant downgrading of the UK's commitment to such transnational initiatives. Under the banner of reasserting state sovereignty, these changes may reverse the direction of travel in terms of transnational crime control, creating instead a more divergent and potentially conflictual patchwork of national standards and practices. In other words, one the most important issues facing scholars of cyber-crime is the prospect that the state is 'striking back' when it comes to social control over online behavior.

Conclusions

This chapter has sought to address issues of transnational governance and crime control as they relate to the Internet and the unlawful acts that it facilitates. Research in this area has focused upon the de-spatializing and border-transcending character of digital communications technologies, and has emphasized the challenges that the Internet presents for crime control and criminal justice systems that have been historically configured around territorially-bounded governance practices of sovereign nation states. Seeing pre-existing arrangements for law-making, regulation, policing and enforcement as inadequate to the challenges of globally-integrated networks of electronic action and interaction, researchers have explored what they see as an emerging architecture of transnational crime control, effected through international public law, IGOs, NGOs, businesses and cooperation by criminal justice agencies and judicial authorities across countries. However, this chapter has sought to challenge some of the assumptions about the attenuation of state authority and the rising power of non-state and transnational actors when it comes to controlling and countering cybercrime. Rather, it has pointed out a number of reasons for not only rethinking the role of the state, but also for developing a criminological research agenda that pays due attention to present counter-trends that may 'roll back' (in whole or part) the ceding of governance functions by states to non-state and/or supra-state actors. It may be that, in the coming years, cybercrime control becomes increasingly recuperated by states which, in the current ideological and political climate, are resistant to political and economic globalization.

References

Aas, Katja Franko (2007), *Globalization & Crime*, London: Sage.

Annicelli, Cliff (2017), 'Facebook the focus of UK ire over illegal content', accessed 27 April 2018 at: https://www.emarketer.com/Article/Facebook-Focus-of-UK-Ire-Over-Illegal-Content/1015794

Banks, James (2010), 'Regulating hate speech online', *International Review of Law, Computers & Technology*, 24(3), 233–239.

Broséus, Julian, D. Rhumorbarbe, M. Morelato, L. Staehli and Q. Rossy (2017), 'A geographical analysis of trafficking on a popular darknet market', *Forensic Science International*, 277, 88–102.

Cairncross, Frances (2000), *The Death of Distance*, Cambridge, MA: Harvard University Press.

Castells, Manuel (1996), *The Information Age: Economy, Society, and Culture. Volume I: The Rise of the Network Society*, Oxford: Blackwell.

Castells, Manuel (1997), *The Power of Identity: The Information Age: Economy, Society, and Culture* (Vol. 2), Oxford: Blackwell.

Castells, Manuel (1998), *End of Millennium: The Information Age: Economy, Society, and Culture* (Vol. 3), Oxford: Blackwell.

Clough, Jonathan (2014), 'A world of difference: the Budapest convention of cybercrime and the challenges of harmonisation', *Monash University Law Review*, 40, 698–736.

COE (Council of Europe) (2017), 'Chart of signatures and ratifications of Treaty 185 *Convention on Cybercrime:* Status as of 19/11/2017', accessed 27 April 2018 at: https://www.coe.int/en/web/conventions/full-list/-/conventions/treaty/185/signatures

Cohen, Scott A., T. Duncan and M. Thulemark (2015), 'Lifestyle mobilities: the crossroads of travel, leisure and migration', *Mobilities*, 10(1), 155–172.

Cohen, Stan (1985), *Visions of Social Control: Crime, Punishment and Classification*, Cambridge: Polity Press.

Drezner, Daniel W. (2004), 'The global governance of the internet: bringing the state back in', *Political Science Quarterly*, 119(3), 477–498.

Elgot, Jessica (2017), 'Facebook's response over sexualised child images is "extraordinary"', *The Guardian*, 7 March.

Europol (2017), 'European Cybercrime Centre – EC3', accessed 27 April 2018 at: https://www.europol.europa.eu/about-europol/european-cybercrime-centre-ec3

Facebook (2017), 'Community standards', accessed 27 April 2018 at: https://en-gb.facebook.com/communitystandards/

Feeley, Malcolm and J. Simon (1994), 'Actuarial justice: the emerging new criminal law', in D. Nelken (ed.) *The Futures of Criminology*, London: Sage.

Finkelstein, Lawrence S. (1995), 'What is global governance?', *Global Governance*, 1(3), 367–372.

Foucault, Michel (1991), *Discipline and Punish*, Harmondsworth: Penguin.

Foucault, Michel (2000), 'Truth and Power', in J.D. Faubion (ed.) *Power: Essential Works of Michel Foucault 1954–1984 v. 3*, New York: New Press.

Giddens, Anthony (1990), *The Consequences of Modernity*, Cambridge: Polity.

Gottfredson, Michael and T. Hirschi (1990), *A General Theory of Crime*, Palo Alto, CA: Stanford University Press.

Harvey, David (1991), *The Condition of Postmodernity: An Enquiry into the Conditions of Cultural Change*, Oxford: Blackwell.

Held, David, A. McGrew, D. Goldblatt and J. Perraton (2000), *Global Transformations: Politics, Economics and Culture*, Cambridge: Polity Press.

House of Commons Home Affairs Committee (2017), *Hate Crime: Abuse, Hate and Extremism Online*, London: House of Commons.

ICANN (2013), *A Quick Look at ICANN*, Los Angeles: ICANN.

Interpol (2016), *Interpol Annual Report 2016*, Lyon: Interpol.

Jewish News Online (2015), '20,000 Israelis sue Facebook over failure to moderate incitement of violence', 27 October, accessed 27 April 2018 at: http://jewishnews.timesofisrael.com/20000-israelis-sue-facebook-over-failure-to-moderate-incitement-of-violence/

Kalathil, Shanti and Taylor C. Boas (2010), *Open Networks, Closed Regimes: The Impact of the Internet on Authoritarian Rule*, Washington, DC: Carnegie Endowment for International Peace.

Kramer, Andrew E. (2016), 'How Russia recruited elite hackers for its cyberwar', *New York Times*, 29 December, accessed 27 April 2018 at: https://www.nytimes.com/2016/12/29/world/europe/how-russia-recruited-elite-hackers-for-its-cyberwar.html

Kuchler, Hannah (2017), 'Facebook to hire 3,000 more moderators to check content', *Financial Times*, 3 May.

Leukfeldt, Rutger and E. de Pauw (2012), 'Fighting cyber crime: an integral approach', in E.R. Leukfeldt and W.Ph. Stol (eds) *Cyber Safety: An Introduction*, The Hague: Eleven International Publishing.

Maddox, Alexia, M.J. Barratt, M. Allen and S. Lenton (2016), 'Constructive activism in the dark web: cryptomarkets and illicit drugs in the digital "demimonde"', *Information, Communication & Society*, 19(1), 11–126.

Manjoo, Farhan (2017), 'The internet is dying. repealing net neutrality hastens that death', *New York Times*, 29 November.

Mueller, Milton (1999), 'ICANN and internet governance: sorting through the debris of "self-regulation"', *info*, 1(6), 497–520.

Mueller, Milton and B. Kuerbis (2014), 'Towards global internet governance: how to end US control of ICANN without sacrificing stability, freedom or accountability', 27 August 2014. 2014 TPRC Conference Paper. Available at SSRN: https://ssrn.com/abstract=2408226

Mueller, Milton, J. Mathiason and H. Klien (2007), 'The internet and global governance: principles and norms for a new regime', *Global Governance*, 13, 237–254.

Murphy, Hannah and A. Kellow (2013), 'Forum shopping in global governance: understanding states, business and NGOs in multiple arenas', *Global Policy*, 4(2), 139–149.

MUSO (2017), *MUSO Global Piracy Report 2017*, London, Los Angeles and Paris: MUSO.

Omand, David (2015), 'The dark net policing the internet's underworld', *World Policy Journal*, 32(4), 75–82.

Rhodes, R.A.W. (1996), 'The new governance: governing without government', *Political Studies*, 44, 652–657.

Rhodes, R.A.W. (2007), 'Understanding governance: ten years on', *Organization Studies*, 28(8), 1243–1264.

Rioux, Michele and Fontaine-Skronski, K. (2015), 'Conceptualizing institutional changes in a world of great transformations: from the old telecommunications regime to the new global internet governance', in *Global Governance Facing Structural Changes*, New York: Palgrave Macmillan, pp. 59–78.

Savchenko, I.I. and O.Y. Gatsenko (2015), 'Analytical review of methods of providing internet anonymity', *Automatic Control and Computer Sciences*, 49(8), 696–700.

Smith, Cooper (2013), 'Facebook users are uploading 350 million new photos each day', accessed 27 April 2018 at: http://www.businessinsider.com/facebook-350-million-photos-each-day-2013-9?IR=T

Timofeeva, Yulia A. (2003), 'Hate speech online: restricted or protected-comparison of regulations in the United States and Germany', *Journal of Transnational Law & Policy*, 12, 253–286.

Twitter (2017), 'The Twitter Rules', accessed 27 April 2018 at: https://support.twitter.com/articles/18311

UNODC (2016), *UNODC Annual Report: Covering Activities During 2016*, Vienna: UNODC.

Wall, Davis S. (2001), 'Introduction', in D.S. Wall (ed.) *Crime and the Internet: Cybercrimes and Cyberfears*, London: Routledge, pp. 1–17.

Wall, David S. (2007), *Cybercrime: The Transformation of Crime in the Information Age*, Cambridge/Malden, MA: Polity.

Warf, Barney (2011), 'Geographies of global internet censorship', *GeoJournal*, 76(1), 1–23.

Weimann, Gabriel (2016), 'Going dark: terrorism on the dark web', *Studies in Conflict & Terrorism*, 39(3), 195–206.

Weinberg, Jonathan (2000), 'ICANN and the problem of legitimacy', *Duke Law Journal*, 50, 187–260.

Williams, Katherine (2010), 'Transnational developments in Internet law', in Y. Jewkes and M. Yar (eds) *Handbook of Internet Crime*, Abingdon: Routledge, pp. 466–491.

Williams, Matthew (2006), *Virtually Criminal: Crime, Deviance and Regulation Online*, Abingdon and New York: Routledge.

Williams, Steve, H. Bradley, R. Devadson and M. Erickson (2013), *Globalization and Work*, Cambridge: Polity Press.

Wong, Julia C., M. Safi and S.A. Rahman (2017), 'Facebook bans Rohingya group's posts as minority faces "ethnic cleansing"', *The Guardian*, 20 September.

Yar, Majid (2005), 'The novelty of "cybercrime": an assessment in light of routine activity theory', *European Journal of Criminology*, 2(4), 407–427.

8 The demand for counterfeiting on the criminological research agenda

Jo Large

The problem of counterfeiting

Counterfeit goods are fake items deliberately made to look genuine. These can range from clothes, bags, watches, perfume, cosmetics and electrical items as well as pirate DVDs, CDs, computer software and games. Although the crime of counterfeiting is not new, the sale of fake goods is increasing. More counterfeit items are now being sold online and spotting copies is becoming much harder.

More and more people are now prepared to knowingly buy fake items; however there are serious risks involved with counterfeit goods.

Why you should avoid buying counterfeit goods

There are many risks involved with buying fake goods:

Breaking the law

It is a criminal offence to try to financially gain by using a trademark without the owner's permission.

Your safety

Fake goods are often bad quality and in most cases unsafe. Counterfeit electrical goods are not put through the same vigorous safety checks as legitimate items and are often very dangerous. Fake cosmetics and fragrances have been found to contain toxic levels of chemicals and unpleasant substances, such as arsenic, mercury and even urine, that could seriously harm your health.

Consumers also need to be aware that by accessing websites like this they are running the risk of their personal details being compromised and being used for other fraudulent scams, as well as exposing their computer to malware and viruses.

Funding organised crime

Many fraudsters will use the proceeds from selling counterfeit goods to fund other types of serious organised crime.

Affecting genuine businesses and the economy

Buying fake goods affects legitimate businesses as counterfeit sales drive the profit away from the genuine manufacturer which could result in job losses and in turn affecting the economy.

(Police Intellectual Property Crime Unit, 2017)

Counterfeiting, along with piracy, has been described as the most financially valuable global criminal market – more so than drug trafficking and illegal logging (May, 2017). In April 2016 the Organisation for Economic Co-Operation and Development (OECD) suggested that the global import trade in counterfeit goods amounts to nearly half a trillion US dollars (OECD and EUIPO, 2016). Unsurprisingly, given the scale of these estimations, national and international attention is increasingly being afforded to dealing with the problem of the trade in counterfeit products. As the excerpt above from the Policing Intellectual Property Crime Unit's (PIPCU)[1] – the United Kingdom's specialist national policing unit for intellectual property issues – website suggests, counterfeiting is of a concern to law enforcement and policy makers. Also emphasized is the role of the public in their complicity of the counterfeit trade. Evidently, although there is concern regarding supply, there is also concern regarding the demand for popular consumer products.

Although questions remain about the data that underpins the suggested increase in counterfeiting, recent years have witnessed a movement away from a small-scale localized 'cottage industry' (Vagg and Harris, 1998: 189) to a rapidly developing complex global market, that produces, distributes and retails counterfeits. Technological advances, most notably the expansion of Internet banking, online shopping and social media, have transformed the nature of the market(s) for counterfeit goods. It is easier than ever to distribute, retail and manufacture goods (Antonopoulos et al., 2018, 2017; Hall and Antonopoulos, 2016; Heinonen et al., 2012; Treadwell, 2012; Wilson and Fenoff, 2014). It is also easier than ever for consumers to get hold of these goods – intentionally or otherwise (Antonopoulos et al., 2018; Hall and Antonopoulos, 2016; Heinonen et al., 2012; Large (2019a); Lavorgna, 2014; Rojek, 2017; Treadwell, 2012; Wilson and Fenoff, 2014). Although there is a growing discussion around social, cultural and technological changes as part of the attempts to reduce demand for more consumer orientated counterfeit goods there remains the more clandestine markets for aircraft and auto component parts (see Yar, 2005) that appear to be often overlooked in examinations of counterfeiting.

---

1 Based within the Economic Crime Directorate of the City of London Police the unit was launched in 2013 as an operationally independent unit. The unit is funded by the Intellectual Property Office.

Despite counterfeiting being one of the biggest illicit markets globally, it is a topic only recently gaining notable attention in criminological research and as such remains an area which requires further development.

Much of what we know about the global nature of counterfeiting comes from various official, trade and industry sources. In terms of the global flows of counterfeit goods, China is recognized as the main source for counterfeit goods which enter the European Union (EU) with Chinese counterfeits making up 66 per cent of the volume of the goods detained at EU borders (European Commission DG TAXUD[2]). Other countries of special concern to the European Commission include India for pharmaceutical products and Turkey for cosmetics and perfume. In 2013, customs seized EUR 26.1 million worth of cosmetics and perfumes originating from Turkey alone. Turkey's importance in the illicit goods market should not be underestimated given its proximity to the EU, its role in manufacturing and its importance for trading with the EU (European Commission, 2017). Despite recognizing the problems with financial estimations based on seizure data (as discussed more thoroughly later in this chapter) these official data sources reinforce that even though China may well remain the biggest player in the production of counterfeit goods, it is far from the only source of goods. Of interest with regards to China is that while it is suggested to be the source country for over two-thirds of counterfeit goods circulating in the EU (Europol and OHIM, 2016) it is also where most of the legal goods circulating in the EU are produced. The prominence of both China and Turkey as legitimate importers is notable and the relationship between the legitimate and illegitimate production of products should not be ignored in an assessment of the illicit market. Here it is useful to draw upon the work of Hudson (Chapter 2, this volume) who suggests that links between illegal and legal markets are 'endemic' in global capitalist economies. A position, as outlined by Hudson, that recognizes the blurred boundaries of licit and illicit markets is adopted from the outset of this chapter.

This chapter will argue the need for criminology to take more ownership in developing an understanding of counterfeiting. This includes issues related to design, manufacture, production, supply *and* in examining the intricacies of demand. The next section will examine existing themes of research on counterfeiting and highlight challenges criminologists face. Following this, an agenda for developing research on counterfeiting will be discussed, arguing that criminologists must examine counterfeiting as a phenomenon within a broader understanding of global supply and demand, recognizing the overlapping nature of licit and illicit economies and problematizing forcing a distinction between these. The chapter will conclude by suggesting that although counterfeiting provides numerous research challenges for criminologists, as a phenomenon it creates a whole range of issues which criminologists, utilizing a range of disciplinary expertise, should be at the forefront of explaining.

---

2 Directorate General for Customs and Taxation Union, European Commission.

Existing research on counterfeiting

The paucity of criminological research on counterfeiting identified by Yar in 2005 appears to remain an issue as despite a growing interest among a small number of criminologists. Sullivan et al. (2016: 340) suggest that 'product counterfeiting research is still at a primitive stage compared to other types of crime'. After conducting a content analysis of articles in crime- or criminal justice-focused journals published up until 2014, Sullivan et al. (2016: 340) highlight 'the infrequent and sporadic publication of product counterfeiting studies, the diverse range of publication outlets for this research, and the breadth of coverage with limited depth of discourse in any subarea of product counterfeiting'.

As part of an attempt to draw attention to counterfeiting as a criminological issue and provide a coherent space for publications, in 2017 we saw the publication of a Special Issue on Counterfeiting in the journal *Trends in Organised Crime* (Antonopoulos et al., 2017). Although demonstrating some of the ranges of approaches in researching counterfeiting and highlighting important work in the field, the special issue also reinforces the need for greater attention to be paid to counterfeiting in many respects, not least theoretically, in an area that remains dominated by official accounts, marketing or brand-focused perspectives. Even within criminology, despite growing interest, much of the work tends to focus on methods of crime prevention (see Sullivan et al., 2016: 338) or to place considerable reliance on industry and official data in assessments of nature and prevalence.

Both seizure data and criminological research highlight the nature of the scope of goods counterfeited, and these tend to be categorized as 'safety critical' or 'non-safety critical'. Here it is clear that the emphasis of concern relates to the potential for physical harm to the consumer ('victim') of the counterfeit product. Even though distinctions of these as two delineable categories should be noted as problematic (Large, 2015; Large, forthcoming a), they do provide a broad, albeit simplistic, contextual understanding of the nature of counterfeit products. Non-safety critical goods such as clothing and fashion items (Large, 2015, 2019a; Treadwell, 2012; Wall and Large, 2010) which appear relatively harmless to the consumer flood the market, as do safety critical goods which can pose serious health consequences such as vehicle/airline parts (Yar, 2005); defence products (Sullivan and Wilson, 2017); food, alcohol and tobacco (Antonopoulos, 2009; Lord et al., 2017; McEwan and Straus, 2009; Shen and Antonopoulos, 2017; Shen et al., 2010) and pharmaceuticals (Hall and Antonopoulos, 2016; Hall et al., 2017) among other things.

In addition to research that examines specific types of counterfeiting, areas of focus also include the role of the Internet (Hall and Antonopoulos, 2016; Heinonen and Wilson, 2012; Lavorgna, 2014; Treadwell, 2012; Wilson and Fenoff, 2014), media representations (Sullivan and Chermak, 2013), the relationship between counterfeiting and terrorism (Ganor and Wernli, 2013) and general assessments of counterfeiting, crime and crime control (Beresford et al., 2005; Nasheri, 2005; Wall and Large, 2010; Yar, 2005). Those such as Mackenzie (2010) and Rojek (2017) have sought to theorize counterfeiting in how it relates to legitimate global economies and industry, with Rojek (2017) further expanding on the nature of counterfeit consumption. Finally, recent work by Antonopoulos et al. (2018) has sought to provide an empirical interdisciplinary investigation into the financial aspects and management of counterfeit businesses in the context of the United Kingdom and China. Despite these important contributions to the field, more work is needed to develop a cohesive and solid exploration of counterfeiting from a critical criminological perspective.

The challenges of researching counterfeiting

Much of the research literature on counterfeiting places a primary reliance on analysing official data or interview data of policy makers, law and regulatory enforcement or industry representatives. While this provides important insights, it can only provide part of the picture as it focuses on activities which have come to the attention of authorities. As acknowledged previously, much of what we know about the extent and prevalence of counterfeiting comes from official estimates which tend to rely on customs seizure data. This forms the basis for estimations regarding the size of the counterfeit market globally – which is currently claimed to be 4–7 per cent of all world trade (International Chamber of Commerce cited in UNODC, 2013). Although those such as the OECD have developed sophisticated analysis and techniques for quantification of the economic impact of counterfeiting (see OECD and EUIPO, 2016), relying on these kinds of estimations is problematic for a number of reasons (see Spink and Fejes, 2012), not least because they tend to, by their very nature, place the main emphasis on financial and economic impacts (see for example OECD and EUIPO, 2016). An absence of the counter-narratives of producers and retailers in economies where counterfeit manufacturing is high, for example, is notable. Criminologists have an important role in the need to be addressing the 'gaps' and examining the data and basis for such claims.

Where access is permitted, criminologists can also analyse case files and transcripts of interviews with counterfeiters. Again, this can provide fruitful detailed information but still relies on incidents or offenders who are known to the authorities. Those such as Treadwell (2012), Hall and Antonopoulos (2016), and Antonopoulos et al. (2018) have sought to address some of these limitations and conduct ethnographic research with those actively involved in the counterfeit trade. The nature of a clandestine industry and the illegal activities being undertaken means that there will be inevitable access issues and challenges to overcome. This means that even when access is possible, projects tend to be small scale and sample sizes tend to be low, often limited to a particular geographical area and constrained to the language(s) spoken by the researcher, which may fail to recognize important issues in relation to the global trade.

Further, the mutating nature of crime and criminal markets enabled and exacerbated by technological developments provide challenges for the scope and nature of research. Treadwell's (2012) work with 'professional criminals' highlighted the overlapping nature of their illicit and licit business activities and the problem with assuming that criminals will not be willing to adapt their business (in this case embracing the Internet) as a way of maximizing profit. Further Treadwell's work, along with other qualitative studies of 'criminal entrepreneurs' in the counterfeit trade, such as Hall and Antonopoulos (2016) and Antonopoulos et al. (2018), refute the notion that crimes committed via the Internet require a high level of sophistication or technological skill. Therefore, criminologists must utilize both old and new methods to capture new and changing criminal markets at a local level and how criminal markets adapt, mutate and evolve within a global context. In line with Hudson (this volume) criminologists should also investigate intricacies and overlaps in licit and illicit economies and recognize the problems with considering these as separate entities. This calls into question notions of 'shadow' or 'black' markets, and further criminality, when illicit activities are likely to be happening within the 'licit' economy.

Although counterfeiting has local peculiarities that need exploring, it is also a globally complex and shifting phenomenon. Drawing on the challenges which von Lampe (2012) identifies with research on 'transnational organized crime' is relevant. The nature of global supply and demand connections means that interactions to facilitate the supply will happen in different countries and across legal and illegal boundaries. Researchers face challenges in understanding the detail of these interactions, the nature of interactions in origin, transit and destination countries, and localized peculiarities. Language and cultural barriers further hamper access and even when access is gathered, localized differences in law, regulations and the collection of data may all further exacerbate the challenges faced.

In a research field which remains dominated by business management, economic or psychological 'willingness' style studies, a small number of criminologists have paid attention to understanding the consumer of counterfeit goods. This may be to understand their behaviour, or to assess their level of harm experienced within the framework of victimization. Research so far tends to be localized, compounded by many of the issues outlined above in relation to suppliers. Although the focus on this aspect of the transaction might appear to be less problematic, there might be a number of reasons why a consumer of counterfeit goods might be unwilling to come forward or take part in research. This might include concerns about the legal status of their behaviour, stereotypical associations with counterfeit buying, and overlapping statuses of consumer and seller. There will also be the challenge of addressing the problem that many consumers are deceived into buying counterfeit goods and may therefore never be aware that they have been 'victims' of counterfeiting. As a result, this area remains under-examined and under-theorized. Understanding victimization and victims of counterfeiting, something that tends to be framed within a static view of legal status, is generally an area that needs more attention and is a point returned to shortly.

Setting the agenda for a critical perspective on counterfeiting

As evidenced by the review of much of the criminological literature on counterfeiting above, excellent headway is being made by a small but growing number of academics. However, despite the commendable intentions to seek to inform and influence policy and assist law enforcement departments in tackling the growing counterfeit goods market – in an era where academic research is pressured to show its demonstrable impact and policy relevance (MacDonald, 2017) – there is a danger that the predominant focus of counterfeiting research becomes an applied or administrative attempt at designing out crime. Counterfeiting, which as a topic sits at the border of traditional criminological boundaries (Large, 2015; Wall and Large, 2010), generates a number of questions and issues criminologists should be at the forefront of addressing. Situating counterfeiting within developments in (and adjacent to) criminology will both cement the importance of counterfeiting as a criminological topic and contribute to and help expand recent theoretical developments.

The importance of measuring and assessing counterfeiting

The current approaches to assessing the scale and extent of counterfeiting rely on official estimations, and especially data from customs seizures. This means that it is common in a variety of sources, academic and otherwise, to hear similar statements regarding the scope and economic impact of counterfeiting. Spink and Fejes (2012) have explored this issue and found that across the board references to statements about the size of the industry could generally be traced back to three documents. Further, they conducted a detailed review of these three 'core reference documents (CIB, 1997; OECD, 2007; FBI, 2002)' and noted:

> The two full reports – CIB 1997 and OECD 2007 – emphasized the challenges of developing both a sound methodology and a data gathering process to provide a statistically supported estimate. The FBI (2002) reference was a one-page release with no reference to the methodology used for the estimate. Conversely, while the two full reports were substantial and had a developed methodological foundation, they clearly stated that the methodology was, at best, an educated guess. (Spink and Fejes, 2012: 265)

The OECD has recently updated its estimates of the counterfeit economy (OECD and EUIPO, 2016) drawing largely upon the methodology and lessons learned from the previous exercise. While these estimations based on seizure data can give an idea of goods seized and frequency of seizure, for example, caution needs to be exercised in how much reliance criminologists place on taking this data as fact. Further, seizure data does not help us understand the domestic market for counterfeit goods, nor characterize its size and scope. Further still, given what is discussed next regarding free trade zones (FTZs), seizure data has the potential to be highly skewed or based on inaccurate information. Criminologists have an important role in interrogating the assumptions which underpin this kind of data and assisting in developing new methodologies. Huge potential lies in exploring opportunities of working with organizations to examine existing sets of data for secondary data analysis. The prevalence of online activity for counterfeiting further creates opportunities for examining web data, algorithms and social media interactions – beyond existing small-scale virtual ethnographic studies such as that of Hall and Antonopoulos (2016).

The importance of legitimate supply and trading routes for counterfeiting

Research into the supply of counterfeit goods demonstrates how so much of the global trade in counterfeit goods relies on the processes of existing and legitimate trade and supply chains. As Hudson (this volume) discusses in more depth, it is more useful to consider the economic nature of illicit and licit economies as fluid and overlapping and spatially and temporally constrained. Although the focus here is on the illicit counterfeit economy, criminologists should be mindful of the potential for illegal activity within the 'legitimate' parallel economy. This is a point returned to shortly in a discussion regarding harm and victimization. The more globalized connectivity of trading develops, the more opportunities there are for counterfeiters to take advantage of the legitimate supply chain. A good example of this relates to FTZs. A number of major shipping hubs exist globally which sit within large FTZs. Items which originate in Southeast Asia and the Far East tend to transit through major hubs such as Morocco, Hong Kong, Egypt and the United Arab Emirates (UAE) (Europol & OHIM, 2016). FTZs are designed to encourage and incentivize foreign investment, localized employment opportunities and the development of exports. This may mean far simplified processes, imports which are duty free and various other exemptions from taxes and duty. These can all create a lack of transparency over businesses' transactions and operations within these zones. Concerns from authorities and other organizations highlight the attractive nature of FTZs for 'organized crime groups' and, of concern here, counterfeiters. Europol and OHIM (2016) document how FTZs provide opportunities for counterfeiters to change documentation concealing their origin (to reduce the likelihood of customs suspicion), contents and destinations. Importantly, this can impact on what we think we know about the origin of counterfeit goods. This relates back to the importance of criminologists seeking to understand the nuances and intricacies of supply chains at different points. The World Economic Forum (WEF) highlights counterfeiters as the main group of criminals who take advantage of such existing global trade structures (see Europol and OHIM, 2016).

This is just one example of counterfeiting as a 'parasitic' (Rojek, 2017) industry, and research that has examined the supply side of counterfeit goods (see Antonopoulos et al., 2011; Antonopoulos et al., 2018; Hall and Antonopoulos, 2016; Treadwell, 2012, for good examples) highlights the overlap and entangled nature of the counterfeit business with licit modes of manufacture, supply and retail. As pointed out by Hobbs (2012: 265), '[we] should not [be] blind to the attractions of market behaviour that makes nonsense of the often arbitrary distinctions between legal and illegal business'.

Thus, this demands a truly interdisciplinary approach to studying counterfeiting and problematizes understanding counterfeiting as an issue which is specific to criminals. Only focusing on the criminal aspects of counterfeiting misses out the importance of geography and economics for example in understanding global trade (Hudson's chapter is an excellent example here), and likewise the problem of counterfeiting being approached from an economics or geography or business management perspective, for example, is that they fail to interrogate the relationship with crime and harm in the sophisticated manner of critical criminologists. Simply focusing on counterfeiting as a crime problem lacks depth – and as also demonstrated throughout many of the chapters in this volume – there is a real need to develop theoretically strong interdisciplinary approaches to studying contemporary issues of crime and harm.

The importance of harm in the counterfeiting debate

Conceptually, an issue that needs further attention is the underlying rhetoric of much of the debate about counterfeiting. Beyond acknowledging it as a crime issue, certainly much of the literature outside of criminology highlights counterfeiting in relation to harm. This tends to be either physical or criminal when explicitly discussed in terms of harm, but when other terms such as costs or impacts are used there is further a recognition of a varying degree of other harms. These might be to society, to industry or to the economy. However, this aspect appears to be much under-considered within criminological accounts. It can therefore be suggested that, due to the focus on criminal activities and criminal markets, framing counterfeiting as a crime may in itself be limiting and problematic. This is not to dispute or take less seriously the real harms of many of the criminal acts (Hall and Winlow, 2015) counterfeiting is associated with, but to reinforce there is a need to go beyond legal definitions of crime when examining counterfeiting. This brings us to the importance of recent developments in critical criminology and zemiology (the study of harm), not least tapping into one of the fundamental questions of what should be the core focus of the discipline.

Criminologists need to develop an understanding of counterfeiting which takes account of the motivations, techniques and rapidly changing nature of counterfeit supply and at the same time establish a much better understanding of the victimization and harm associated with counterfeiting. This should go beyond seeking to identify typical victim or offender characteristics and not be constructed within a framework which prioritizes crime. Applying a broad framework of harm which can capture social harms (see Pemberton, 2016), environmental harms (see White, 2013; and see also Altopiedi, Chapter 6 this volume) and harm as an embedded feature of the social order (see Hall, 2012; Hall and Winlow, 2015; Smith and Raymen, 2016) will allow criminologists to think differently about counterfeiting. Two examples seem pertinent here. The first is with the common claim that counterfeiting is associated with 'wider criminality'. On a small scale, the Intellectual Property Crime Group (IPCG) suggests that a range of links exist with 'lower level' types of criminal and antisocial behaviour, and especially benefit fraud (IPCG, 2010: 16). Yet, we know that there are:

> people who are involved in selling counterfeit goods because they want to make a bit of extra money. They are trying to supplement their income and they're more likely to be in receipt of benefit payments . . . That's the nature of the situation, unfortunately, they find themselves in and they're trying to supplement their income or benefit income. (Interview with Police Intellectual Property Crime Unit officer, cited in Antonopoulos et al., 2018)

Although not to suggest that benefit fraud is acceptable or desirable, if we approach questions about the impact of counterfeit goods – even just at an economic level – from a harms-based perspective we do not start with the implicit assumption that the person breaking the criminal law is the problem. We can also draw upon recognition of the spatial and temporal nature of what is (il)legal and socially acceptable (Hudson, this volume). Instead we could more carefully tease out the implications of the counterfeit trade in relation to harm and ethics. Further, once we move away from a focus on 'crime' and towards a focus on harm, we are able to assess the counterfeit industry within the context of the legitimate industry.

A second example draws upon the work I have explored in more depth elsewhere (Large, 2018, 2019a) using the example of fashion counterfeiting – a form of counterfeiting which appears to be the most problematic when approached from a perspective that only addresses crime (see Large, 2015; Wall and Large, 2010). General common complaints about the harms of the counterfeit industry also highlight labour exploitation, substandard goods and the morally harmful cause of 'lining criminals' pockets'. However, if criminologists were to cast a more critical eye over the fashion industry (or any other consumer industry) serious concerns most likely would be raised. High-profile events such as factory collapses have brought global scrutiny on the fashion industry, generating questions about labour-related harms and corruption among other things. Placing the emphasis on harm also recognizes the polluting and environmentally harmful nature of consumer industries such as fashion. Research by Brooks (2015) highlights the exploitative nature of the clothing industry, with its failure to do much for poverty alleviation in global economies. Further (along similar arguments to Large, 2019b, on charity tourism), Brooks (2015) additionally explores the problems with even so called 'socially responsible' or ethical fashion initiatives, which he argues tend primarily to serve the consumer, rather than making any substantial impact in reducing harm. This is not to say that recognizing the harmful nature of the fashion industry excuses or justifies counterfeiting. On the one hand it is likely that the nature of a clandestine shadow counterfeit industry completely free from regulation and scrutiny will exacerbate various social and environmental harms. However, if we want to provide a thorough and advanced understanding of counterfeiting we need to move beyond the trap of 'crime' and examine closely the harms of the illegitimate industry within the context of the legitimate. We should also not shy away from the notion that the legitimate industry has to take at least some responsibility for the shadow counterfeit industry (see Hall and Antonopoulos, 2016; Hilton et al., 2004; Large, 2018, 2019a; Mackenzie, 2010; Rojek, 2017).

Discussions about counterfeiting framed within a context of harm and ethics will also call into question the role and nature of the legitimate industry. In short, the very nature of fashion is one which at its core relies on imitation and copying (see Large, 2018, forthcoming 2018a). This has the dual effect of both blurring the boundaries of acceptable and non-acceptable copying (i.e. counterfeits) and perpetuating the pressure to consume. Fashion is the quintessential model for capitalism and a core industry for the success of global economies (Hoskins, 2014). Hyper-levels of consumption take place among a social and economic backdrop which is characterized with precarity, anxiety and insecurity (Hall et al., 2008; Lloyd, 2013), not to mention a growing consumer debt market (Horsley, 2015). Given that the nature of fashion and the industry essentially exacerbates – and is reliant on – consumer anxieties, about not having the 'right' product, or not having the right body shape, or not having clothes that are the latest trend, we could consider this as harmful. As Smith and Raymen's (2016) work on 'deviant leisure' highlights, we should be mindful of the harms of 'legitimate and socially accept-able' leisure activities. In this framework, from a consumer perspective at least, there is room for the argument that counterfeit fashion can provide an important route of consumption. Certainly, the fashion industry can be positioned as harmful and there is a need to emphasize it is about more than clothing or accessories. Underpinning fashion is an inevitable focus on the body (Entwistle, 2000) which in itself stimulates a huge health industry, with quick-fix diets and self-proclaimed 'lifestyle coaches' existing alongside an ever-growing beauty and cosmetics industry that enable consumers to manipulate their bodies into the latest fashionable craze. With this comes further anxiety, insecurity and harm; not to mention a booming illicit pharmaceutical and cosmetic trade with the potential for further repercus-sions for the consumer (see Hall, 2019; Hall and Antonopoulos, 2016). Addressing counterfeiting from a perspective of harm – while recognizing the spatial and tem-poral nature of what is 'legal' or socially acceptable (Hudson, this volume; see also Smith and Raymen, 2016) – is essential.

The importance of considering demand

The final call is that criminologists must engage critically with an understanding of why counterfeit markets exist when we know that many consumers knowingly buy counterfeit products (Large, 2019a). This is particularly important when one of the emphases of policy is to place the onus on the consumer, or the public, to take responsibility and not purchase counterfeits (see Large, 2015). Thus, there is a need to consider demand for counterfeit goods which goes beyond super-ficial understandings of purchase intentions common in brand marketing style research. Firstly, as argued elsewhere (Large, 2019a), given the huge market for counterfeit goods we need to abandon the assumption that counterfeit consump-tion can be typified demographically or as deviant. Of relevance is the fact that the sustainability of illegal markets, such as that of counterfeits, is inherently reliant on the consumption of products (counterfeit or not). This is the case for the counterfeit products which consumers are deceived into buying, as much as it is the case for counterfeits consumers knowingly buy. Yet, we remain in a situation where, despite increased attention from criminologists towards understanding the *supply* of counterfeit goods, much of what is known about the consumption (or *demand*) of these goods tends to come from industry sources or outside of criminology. As a result, the consumption of counterfeit products tends to be understood as something outside of usual consumer behaviour, with an implication that the practice is deviant. Existing research on the demand for counterfeit fashion (Large, 2015, 2019a) and counterfeit pharmaceuticals (Hall and Antonopoulos, 2016) explores and highlights why this assumption is inherently problematic. Criminologists need to go beyond engaging in superficial 'purchase intention' styles of research and drill down to understanding motivations and how these relate to behaviours and values. If criminologists truly wish to inform policy which seeks to change consumer behaviour, then a much better understanding of motivation and behaviour within a broader context of consumption and contemporary society is required.

Conclusion

The evolving nature of technological advances – especially the Internet – coupled with consumer capitalism in a global economy has contributed to the rapidly changing nature of counterfeit markets, to the point where counterfeiting is now a primary international law enforcement concern. Therefore, given this context, this chapter has argued the need for criminology to take more ownership in developing a critical understanding of counterfeiting. This includes issues related to design, manufacture, production, supply *and* the nature of demand. This needs to go beyond a focus on demand in the sense of consumers and consumer products and engage with discussions around harm and victimization. While recognizing that there are a number of barriers and challenges to researching this globally complex field, this chapter has identified a number of areas in which criminologists need to develop research. At the same time, if criminologists wish to provide a meaningful analysis of the phenomenon of counterfeiting, research needs to recognize the broader context of global supply and demand and recognize the overlapping nature of licit and illicit economies. Additionally, moving towards a perspective centred on harm, as opposed to crime, is essential. Research which is able to capture global trends and patterns must at the same time recognize nuances and complexities both locally and globally. Recognizing, examining and challenging taken-for-granted assumptions is important, as is moving beyond disciplinary silos to develop and refine methods and frameworks that are able to explore a complex, contemporary global phenomenon such as that of the manufacture of and trade in counterfeit goods.

References

Antonopoulos, G. A (2009), 'Cigarettes of "ambiguous quality" in the Greek black market?: findings from an empirical study on cigarette smuggling', *Trends in Organised Crime*, 12 (3–4), 260–266.

Antonopoulos, G. A., D. Hobbs and R. Hornsby (2011), 'A soundtrack to (illegal) entrepreneurship: pirated CD/DVD selling in a Greek provincial city', *British Journal of Criminology*, 51 (5), 804–822.

Antonopoulos, G. A., A. Hall, J. Large and A. Shen (2017), 'An introduction to the special issue on counterfeiting', *Trends in Organised Crime*, 20 (3–4), 247–251.

Antonopoulos, Georgios A., Alexandra Hall, Joanna Large, Anqi Shen, Michael Crang and Michael Andrews (2018), *Fake Goods, Real Money: The Counterfeiting Business and its Financial Management*, Bristol: Policy.

Beresford, A. D., C. Desilets, S. Haantz, J. Kane, and A. Wall (2005), 'Intellectual property and white-collar crime: report of issues, trends, and problems for future research', *Trends in Organised Crime*, 8 (4), 62–78.

Brooks, Andrew (2015), *Clothing Poverty: The Hidden World of Fast Fashion and Second-Hand Clothes*, London: Zed Books.

CIB (1997), *Countering Counterfeiting. A Guide to Protecting & Enforcing Intellectual Property Rights*, London: Counterfeiting Intelligence Bureau [CIB], International Chamber of Commerce [ICC].

Entwistle, Joanne (2000), *The Fashioned Body: Fashion, Dress and Modern Social Theory*, London: Polity.

European Commission (2017), *Trade Policies – Countries and Regions – Turkey*, accessed 30 November 2017 at http://ec.europa.eu/trade/policy/countries-and-regions/countries/turkey/

Europol and OHIM [Office for Harmonisation in the Internal Market] (2016), '2015 Situation report on counterfeiting in the European Union' [EXCERPT], *Trends in Organised Crime*, 20 (3–4), 370–382.

FBI [Federal Bureau of Investigation] (2002), *The FBI and the U.S. Customs Service Announce the National Intellectual Property Rights Coordination Center's First Conference for Members of Congress and Industry in Washington July 17 2002*, accessed 30 November 2017 at https://archives.fbi.gov/archives/news/pressrel/press-releases/the-federal-bureau-of-investigation-and-the-u.s.-customs-service-today-announced-the-national-intellectual-property-rights-coordination-centers-first-conference-for-members-of-congress-and-industry-in-washington

Ganor, B. and M. H. Wernli (2013), 'The infiltration of terrorist organizations into the pharmaceutical industry: Hezbollah as a case study', *Studies in Conflict and Terrorism*, 36 (9), 699–712.

Hall, A. (2019), 'Lifestyle drugs and late capitalism: a topography of harm', in Smith, Oliver and Thomas Raymen (eds), *Deviant Leisure: Contemporary Perspectives on Leisure and Harm*, London: Palgrave Macmillan.

Hall, Alexandra and Georgios A. Antonopoulos (2016), *Fake Meds Online: The Internet and the Transnational Market in Illicit Pharmaceuticals*, Basingstoke: Palgrave Macmillan.

Hall, A., R. Koenraadt and G. A. Antonopoulos (2017), 'Illicit pharmaceutical networks in Europe: organising the illicit medicine market in the United Kingdom and the Netherlands', *Trends in Organised Crime*, 20 (3–4), 296–315.

Hall, Steve (2012), *Theorizing Crime and Deviance: A New Perspective*, London: Sage.

Hall, Steve and Simon Winlow (2015), *Revitalizing Criminological Theory: Towards a New Ultra Realism*, London: Routledge.

Hall, Steve, Simon Winlow and Craig Ancrum (2008), *Criminal Identities and Consumer Culture: Crime, Exclusion and the New Culture of Narcissism*, Devon: Willan.

Heinonen, J. A., T. J. Holt and J. M Wilson (2012), 'Product counterfeits in the online environment: an empirical assessment of victimization and reporting characteristics', *International Criminal Justice Review*, 22 (4), 353–371.

Hilton, B., C. J. Choi and S. Chen (2004), 'The ethics of counterfeiting in the fashion industry: quality, credence and profit issues', *Journal of Business Ethics*, 55, 345–354.

Hobbs, D. (2012), '"It was never about the money": market society, organised crime and UK criminology', in Hall, Steve and Simon Winlow (eds), *New Directions in Criminological Theory*, London: Routledge.

Horsley, Mark (2015), *The Dark Side of Prosperity*, Farnham: Ashgate.

Hoskins, T. E. (2014), *Stitched Up: The Anti-Capitalist Book of Fashion*, London: Pluto.

IPCG (2010), *Intellectual Property Crime Report 2009–2010*. Intellectual Property Crime Group [IPCG], UK Intellectual Property Office, accessed 15 August 2011 at http://www.ipo.gov.uk/ipcreport09.pdf

Large, Joanna (2015), '"Get real don't buy fakes". Fashion fakes and flawed policy: the problem with taking a consumer – responsibility approach to reducing the problem of counterfeiting', *Criminology and Criminal Justice*, 15 (2), 169–185.

Large, Joanna (2018), 'Spot the fashion victim: the importance of rethinking harm within the context of fashion counterfeiting', in Boukli, Avi and Justin Kotze (eds), *Zemiology: Reconnecting Crime and Social Harm*, London: Palgrave Macmillan.

Large, Joanna (2019), *The Consumption of Counterfeit Fashion*, London: Palgrave Macmillan.

Large, Joanna (2019), 'Conspicuously "doing" charity: exploring the relationship between doing good and doing harm', in Smith, Oliver and Thomas Raymen (eds), *Deviant Leisure: Contemporary Perspectives on Leisure and Harm*, London: Palgrave Macmillan.

Lavorgna, A. (2014), 'The online trade in counterfeit pharmaceuticals: new criminal opportunities, trends and challenges', *European Journal of Criminology*, 12 (2), 226–241.

Lloyd, Anthony (2013), *Labour Markets and Identity on the Post-Industrial Assembly Line*, Farnham: Ashgate.

Lord, N., J. Spencer, E. Bellotti and K. Benson (2017), 'A script analysis of the distribution of counterfeit alcohol across two European jurisdictions', *Trends in Organised Crime*, 20 (3–4), 252–272.

MacDonald, R. (2017), '"Impact", research and slaying zombies: the pressures and possibilities of the REF', *International Journal of Sociology and Social Policy*, 37 (11–12), 696–710.

Mackenzie, S. (2010), 'Counterfeiting as corporate externality: intellectual property crime and global insecurity', *Crime, Law and Social Change*, 54 (1), 21–38.

May, C. (2017), *Transnational Crime and the Developing World*, Washington, DC: Global Financial Integrity [GFI].

McEwan, A. and L. Straus (2009), 'Counterfeit tobacco in London: local crime requires an international solution', *Trends in Organised Crime*, 12 (3), 251–259.

Nasheri, H. (2005), 'Addressing the global scope of intellectual property crimes and policy initiatives', *Trends in Organised Crime*, 8 (4), 79–108.

OECD (2007 [2008]), *The Economic Impact of Counterfeiting and Piracy*. Organisation for Economic Co-Operation and Development [OECD], accessed 30 November 2017 at http://www.oecd.org/sti/ind/theeconomicimpactofcounterfeitingandpiracy.htm

OECD and EUIPO (2016), *Global Trade in Fake Goods Worth Nearly Half A Trillion Dollars A Year*. Organisation for Economic Co-Operation and Development [OECD] and European Union Intellectual Property Office [EUIPO], accessed 20 November 2017 at http://www.oecd.org/industry/global-trade-in-fake-goods-worth-nearly-half-a-trillion-dollars-a-year.htm

Pemberton, S. (2016), *Harmful Societies: Understanding Social Harm*, Bristol: Policy Press.

Police Intellectual Property Crime Unit [PIPCU] (2017), *Counterfeit Goods*. City of London Police, accessed 20 November 2017 at https://www.cityoflondon.police.uk/advice-and-support/fraud-and-economic-crime/pipcu/Pages/counterfeit-goods.aspx

Rojek, C. (2017), 'Counterfeit commerce: relations of production, distribution and exchange', *Cultural Sociology*, 11 (1), 28–43.

Shen, A. and G. A. Antonopoulos (2017), '"No banquet can do without liquor": alcohol counterfeiting in the People's Republic of China', *Trends in Organised Crime*, 20 (3–4), 273–295.

Shen, A., G. A. Antonopoulos and K. von Lampe (2010), '"The dragon breathes smoke": cigarette counterfeiting in the People's Republic of China', *British Journal of Criminology*, 50 (2), 239–258.

Smith, O and T. Raymen (2016), 'Deviant leisure: a criminological perspective', *Theoretical Criminology*. Article first published online 11 August 2016, accessed at https://doi.org/10.1177/1362480616660188

Spink, J. and Z. L. Fejes (2012), 'A review of the economic impact of counterfeiting and piracy methodologies and assessment of currently utilized estimates', *International Journal of Comparative and Applied Criminal Justice*, 36 (4), 249–271.

Sullivan, B. A. and S. M. Chermak (2013), 'Product counterfeiting and the media: examining news sources used in the construction of product counterfeiting as a social problem', *International Journal of Comparative and Applied Criminal Justice*, 37 (4), 295–316.

Sullivan, B. A. and J. M. Wilson (2017), 'An empirical examination of product counterfeiting crime impacting the U.S. military', *Trends in Organised Crime*, 20 (3–4), 316–337.

Sullivan, B. A., F. Chan, R. Fenoff and J. M. Wilson (2016), 'Assessing the developing knowledge base of product counterfeiting: a content analysis of four decades of research', *Trends in Organised Crime*, 20 (3–4), 338–369.

Treadwell, J. (2012), 'From the car boot to booting it up? eBay, online counterfeit crime and the transformation of the criminal marketplace', *Criminology and Criminal Justice*, 12 (2), 175–192.

UNODC [United Nations Office on Drugs and Crime] (2013), 'Counterfeit products. Excerpt from The Globalization of Crime: A Transnational Organized Crime Threat Assessment, 2010', *Trends in Organised Crime*, 16, 114–124.

Vagg, J. and J. Harris (1998), 'Bad goods: product counterfeiting and enforcement strategies', in Gill, M. (ed.), *Crime at Work*, London: Palgrave Macmillan.

von Lampe, K. (2012), 'Transnational organised crime challenges for future research', *Crime, Law and Social Change*, 58 (2), 179–194.

Wall, D. S and J. Large (2010), 'Jailhouse frocks: locating the public interest in policing counterfeit luxury fashion goods', *British Journal of Criminology*, 50 (6), 1094–1116.

White, Robert (2013), *Environmental Harm: An Eco-Justice Perspective*, Bristol: Policy Press.

Wilson, J. M and R. Fenoff (2014), 'Distinguishing counterfeit from authentic product retailers in the virtual marketplace', *International Criminal Justice Review*, 24 (1), 39–58.

Yar, M. (2005), 'A deadly faith in fakes: trademark theft and the global trade in counterfeit automotive components', *Internet Journal of Criminology*, accessed at www.internetjournalofcriminology.com

9 State, society and violence in Russia: towards a new research agenda

Svetlana Stephenson

Introduction

The development of capitalism in Russia coincided with an enormous explosion of illegality and violence, with high incidence of many types of crime lasting throughout the 1990s (Galeotti, 2002; Zvekic, 1998). All over Russia battles raged over appropriation of state property, with both illegal and legal entrepreneurs using violence and coercion in the capture of assets, while an inefficient police force was unable to control crime. Towards the end of the 1990s and the beginning of the 2000s new contours of stability began to emerge. The state became credited with restoring order (Volkov, 2002). The nightmare of the 1990s seemed to be over. However, as the new order has solidified, it has become apparent that the use of private force has not gone away, and that state and private violent actors often act together, protecting each other from economic competition and political opposition (Briquet and Favarel-Garrigues, 2010; Stephenson, 2017). With violent vigilantism co-existing and often overlapping with state violence, the challenge of explaining the social order in modern Russia is that the Russian state is clearly not weak and can pursue its objectives very effectively, but it willingly delegates violence to private agents, and often encourages violence in society.

So far the study of the relationship between the state and agents of organized non-state violence has been heavily influenced by the tradition going back to Max Weber and later Charles Tilly. This tradition sees states as seeking to monopolize the legitimate use of force (Tilly, 1975; Weber, 1970). Only when states lack capacity to become the sole agents of violence can they be forced to form alliances with a variety of non-state actors, such as organized crime groups, gangs and vigilante militias, thus sharing their sovereignty and order-making role. It is assumed that while in most contemporary Western societies the state is strong enough to achieve a monopoly on violence, there are also under-institutionalized societies around the world where state and non-state actors may develop improvised solutions to the problems of social order (Streeck, 2016). Generally, it is the absence rather than the presence of the state that is seen to breed societal violence and give rise to the unchecked power of organized crime, gangs or vigilante groups.

This assumption is currently being questioned by global research that shows that the existence of interpenetrating networks and alliances of the state with a variety of shadow and criminal agents of power is not necessarily a sign of state failure but can be an intrinsic part of social order (Arias, 2013; Hibou, 1999; Nordstrom, 2000, see also Mitchell, Chapter 5 this volume). The state can collude with criminal actors, exchanging information, goods and services. Research into the state and vigilante violence has also shown that in certain conditions it is not so much the weakness of the state but the interests of the dominant groups that push them towards condoning or encouraging violence outside the state. A famous historical case was the rise of German fascism, where, according to Barrington Moore (Moore, 1967), the ruling groups, unwilling to implement reforms that would threaten their power, chose to cooperate with the Nazi Party. Similarly, as Richard Brown attested in his overview of the history of vigilante violence in America, much of the violence 'has represented the attempt of the established Americans to preserve their favored position in the social, economic and political order' (Brown, 1975: 5). Also, in America, as Skocpol showed, by outsourcing violence to private agencies or militias the state aimed to reproduce its authority and control, and fight off any challenges (Skocpol, 1985: 15).

Agents of state and societal violence are often considered to be distinct from each other and even in competition. By bringing the state back into the study of societal violence, we can also investigate how it influences through its actions, as Elias proposed, 'the patterning of the whole libidinal economy – drives, affects, emotions, and all' (Elias, 1978: 239). The growth of state capacity, which is often seen as associated with the decline of interpersonal violence (Pinker, 2012), may not guarantee internal pacification and may be conducive to violence. Using a language of violence which appeals to a range of affective and moral emotions, the state may attempt to mask the hollowness of its political agenda and promote social cohesion by directing anger onto a range of scapegoats and enemies.

In what follows I problematize the relationship between the state and societal violence in Russia (albeit without attempting a full literature review on this subject). I first discuss the ways in which we can analyze the relationship between the state and organized crime by looking at territorial social orders where representatives of both form intersecting networks of wealth and power, where violence helps sustain social order and provides avenues for economic accumulation and social mobility. I then move on to discuss the relationship between vigilante groups and the state and propose a research agenda that would look at how private violence is used to reinforce the state agenda while at the same time providing legitimate social identities for vigilantes and promoting their economic interests. Finally, I suggest ways in which we can study how the state encourages conflict in society through the sphere of emotions.

The state and organized crime

The analysis of the relationship between the state and organized crime often rests on two propositions. The first states that the criminals mainly aspire to clandestine material accumulation, aiming to make illegal profits. The second asserts that they may also aspire to become agents of criminal governance, establishing independent power enclaves and adopting the regulatory and justice roles not fulfilled by absent or deficient state power. When it comes to the state, in both cases it is seen as fundamentally antagonistic to organized crime, although at times it can be corrupted, infiltrated and subverted by it. The Russian experience, however, demonstrates that criminals may have wider aspirations, seeking to achieve legitimate social positions in business and government, while at the same time allowing the representatives of the state to use their criminal resources and competencies and social networks to defend and further their interests (Stephenson, 2017). This phenomenon does not only exist in Russia, being described in many areas across the world (North, Wallis, and Weingast, 2009; Sergi, 2015) where there is a fusion of the economic and political power of state-based groups and organized crime, as those who control the state can use criminal connections to develop their business interests, while criminals become politicians to protect and expand their and their groups' criminal business.

In Russia, the interpenetration of the state and organized crime started before the arrival of capitalism (see, for example, Finckenauer and Voronin, 2001; Handelman, 1994), but it was the capitalist transformation that allowed criminals to achieve spectacular social mobility. As the previous social structure collapsed, new fortunes and careers were launched by means that were on the fringes, or beyond the fringes, of legality. Members of the state apparatus and aspiring bourgeoisie, as well as leaders of organized crime groups and representatives of ethnic formations, and even urban sub-proletariat, assembled in various street gangs, and became involved in the process of social mobility (Derluguian, 2005: 309; Volkov, 2002: 125) using their different networks and resources.

To use Gramscian language, members of 'political society' – i.e., the state – and 'civil' society – i.e., the 'ensemble of organisms commonly called "private"' (Gramsci, 1971: 12), including its criminal elements – were both involved in a quest for hegemonic power. In Russia the process that Gramsci called the 'reciprocal fusion and assimilation' of elites (Gramsci, 1971: 221) can be observed in the way that actors from the state and civil society have jointly accumulated material resources and formed intersecting social networks where favors and economic opportunities are exchanged, and alliances built, through joint membership in charities, cultural institutions and political parties. This process has not been smooth, especially for the criminal elements, and many have failed, or been disqualified by vigilant security services and electoral authorities. Yet others have succeeded and joined state power structures – without necessarily abandoning their criminal business. This process of the straddling of social positions of criminal entrepreneurs and members of local and regional political elites has been documented in Tatarstan (Stephenson, 2015), in the Krasnodar region in the case of the infamous Kushchevskaia gang (see

Kostiuchenko, 2015 for a journalistic account) and in several other areas of Russia (Volkov, 2002). The analysis of criminal cases in several Russian regions conducted by Alexander Sukharenko showed that state representatives deliberately bring people with criminal connections into government structures in order to use their violent resources in illegal schemes (Sukharenko, 2015), while Michael Rochlitz demonstrated a clear correlation between the use of illegal methods to take over businesses by local officials and their ability to assure votes for Putin (Rochlitz, 2014).

Generally, though, while both the state (Ledeneva, 2013) and organized crime structures in Russia (Galeotti, 2000: 37; Varese, 2001, 2013) consist of a multitude of fragmented and flexible networks, so far discussions of the state and organized crime have too often focused on a monolithic state – in the form of a single clan of *siloviki* (state security or military services personnel), or Putin's kleptocracy – and seemingly monolithic organized crime. There is a need for case studies into territorial networks of power which would investigate the symbiotic relationship between state and criminal operators that takes place via personal and business networks, and a complex political economy, in which individual members of the state bureaucracy and the police build coalitions with members of criminal organizations wherever their interests are threatened or where they want to use the criminals' violent resources or competences to gain access to sources of revenue. Study of the evolution of collaborations at local and regional levels would allow us to see specific dynamics of assimilation between state actors and organized crime in Russia (Gilinskiy, 2006).

Vigilante violence and the state

Another area where issues of intersection of state and societal violence can be fruitfully explored is that of vigilantism. Although vigilantism is a highly debated concept (Moncada, 2017), it is commonly seen as a form of political violence that is aimed at eradication of transgression (or potential transgression) of institutionalized norms (Johnston, 1996: 229). In modern societies, where the state acts as the main guarantor of social order, vigilantism typically emerges as a citizens' reaction to a perceived deficit of justice, to the absence or ineffectiveness of state efforts to fight deviant behavior (Pratten and Sen, 2007). It is commonly thought that by using force to establish order, vigilantes effectively undermine the state's monopoly on violence (Rosenbaum and Sederberg, 1976: 7), leading the latter to try to eliminate unwanted competitors (although sometimes also co-opting those who might otherwise oppose it).

All over the world vigilante groups tend to be autonomous from the state, their activities being voluntary rather than state-directed or supported (Johnston, 1996), and generally vigilantism takes place in contexts of limited state presence. When it comes to Russia, however, the relationship between vigilantism and the state seems to deviate from the international pattern. Here, rather than representing the fracturing or erosion of the state's monopoly on violence, vigilantism frequently can be seen as a part of state capacity, with the political establishment encouraging and often actively supporting citizens' assaults on deviants. This mode of relationship between the state and agents of private violence can be partly attributed to Soviet tradition. Under state socialism autonomous vigilantism did not exist, but the state nevertheless organized citizens' groups to help achieve its purposes. Research into Soviet vigilantism has demonstrated that whether these were members of communist youth organizations who fought cultural deviations among their peers, or activists fighting antisocial behavior through the industrial and residential 'comrades' courts,' they did so within the ideological and legal limits set by the Soviet regime (LaPierre, 2012; Stephenson, 2006: chapter 5). The Soviet tradition was broken in the 1990s with the weakening of state control and the emergence of independent vigilante groups, such as Cossacks and ultra-nationalist associations (see, for example, Derluguian and Cipko, 1997).

With the strengthening of the state towards the end of the 1990s, vigilantism did not disappear, and many new groups have emerged. Some of these are overtly political, often sharing 'patriotic' and nationalist agendas; others engage in seemingly depoliticized activities. Often the activities merge in digital and physical space in a process that Trottier called 'digital vigilantism,' whereby 'citizens are collectively offended by other citizen activity, and coordinate retaliation on mobile devices and social platforms' (Trottier, 2017: 56). Citizens' groups police the territory, conduct anti-littering campaigns, organize 'actions' against public alcohol consumption, expose shops selling expired products, interfere in parking violations, attack suspected pedophiles or brothel keepers, or make raids against illegal immigrants. They also engage in assaults on people perceived as enemies of Russia and its 'traditional values.' The latter can include contemporary artists, independent journalists, human rights defenders and oppositional politicians. These people are subjected both to physical assaults and 'status degradation ceremonies' (Garfinkel, 1956), including spraying them with paint or urine, public flogging (suffered, for example, by the members of the protest group Pussy Riot in Sochi in 2014, at the hands of Cossacks), making degrading inscriptions on the walls of their homes or offices, or public destruction of their portraits. All these actions effect ritual destruction of the denounced persons and are ultimately intended to reinforce social solidarity and defend the values 'undermined' by those who are being denounced.

Investigating the activities of state-run youth organizations (such as the pro-Putin youth movement 'Nashi'), Julie Hemment (2015) documented a range of vigilante 'projects' developed by the activists. Young people policed their territories against various deviants, such as beggars, street drinkers or drug addicts; engaged in the naming and shaming of oppositional activists; and conducted campaigns of harassment and physically attacked those whom they saw as 'enemies of Russia,' including foreign diplomats. The Nashi activists showed a peculiar combination of belligerent and defensive xenophobia and entrepreneurial capitalist spirit. They saw their vigilante activities as opportunities to boost their CVs and acquire connections with influential people in government and affiliated businesses, looking for concrete rewards such as jobs, skills and connections (Hemment, 2015: 21).

Similar motivations seem to be behind the activities of other groups that engage in civil society activism with clear violent agendas (Favarel-Garrigues, 2016). One such group is the Night Wolves Motorcycle Club (*Nochnye Volki*). This countercultural group of motorcycle enthusiasts and rock music fans emerged at the end of the 1980s, made their money through protection rackets in the 1990s and towards the end of the 2000s transformed themselves into ultra-Russian patriots, Orthodox believers and staunch supporters of Russia's leadership. While the trend towards the politicization of biker organizations is not limited to Russia, the Night Wolves support the political establishment rather than fringe far-right movements. The club participates in political and religious events and celebrations and promotes Putin's policies in Russia and abroad. In return it receives substantial government funding, awards, grants and assets. Its leadership combines a fierce ideological agenda with ambitious business interests. As well as a number of commercial ventures, the club has a large portfolio of violent services, from private security companies that it owns, to security training of radical pro-Russian groups abroad and military support to pro-Russia rebels in Ukraine (Zabyelina, 2017). The Night Wolves have been among a plethora of paramilitary organizations (including former officers of Spetsnaz, Russia's Special Purpose Military Units and representatives of neo-Nazi groups) that have been training members of right-wing movements in Slovakia, the Czech Republic and Hungary (Shekhovtsov, 2018).

Russian vigilantism poses important questions about the relationship between state and society, and yet so far there has been limited research into its social organization and targets, its repertoires of violence, its justification and motivation – all the aspects of vigilantism, that, according to the helpful analysis by Moncada, constitute its definitional characteristics and can be used for comparative research (Moncada, 2017). Little is known about the uses of vigilante activism by the state and how it encourages, mobilizes and funds such groups and provides legitimate identities for their members, or, in some cases, willingly turns a blind eye to their violent activities. Likewise, the use of vigilantes by 'moral entrepreneurs' (Becker, 1963) within the central government and local authorities, by parliamentarians, and by the Orthodox Church and private commercial interests associated with the state all require exploration.

In addition to the motives of the state or separate strands within it, not much is known about the motivations of the activists cooperating with it. So far, there has been limited research on the benefits that accrue to people involved in various state-organized or state-encouraged vigilante practices. Instead of seeing vigilante violence as a set of autonomous civil society activities that are directed at perceived transgressions and injustices, we can see a substantial part of it as an example of cooperation between the state and violent groups. There is a need for research that would investigate how the flames of moral indignation may be fed not just by perceived harm to society, but by the members' material interests and opportunities to enter prestigious networks of power and influence. We can explore whether and how vigilantes may aspire to acquire legitimate identities alongside insurgent and outlaw identities, as well as whether their fight against perceived deviants runs alongside illicit and criminal activities.

Emotions, violence and the state

Organized violence in civil society feeds on moral emotions, such as moral indignation, and affective emotions such as hate, distrust, disrespect or solidarity that are linked to the construction of collective identities ('us' versus 'them'). Over recent years, the association between emotions and violence has become a matter for much research in sociology, cultural criminology and political science (Collins, 2008; Goodwin and Jasper, 2004; Presdee, 2000; Scheff, 1990; Scheff and Retzinger, 1991). What is still missing, particularly in the analysis of the Russian state and society, is an analysis of the relationship between emotions, violence and state power.

A number of theoretical approaches can be applied to the study of how the Russian political regime uses the emotional sphere to achieve social cohesion and mobilize support. We can address these policies as a part of the post-ideological political project. Instead of the common ideologies or values of progress and the goal of positive social transformation that characterized the formal politics of the twentieth century both in the liberal West and the socialist Soviet Union (Lyotard, 1984), the current regime prioritizes negative mobilization against perceived internal and external enemies. With the dream of progress now appearing hollow, the political class can instead appeal to what Nietzsche (1996) called a slave morality, where, lacking the will or capacity to change their material conditions, individuals settle for politics directed at blaming the Other. Slave morality involves judging the actions of others by their presumed intentions rather than consequences, by intolerance, envy towards those who have achieved success, and suspicion that they did so using dishonest means. Those in power use manipulation to stoke feelings of hurt and animosity towards the appointed scapegoats (see also Mitchell, this volume). Instead of social transformation, the masses are offered the rhetoric of *ressentiment* both in relation to internal enemies (atheists, intellectuals, oppositional politicians, members of the LGBT community, etc.) and external foes.

The demonization and scapegoating of these 'enemies' by the state-controlled media runs in parallel with the efforts of government-paid 'trolls' in social networks to act as moral police. Insufficient grief shown by 'liberals' or 'the fifth column' for victims of terror acts or plane crashes, or a lack of respect shown to heroic historical figures or war veterans, for example, become subjects of orchestrated moral outrage. By claiming that the perpetrators shock the common conscience,[1] the

---

1 As Durkheim famously said, 'we must not say that an action shocks the common conscience because it is criminal, but rather that it is criminal because it shocks the common conscience' (Durkheim, 1964 [1893]: 81).

community of the 'outraged' designates them as criminals who need to be punished for their transgression.

The political use of emotions by the state is increasingly facilitated by legislation aimed at protecting the 'dignity' of individuals and groups. One salient example is the state's mobilization of groups that present grievances against oppositional groups and individuals on the basis of 'violated dignity' and 'insulted religious sentiments,' providing the state with justification for political persecution and cultural censorship. The Russian anti-extremist and anti-blasphemy laws, together with legislation that criminalizes 'incitement to hatred and enmity' in relation to 'any social group,' have led to severe restrictions on freedom of expression, particularly among groups and individuals oppositional to the political regime (Bogush, 2017). The legislation has given rise to an avalanche of criminal prosecutions, in which the victims (from Orthodox believers to policemen and public officials) claim that their and their 'social group's' dignity or religious sentiments have been offended by publications in mass media or social networks.

Investigating how this legislation acts to bring together new groups of 'victims,' and how this relates to identity formation and collective mobilization, can shed light on the broader processes of political uses of moral conflict. Globally, the conflicts around harmful speech that results in 'violated dignity' and 'insulted sentiments' have been partly shaped by national and international human rights legislation, particularly around the right to dignity, and by hate crime legislation. While appeals to violated dignity and insulted sentiments may seek to redress serious violations, abuse, neglect and degrading treatment, there has also emerged criticism of their potential to confer the status of serious harm on what are often only minor incivilities, and their potential encouragement of a new culture of victimhood (Campbell and Manning, 2014).

Criminalization of speech acts, while in some contexts helping to confront abuses of dignity and protect damaged sensitivities, can thus also serve the purposes of oppression, becoming a conduit for 'capillary' power of modern states. Foucault suggested that in modern societies power, rather than being predominantly exercised from the top down, is diffused and circulates in the entire social body (Foucault, 2003: 94). It reaches everywhere in society through to its most private parts. By appealing to emotions and instigating conflicts that serve its agenda among citizens, the state no longer needs to execute heavy-handed top-down control, leaving it to members of society to police the moral boundaries. Investigating the ways in which the state exercises its power by instigating moral conflict, devising legislation around speech acts that are deemed to adversely affect the emotional states of citizens, and mobilizing civil society groups against appointed perpetrators, would help us to reach a better understanding of the relationship between state and society, particularly in authoritarian regimes.

Conclusion

There is a long scholarly tradition of seeing the state as the main agent of societal pacification, and the state law and order institutions as bulwarks against disruptive private violence. The strengthening of state institutions is seen as a key to fighting crime and violence, and to establishing the legitimacy of a political system that can effectively protect citizens against threats and dangers. Yet, analysis of cooperation between the state and groups that pursue, through violent means, a variety of their own projects – be this in the service of their own social mobility, economic accumulation or some ideological crusades – shows that political regimes can be complicit or actively involved in the unleashing of non-state violence. While this chapter has looked at Russia, there are many other examples from around the world – from the use of private anti-drug squads by the South African authorities in Cape Town (Moncada, 2017: 414), to the mobilization of violent 'colectivos' by the Venezuelan political regime (Werlau, 2014) and to legitimation of fringe ideas and groups by Donald Trump in the USA, thus leading to an increase in possibilities of violence (Barkun, 2017).

While in some cases we do indeed see weak state capacity propelling such cooperation, in others the political regimes are far from weak and they deliberately instigate and promote private violence as an instrument of their power. Non-state violence, which has long been seen as undermining or challenging the existing social order, can be used to sustain it. Investigating the arrangements that the state establishes with agents of organized violence can elucidate important questions about the nature of social order, the exercise of sovereignty and state-society relations, as well as the distribution of policing functions and the changing mechanisms of social control.

References

Arias, E. D. (2013), 'The impacts of differential armed dominance of politics in Rio de Janeiro, Brazil', *Studies in Comparative International Development*, 48 (3), 263–284.

Barkun, M. (2017), 'President Trump and the "fringe"', *Terrorism and Political Violence*, 29 (3), 437–443.

Becker, H. S. (1963), *Outsiders: Studies in the Sociology of Deviance*, New York: Glencoe.

Bogush, G. (2017), 'Criminalisation of free speech in Russia', *Europe-Asia Studies*, 69 (8), 1242–1256.

Briquet, J.-L. and Favarel-Garrigues, G. (2010), 'Introduction', in J.-L. Briquet, G. Favarel-Garrigues and R. Leverdier (eds), *Organized Crime and States: The Hidden Face of Politics*, Basingstoke: Palgrave Macmillan, pp. 5–13.

Brown, R. M. (1975), *Strain of Violence: Historical Studies of American Violence and Vigilantism*, New York: Oxford University Press.

Campbell, B. and Manning, J. (2014), 'Microaggression and moral cultures', *Comparative Sociology*, 13 (6), 692–726.

Collins, R. (2008), *Violence: A Micro-sociological Theory*, Princeton, NJ and Woodstock: Princeton University Press.

Derluguian, G. M. (2005), *Bourdieu's Secret Admirer in the Caucasus: A World-System Biography*, Chicago, IL and London: University of Chicago Press.

Derluguian, G. M. and Cipko, S. (1997), 'The politics of identity in a Russian borderland province', *Europe-Asia Studies*, 49 (8), 1485–1500.

Durkheim, E. (1964 [1893]), *The Division of Labor in Society*, New York: The Free Press.

Elias, N. (1978), 'On transformations of aggressiveness', *Theory and Society*, 5 (2), 229–242.

Favarel-Garrigues, G. (2016), 'Kto prishel na smenu sovetskim druzhinnikam?', accessed 20 March 2018 at https://openpolice.ru/news/kto-prishyol-na-smenu-sovetskim-druzhinnikam

Finckenauer, J. O. and Voronin, Y. A. (2001), *The Threat of Russian Organized Crime*, Washington, DC: U.S. Department of Justice.

Foucault, M. (2003), *"Society Must be Defended": Lectures at the College de France, 1975–76*, London: Allen Lane.

Galeotti, M. (2000), 'The Russian mafiya: economic penetration at home and abroad', in A. V. Ledeneva and M. Kurkchiyan (eds), *Economic Crime in Russia*, Hague and London: Kluwer Law International, pp. 31–42.

Galeotti, M. (2002), *Russian and Post-Soviet Organised Crime*, Aldershot and Dartmouth, MA: Ashgate.

Garfinkel, H. (1956), 'Conditions of successful degradation ceremonies', *American Journal of Sociology*, 61 (5), 420–424.

Gilinskiy, Y. (2006), 'Crime in contemporary Russia', *European Journal of Criminology*, 3 (3), 262–292.

Goodwin, J. and Jasper, J. M. (2004), *Rethinking Social Movements: Structure, Meaning, and Emotion*, Lanham, MD: Rowman and Littlefield Publishers.

Gramsci, A. (1971), 'The intellectuals', in A. Gramsci, Q. Hoare, and G. N. Smith (eds), *Selections from the Prison Notebooks*, New York: International Publishers, pp. 3–23.

Handelman, S. (1994), *Comrade Criminal: The Theft of the Second Russian Revolution*, London: Michael Joseph.

Hemment, J. (2015), *Youth Politics in Putin's Russia: Producing Patriots and Entrepreneurs*, Bloomington, IN: Indiana University Press.

Hibou, B. (1999). 'The "social capital" of the state as an agent of deception, the ruses of economic intelligence', in J.-F. Bayart, S. Ellis and B. Hibou (eds), *The Criminalization of the State in Africa*, Oxford: J. Currey, pp. 69–113.

Johnston, L. E. S. (1996), 'What is vigilantism?', *The British Journal of Criminology*, 36 (2), 220–236.

Kostiuchenko, E. (2015), *Nam zdes' zhit'*, Moscow: AST.

LaPierre, B. (2012), *Hooligans in Khrushchev's Russia: Defining, Policing, and Producing Deviance during the Thaw*, Madison, WI: University of Wisconsin Press.

Ledeneva, A. V. (2013), *Can Russia Modernise?: Sistema, Power Networks and Informal Governance*, Cambridge: Cambridge University Press.

Lyotard, J.-F. (1984), *The Postmodern Condition: A Report on Knowledge*, Minneapolis: University of Minnesota Press.

Moncada, E. (2017), 'Varieties of vigilantism: conceptual discord, meaning and strategies', *Global Crime*, 18 (4), 403–423.

Moore, B. (1967), *Social Origins of Dictatorship and Democracy: Lord and Peasant in the Making of the Modern World*, Boston, MA: Beacon Press.

Nietzsche, F. W. (1996), *On the Genealogy of Morals* (D. Smith, trans.), Oxford and New York: Oxford University Press.

Nordstrom, C. (2000), 'Shadows and sovereigns', *Theory, Culture and Society*, 17 (4), 35–54.

North, D. C., Wallis, J. J. and Weingast, B. R. (2009), *Violence and Social Orders: A Conceptual Framework for Interpreting Recorded Human History*, Cambridge and New York: Cambridge University Press.

Pinker, S. (2012), *The Better Angels of Our Nature: Why Violence has Declined*, New York: Penguin.

Pratten, D. and Sen, A. (2007), 'Global vigilantes: perspectives on justice and violence', in D. Pratten and A. Sen (eds), *Global Vigilantes: Perspectives on Justice and Violence*, New York: Columbia University Press, pp. 1–21.

Presdee, M. (2000), *Cultural Criminology and the Carnival of Crime*, London: Routledge.

Rochlitz, M. (2014), 'Corporate raiding and the role of the state in Russia', *Post-Soviet Affairs*, 30 (2–3), 89–114.

Rosenbaum, H. J. and Sederberg, P. C. (1976), 'Vigilantism: an analysis of establishment violence', in H. J. Rosenbaum and P. C. Sederberg (eds), *Vigilante Politics*, Philadelphia: University of Pennsylvania Press, pp. 1–21.

Scheff, T. J. (1990), *Microsociology: Discourse, Emotion, and Social Structure*, Chicago: University of Chicago Press.

Scheff, T. J. and Retzinger, S. M. (1991), *Emotions and Violence: Shame and Rage in Destructive Conflicts*, Lexington, MA: Lexington Books.

Sergi, A. (2015), 'Mafia and politics as concurrent governance actors: revisiting political power and crime in Southern Italy', in P. C. v. Duyne, A. Maljević, G. A. Antonopoulos, J. Harvey and K. v. Lampe (eds), *The Relativity of Wrongdoing: Corruption, Organised Crime, Fraud and Money Laundering in Perspective*, Oisterwijk: Wolf Legal Publishers, pp. 43–70.

Shekhovtsov, A. (2018), *Russia and the Western Far Right: Tango Noir*, London: Routledge.

Skocpol, T. (1985), 'Bringing the state back in: current research', in P. B. Evans, D. Rueschemeyer and T. Skocpol (eds), *Bringing the State Back In*, Cambridge and New York: Cambridge University Press.

Stephenson, S. (2006), *Crossing the Line: Vagrancy, Homelessness and Social Displacement in Russia*, Aldershot: Ashgate.

Stephenson, S. (2015), *Gangs of Russia: From the Streets to the Corridors of Power*, Ithaca, NY: Cornell University Press.

Stephenson, S. (2017), 'It takes two to tango: the state and organized crime in Russia', *Current Sociology*, 65 (3), 411–426.

Streeck, W. (2016), *How Will Capitalism End?: Essays on a Failing System*, London: Verso.

Sukharenko, A. (2015), 'Kuda Podevalas' Orgprestupnost'?', *Nezavisimaia gazeta*, 27 November, accessed 13 December 2015 at http://www.ng.ru/ideas/2015-11-27/5_criminal.html

Tilly, C. (1975), 'Western-state making and theories of political transformation', in C. Tilly (ed.), *The Formation of National States in Western Europe*, Princeton, NJ: Princeton University Press.

Trottier, D. (2017), 'Digital vigilantism as weaponisation of visibility', *Philosophy and Tecnhology*, 30, 55–72.

Varese, F. (2001), *The Russian Mafia: Private Protection in a New Market Economy*, Oxford and New York: Oxford University Press.

Varese, F. (2013), 'The structure and the content of criminal connections: the Russian Mafia in Italy', *European Sociological Review*, 29 (5), 899–909.

Volkov, V. (2002), *Violent Entrepreneurs: The Use of Force in the Making of Russian Capitalism*, Ithaca, NY: Cornell University Press.

Weber, M. (1970), 'Politics as vocation', in H. Herth and C. W. Mill (eds), *From Max Weber: Essays in Sociology*, London: Routledge.

Werlau, M. C. (2014), 'Venezuela's criminal gangs: warriors of cultural revolution', *World Affairs*, 177 (2), 90–96.

Zabyelina, Y. (2017), 'Russia's Night Wolves Motorcycle Club: from 1%ers to political activists', *Trends in Organized Crime*, accessed at https://doi.org/10.1007/s12117-017-9314-7

Zvekic, U. (1998), *Criminal Victimization in Countries of Transition*, Rome: UNICRI.

10 Riots, protest and globalization

Matt Clement

Introduction

Historians have written extensively on riots and social movements. In fact, the whole tendency to write 'social history' – i.e. to look at events from the bottom up, from the perspective of that majority of people whose lives were considered so little by their rulers – whose perspective is naturally from the top down – has frequently focused on protest movements and explained the 'moral economy' (Thompson 1991, Götz 2015) that surrounds events so often perniciously labelled as 'mob riots' by the powerful and their historians.

Sociologists have also been drawn to the subject of protest. Given Marx's position as one of the founders of the discipline, who so famously pronounced the class struggle to be 'the motor of history', there is a general recognition of the centrality of this phenomenon to their teaching and research. However, much of mainstream sociological thinking has been keen to put Marx 'in the attic' ever since this phrase was first used by the leaders of German social democracy in the early 20th century; and over the decades we have seen regular waves of thinking which have declared 'classical Marxism' outdated and its concepts in need of refreshment, from Max Weber through to Daniel Bell, from Eurocommunism to Manuel Castells. However, it was Castells, in his 1984 work *The City and the Grass Roots*, who revived and popularized the term 'social movement' to capture the way he believed that the traditional locus of conflict in the industrial era – the strike, or class struggle – was becoming less dominant. He could now see 'new social movements' struggling on the streets against the capitalist system to achieve their own goals.

Criminology, of course, takes many theoretical cues from sociology. The heart of much contemporary criminological research still takes its cues from the sociology of deviance – whose thinking on labelling, subcultures, deviance and identity provides the core of much contemporary criminological theory. These ideas were developed, questioned and analysed during a process of evolution whose centre was the crucial decade of civil rights, student riots and labour militancy from 1963 to 1973; a time of rising protest movements and the birth of the 'new left' in Europe and the US. Youth movements of students, anti-war hippies and Black Panthers, womens' and gay liberation fronts, as well as the rising waves of militancy coming out of the ghettos and the prisons, all contributed to a time where for many a 'riot' was a cause for celebration rather than a problem to be solved with effective social control measures (Bingham 2017).

2011 England's summer of discontent

The most recent wave of rioting in the UK, at the time of writing, occurred in August 2011. A detailed review of the response to these events will be presented below, taking in the views of the mainstream media, the government and other political voices as well as sociologists and criminologists. These events are too recent for historical comment to have yet emerged, although many have noted past parallels and precedents for this classic example of citizens demonstrating their riotous reaction to a breach of 'the moral economy of the crowd' (Clement 2014, 2016; Della Porta 2017).

One obvious parallel was that the UK witnessed a similar national wave of rioting in 1981, when 13 cities saw rioting between April and August (Kettle and Hodges 1982). The spark then was the infamous 'Swamp 81' mass stop-and-search operation by the police – targeting young black men in Brixton, South London (Lea and Young 1982). Thirty years later, the Metropolitan Police were conducting a similar exercise under the rubric of their 'Trident' anti-drug dealing initiative. Incidentally, this was being led by Cressida Dick – the officer in charge of the control room in July 2005 that issued the order for armed officers to assassinate suspected terrorist Jean Charles de Menezes – a tragic case of mistaken identity emanating from 'faulty intelligence' which pinpointed the Brazilian electrician as an Islamic terrorist. Dick was subsequently appointed Metropolitan Police Commissioner in 2017. In August 2011, during that 'summer of discontent' (Briggs 2012), armed police confronted a suspect, Mark Duggan, forced him out of a taxi and shot him dead on the streets of Tottenham, North London. His body was visible for several hours lying on the road and images swept across social media of another young black man killed by the police. There was no immediate riot, but the sense of injustice was strong across the city, especially when earlier police and press reports about Duggan being armed and having shot at the police proved to be unfounded. It was only when the family of the dead man and their supporters had gathered outside the police station on Tottenham High Road the following Saturday to receive a promised official communication from the police that events spilled out of control. The failure of the police to issue a communiqué had frustrated the crowd, and when one officer moved in aggressively to arrest one teenager who voiced her anger at their treatment things came to a head.

Footage from the scene captured on a mobile phone shows one person crying out: 'It's a girl, leave her alone it's a fucking girl!' Others stepped in to defend her and as events spiralled, two police cars, a bus and several shops were attacked by members of the crowd. Images of the burning police car then shot across social media, acting as a magnet drawing more bystanders to the scene. Hundreds, and eventually thousands, of people took to the streets. Bystanders described a festive atmosphere, members of Tottenham's Hasidic Jewish community distributed bread to the protesters. Another witness described how some rioters, having seized a case of wine from a local supermarket, were torn between drinking their gains and throwing them at the massed ranks of police now streaming to the scene (Reel News 2011).

Reactions to this phenomenon were predictably variable. Tottenham is a location which symbolizes the tradition of multicultural resistance to racist policing, ever since the Broadwater Farm Riot of 1985 that grew out of the needless death of a black mother at the hands of the police, leading to an uprising on the estate where a police officer was murdered with a machete. One needless death had led to another, only to be compounded by a major miscarriage of justice when Winston Silcott was convicted of the murder of PC Keith Blakelock, a verdict later overturned on appeal due to lack of evidence (Rose 2004). Now, in 2011, the borough was in flames once more due to a well-publicized fatality caused by the police. Unsurprisingly there were many people sufficiently outraged at the turn of events to take to the streets of their locality in more rioting. Social media had spread the message; as Stephanie Baker described, 'a common feature of the 2011 protests was that these forms of "mediated crowd" membership largely emerged in response to a perceived "social tragedy", wherein the interactive online relationships enabled by social media connected aggrieved users into intense relationships that transpired offline' (Baker 2012: 175).

While significant groupings were drawn to the streets, the voices of condemnation were also widespread. The mainstream media were predictably outraged, and the newspaper headlines on Tuesday 9 August 2011 following the initial riots bear this out:

YOB RULE	*Daily Mirror*
RULE OF THE MOB	*The Daily Telegraph*
MOB RULE	*The Independent*
ANARCHY	*The Sun*
ANARCHY IN THE UK	*Daily Star*
THE ANARCHY SPREADS	*Daily Mail*
FLAMING MORONS	*Daily Express*

(Molyneux 2011: 2)

The media reaction reflects the sense of shock that a series of events are shattering the public consensus. This is typical of riots, which generally lead to both condemnation and moral outrage, mixed with a degree of anguish over whether this breach in the social contract requires special methods of reform or repression for its repair. Criminologists should note the language used, especially the return of the epithet of 'the mob' to characterize that collective in riotous assembly. As critical scholars we should avoid reacting to riots in the same fashion as those other institutions – the government, the media and the policing and judicial elements of the criminal justice system – methods so aptly characterized by Stan Cohen as 'moral panics', with the rioting public becoming the mob 'folk devil' (Cohen 2011). Instead of simply condemning their actions we should provide some context for them – which constitutes the moral economy of the situation. The foremost thinker on the concept is the late Edward Thompson, who, when reviewing the many applications of the idea between the 1970s and 1990s, cited the interpretation of another veteran historian of contention, Charles Tilly:

> The term 'moral economy' makes sense when claimants to a commodity can invoke non-monetary rights to that commodity, and third parties will act to support these claims – when, for example, community membership supersedes price as a basis of entitlement. (Tilly, cited in Thompson 1991: 338)

It was the 'moral economy' of justice that lay behind the tendency to riot, combined with an instrumentalist recognition that the right to protest at injustice is best guaranteed collectively. This interpretation also applies to the vast bulk of other phenomena categorized by authorities as riots: from the umbrella protests in Hong Kong in 2014 to the explosion of movements against racist police killings leading to riots in Ferguson, Missouri and Baltimore, and mass protests in New York in 2014–2015. The same could be said since 2017 for the wave of anti-racist and anti-sexist actions provoked by various aspects of the Trump presidency. They are all reactions against perceived injustice. Social movement for social justice as encapsulated by the often-repeated refrain heard on every protest from the Los Angeles riots of 1992 to London's 2017 Grenfell Tower fire: 'No justice: No peace.'

The scale and persistence of 2011's riotous activity throughout the next six days represented a sharp break with the normal pattern of social order in the UK. Geographically, the sheer breadth of locations affected reflected the growth of urban conditions whose populations were likely to identify their situation with those of the heavily policed 'inner-city' locations of the 1980s riots. The phenomenal expansion of London over the last 30 years is often illustrated by pointing to the explosion in property development. This has pushed poorer populations out of much of the capital's inner cities into what was once classified as suburbia (Minton 2017). Thus, besides the 'usual suspects' such as Brixton and Tottenham, riots featured in Hackney and Southwark and outer areas such as Ealing, Clapham, Enfield, Kingston and most notoriously Croydon where a huge fire at a carpet warehouse engulfed TV screens in apocalyptic scenes suggesting much of the capital was 'in flames'. The classical features of Ernest Burgess's 'zone in transition' have been exported to farther-flung regions (Burgess 1967). Fear of an uprising causing an urban conflagration is a potent myth and moral panic that has been around ever since Cicero denounced the 'terror threat' of his political rival Catiline in 63 BC, and also featured in London's Gordon riots of 1780 (Parenti 2003; Clement 2016).

London was undoubtedly the epicentre of the 2011 riots but Bristol, Birkenhead, Birmingham, Gloucester, Kingston upon Thames, Liverpool, Manchester and Nottingham were also affected, alongside smaller outbreaks such as in Reading, or ones that never existed but which people were jailed for organizing on social media even though they did not occur, as happened in Warrington, Lancashire (Briggs 2012: 13−14).

Furthermore, some of the best criminological writing on the riots recognizes the liberating elements encompassed in being caught up in a protest movement, the sense that the participant is involved in a break with the stultifying norms of poverty and dull conformity − seeing it as 'the best three days of our lives' (Newburn et al. 2016: 41). In the words of one teenage UK rioter:

> I got caught up in the moment really . . . It was crazy. It was one of the best moments of my life but one of the worst at the same time, like I'm ashamed of it, but, boy [laughs], it was a real buzz . . . It felt like someone had just, something like someone was holding onto your shoulders in like a hug for a long time and then they just let go, like, no drugs could make you feel like this kinda happened, like it was that, it was that serious man! You sure, you felt invincible in a way. You felt like, ah I can't even describe it . . . It was a good feeling, it was like excitement and fear mixed together. (Newburn et al. 2016: 4−5)

Liberation or consumption?

Unfortunately, for some UK criminologists, this liberatory sense − the power of the riot to shift the consciousness of those involved − is an illusion. Rather, they believe rioters are tools of a dominant system into which the warped values of consumerism have been injected. For the 'ultra-realists' Steve Hall, Simon Winlow, James Treadwell and Daniel Briggs the 2011 riots were a case of 'Shopocalypse Now'. They chose to interpret the widespread looting that took place during the riots as a sign that rioters were conforming to the rules of consumer society rather than breaking them, noting 'the total absence of articulate political opposition . . . The rioters did not demand social justice' (Winlow et al. 2015: 136).

In their award-winning article the authors began by taking a series of quotes gathered from participants in the riots, which they then analysed within this self-fulfilling 'post-political' matrix. I was fortunate enough to debate this issue with Steve Hall at the 2013 British Society of Criminology Conference and suggested that the quotes could plausibly be interpreted within an alternative framework of a political rebellion against consumer society/neoliberalism and its accompanying tools of social control, as demonstrated by the manner of policing adopted during the riots.

The following statements were collected from rioters for the article:

> Will: 'we were trying to get the government back in any sort of way for the killing because there was no reason for it and everyone just thought to join in and take advantage of it'.

> Steve: 'People wanted to get back at the police, but at the same time get some bits . . . I need a bit of money because I am poor'.

Freddie: 'Fuck the police, I am going to get what I can. We arranged to steal stuff . . . we decided on a Corsa and a White van. It was organised bruv'.

'Come on, throw it at them [the police] . . . Fuck off. I'm gonna need this to put through a window. I didn't come here for a protest; I came here for garms [clothes] man'. (Treadwell et al. 2013: 6–7)

Were these statements really an example of what the authors conceptualize as: 'Rioting as a product of objectless dissatisfaction' (Treadwell et al. 2013: 1)? Do they validate the assertion that 'we are not yet convinced by initial empirical accounts of rioters' motivations that centralize dissatisfaction with unequal opportunities, the erosion of welfare or *antagonism towards police*' (Treadwell et al. 2013: 4)? I would argue the contrary. Three of the four statements explicitly condemn the police, while the fourth illustrates an argument about whether the rioters should target the police or prioritize looting goods.

The act of looting, Slavoj Žižek argued, was at the heart of the motivation for the 2011 riots, therefore rendering them 'a blind acting out . . . a meaningless outburst' in his article entitled 'Shoplifters of the world unite' (Žižek 2011). *Guardian* journalist Gary Younge disagreed, stating: 'They were looting, not shop-lifting, and challenging the streets for control of the streets not stealing coppers' hubcaps. When a group of people join forces to flout the law and social convention they are acting politically' (Younge 2011: no page).

Zygmunt Bauman claimed the 2011 riots were an example of 'consumerism coming home to roost', stating 'looting shops and setting them on fire derive from . . . the wrath, humiliation, spite and grudge aroused by NOT having them' (Bauman 2011: no page). Both he and Žižek imply that these were therefore not events triggered by political motivations such as a sense of social injustice. Veteran criminologist John Lea took the contrary view: 'If neoliberalism celebrates the identity of politics and consumption then "shopping" and "taking stuff" could be a very practical critique of neoliberalism!' (Lea 2013: 418). Apparently though, Hall and his colleagues are convinced that people are no longer capable of struggling against the forces that oppress them:

Ultra-realists agree with critical criminologists that lack of social recognition is linked to harm, but it adds the point that neoliberal capitalism has virtually severed the Master-Slave relation. Victims of harmful relations and acts now have very little influence or bargaining position in relation to their exploiters. (Hall 2018: no page)

However, a wide range of criminologists and other social scientists disagree. They have asserted the centrality of the political and social justice elements within these events and challenged the post-political and consumerist interpretation as described above (Clement 2012a, 2012b, 2016; Platts-Fowler 2013; Akram 2014; Sutterluty 2014; Slater 2015). Perhaps this counter-interpretation can be summed up by Klein's explanation: 'Action is triggered by an affront. The violence of the mob then, far from constituting a breach of the law, is a corrective action and, in the view of the rioters at least, to assert a higher justice' (Klein 2012: 134).

This explanation of why crowds gather, get organized through the process of becoming mobilized, and act accordingly is neither simple nor straightforward (Reicher 2011; Clement 2016). The context, as outlined above, is the 'moral economy' of the situation. Appreciation of how this plays out, in all its multi-faceted dimensions in today's media-saturated society, would surely take us further than the description offered in 'Shopocalypse Now' of how 'perpetually marginalized youth populations have become moody and vaguely "pissed off" without ever fully understanding why' (Treadwell et al. 2013: 3). David Matza spells this out definitively in his classic text, *Becoming Deviant*:

> The decision to appreciate . . . delivers the analyst into the arms of the subject who renders the phenomenon . . . to comprehend and to illuminate the subject's view and to interpret the world as it appears to him [sic] . . . to understand the process by which intimate knowledge of deviant worlds tends to subvert the correctional concept of pathology. (Matza 1969: 25)

The politics of contemporary protest movements

Events in Catalonia at the close of 2017 were one of the strongest contemporary examples of collective mobilization against the denial of the right to popular autonomy and forms of national independence. The Spanish state's brutal policing tactics and subversion of the democratic process through polling booth violence have been augmented by a series of dictatorial legal judgments that have led to the incarceration of many leading Catalonian politicians on a spurious and subjective charge of 'rebellion', carrying a devastating 30-year prison sentence. Further state crimes against their own citizens can only exacerbate this increasingly precarious political situation. Those protesters who regularly gathered on the streets in their hundreds of thousands in October and November of 2017 were radicalized by the sheer brutalism of the repression meted out to those campaigning for the right to vote on their national independence.

These events are reviving an awareness that the right-wing Francoist elements of the state and major political parties have retained a significant grip on the Spanish levers of power. After Franco's death in 1975, he

> designated as his successor Juan Carlos, the son of the pretender to the throne, who had been educated by Fascist tutors in Madrid . . . His cabinet was mostly hardened fascists. His armed forces and police were officered by men whose careers had been based on fascist repression. (Harman 1988: 325–326)

Harman's account of the scale of protest that spilled across Spain in the wake of the dictator's death illustrates how any relaxation of repression by the Spanish state risked a rising momentum of popular struggle generating radical regime change – as neighbouring Portugal had seen in its 1974 revolution – and this fear clearly still haunts those in charge. This is not just a case of Hispanic authoritarianism or 'macho' politics engendered by Spain's current leadership's fear of a militant challenge to their rule; the political leaders of the European Union have rushed to endorse the Spanish repression, chiding the Catalonians for incautious leanings towards autonomy and greater democracy. Just as with austerity measures, they appear determined to uphold the neoliberal status quo via economic and political sanctions against all popular movements of resistance (Varoufakis 2016).

The capacity of the state to foment violence in defence of its rule is evident here on a number of levels. In the Catalonian case, representatives of the regional state face violent repression and punishment by the agents of the national state, endorsed by the representatives of the supra-national European state – the financial sentinels protecting the political status quo and economic orthodoxy in the face of mass protest at the necessarily inflicted social harms of welfare and public spending cuts. Many Catalan strikers and protesters were also 'los indignados' who took part in the 'movement of the squares' in 2011–2012, largely protesting against austerity. It is the state violence of austerity that has driven a wave of protest across Europe since 2011, particularly regularly in Greece, Spain and Ireland, but also periodically in France, Romania, Turkey and elsewhere. In that same year, the American 'Occupy' movement was a social movement of the streets in reaction to the 2008 banking crash – a protest at state and corporate violence against the poor in the name of financial stability (Brotherton 2014). The multiple movements constituting the Arab Spring were political uprisings against their tyrannical governments (Farmanfarmalan 2014). These motives have since led to struggles in Bangladesh, Istanbul and Stockholm in 2013, Hong Kong and Ferguson in 2014, Paris and Seoul in 2016 and many more (Pritchard 2014; Clement 2016).

A true appreciation of why protests, including those labelled as riots, occur – i.e. due to a radical reaction against those in power and their acts of oppression – enhances our understanding and suggests that further bouts of repression are likely to foster greater waves of resistance. Of course, the relationship between people and the system they inhabit – the mix of resistance and compliance – is impossible to predict. Marx himself insisted that

> it is always necessary to distinguish between the material transformation of the economic conditions of production, which can be determined with the precision of natural science, and the legal, political, religious, artistic or philosophic—in short, ideological forms in which men [sic] become conscious of this conflict and fight it out. (Marx 1971: no page)

When researching aspects of global crime, it is important to recognize that the level of contention between and across social classes can go up as well as down; factors that appeared to be dying off or evolving into something different can suddenly surge into prominence – shattering theoretical myths in the process. The year of the UK riots – 2011 – was, of course, also the year in which a startling renaissance of class struggle and revolution centred in the Arab world then rippled out across Europe and America. At the time Alex Callinicos (2011) pointed out,

> the Arab revolutions of 2011 have been driven by popular rebellions from below. As commentators have repeated to the point of cliché, they have not been the property of any political party or movement, and have been driven by democratic aspirations given body in the forms of self-organisation that have rapidly emerged in all these struggles.

They also changed notions of what was possible:

> What we are seeing is a renewal of the classical political form of revolution. Innumerable social theorists and media figures have over the past 20 years proclaimed revolution dead, whether because of the definitive triumph of liberal capitalism in 1989 or thanks to the onset of 'postmodernity'. (Callinicos 2011: no page)

Despite the reality that these uprisings were followed by a counter-revolution in Egypt and civil war in Syria, 2011 had vindicated Marxist analysis of social conditions – demonstrating how it still applied in the 21st century. Hence, in 2012, French Marxist Alain Badiou published *The Rebirth of History* which makes a powerful case for the centrality of riots, protests, strikes and social movements; thereby demonstrating the redundancy of the so-called 'End of History' discourse which had envisaged there to be no alternative to neoliberal political economy in the future. Badiou constructs a typology that categorizes riots and protest movements into three different orders of magnitude, illustrated in Table 10.1, and attempts to plot their re-emergence up to the explosion of 2011.

Badiou himself is a '68er', i.e. a veteran radical from the famous French general strike wave in May that year. Other theorists have come up with structures that

Table 10.1   Badiou's (2012) typology of riots and protests

Immediate riot	'[U]nrest among a section of the population, nearly always in the wake of a violent episode of state coercion' (Badiou 2012: 22).
Latent riot	E.g. the various marches and mass strikes against austerity, such as in Greece 2012–2015 or France 2016 and 2018 'contained a latent riotous subjectivity. A single spark, a spectacular incident, a violent escalation, even an ill-understood trade union slogan, would have been enough for the so-called "mobilization" to take a much more resolute turn, to escape locally from the capital-parliamentarian consensus and construct, at least for a time, some impregnable popular sites' (Badiou 2012: 31–32).
Historical riot	E.g. Tahrir Square, Cairo in Spring 2011, 'the construction of an enduring central site, where the rioters install themselves ... asserting that they will stay put until they receive satisfaction ... laying siege to the state ... the threshold of historical riot is crossed' (Badiou 2012: 33–34).

group historical waves of struggle into 'riot' (18th and 19th century), then 'strike' (20th century) and now a new 21st-century era of 'riot prime' (Clover 2016). Theories of 'protest waves' are utilized to explain the persistence and regularity of the emergence of active social movements and the concept of the power of mobilization to change social conditions is growing in popularity (Beck 2015).

The age of Trump

Just after his election in 2017 one acid critic argued that 'many of the great social theorists from Adam Smith and Karl Marx onwards tended to believe that actual capitalists were incapable of effectively running bourgeois nation-states: Trump is a living textbook example of the correctness of their views' (Davidson 2017: no page). By mid-2018, many others would agree, although they often wondered just how he had won. Widespread conspiracy theories abound about Russian money, and an army of 'trolls' working for Vladimir Putin to undermine the US establishment by using social network propaganda to push a maverick leader into the White House. Allegations of state criminality by the new regime are already being documented in some detail even in criminology textbooks. This includes David Simon's *Elite Deviance* (11th edition) which features Trump's portrait on the cover (Simon 2018).

Part of the explanation lies in the fact that, ironically, Trump had campaigned for office dressed in populist colours. What else could be read into his use of claims that if elected he would 'drain the swamp' of corporate lobbying, bribery and corruption in Washington? He made vague promises to rebuild the country's infrastructure through state-funded job creation to 'make America great again'. He was learning from the success in the primaries of left populist Democrat Bernie Sanders who had roundly defeated Hilary Clinton in states such as Wisconsin that Trump needed for victory in 2016. On the eve of the vote Trump even promised voters in Manchester, New Hampshire, 'tomorrow the American working class will strike back' (*Daily Mail* 2016). One year into his term Trump has denied his own 'populism' in economic terms, reserving it for diatribes against migrants he seeks to make scapegoats, and has driven through very unpopular cuts in corporation tax for the rich, while there is as yet no sign of any revived state infrastructure investment.

The recent tsunami of protests against the Trump presidency are a good example of the growing salience of the discourse and practice of resistance in so-called 'advanced economies'. Ever since his inauguration, when hundreds of thousands of women and their supporters demonstrated in city squares across the nation, waves of protest have become normalized in America. In February 2017, airports and many other public spaces were filled with crowds angry at Trump's proposed ban on Muslim immigration. In August, when small numbers of Trump's far-right supporters rallied in Virginia, they became so enraged by the local anti-racist protest that surrounded and outnumbered them that one white supremacist ran down legal assistant Heather Heyer with his car and now faces a murder charge.

Trump infamously refused to condemn the killing, engendering still further waves of anti-racist protest across the country. In December 2017 a month-long trial of inauguration-day protesters concluded with their acquittal. As the *Daily Mail* (2017: no page) reported: 'The six who initially went to trial were charged with destruction of property and participating in a riot, even if there was no evidence connecting them to vandalism.' Their prosecution would have sent a chilling message to anyone opposed to the government. According to a relieved American Civil Liberties Union lawyer, Scott Michelman:

> Today's verdict reaffirms two central constitutional principles of our democracy: first, that dissent is not a crime, and second, that our justice system does not permit guilt by association . . . We hope that the US Attorney's Office gets the message and moves quickly to drop all remaining charges against peaceful demonstrators. (*Daily Mail* 2017: no page)

However, after the verdict, US state prosecutors insisted they would go ahead with plans to try the remaining accused, almost 200, in small groups until the end of summer 2018. On 21 December 2018, the trial of six of the 200 protesters ended in a not guilty verdict. As a pro-Trump news site reported: 'The untimely and disastrous decision by the jury is a triumphant win, not just for the six defendants and their legal advisors, but for other anti-Trump activists' (Blastingnews 2018).

To understand why even conservative politicians, whose natural allies are the economic elite, may wish to polish their popular credentials, we can learn lessons from history. Nick Rogers notes how in London 'the advance of popular Toryism . . . dated from the late seventeenth century when the Whigs [Liberals] shed their radical coat for a more establishment cut' (Rogers 1977: 3). Neoliberal capitalism is now widely viewed as offering little to the impoverished majorities of Europe and the US – something the increasingly detached wealthy minority of 'winners' fails to comprehend. As a recent UK criminology text explaining the rise of the far right pointed out: 'The benefits of our allegedly open, marketised society are the privileges of successful others' (Winlow et al. 2017: 3). Sadly for Trump, although his election was itself a 'protest vote' of sorts – against business as usual corporate neoliberalism advocated by this rival Hilary Clinton, the sheer scale of current anti-Trump protest is matched by his general electoral unpopularity – with only a 32 per cent approval rating (Associated Press/University of Chicago 2017).

It is difficult to be the people's hero when they don't like you, as UK Prime Minister Theresa May has also been finding out. This formerly stable government has seen its hegemony undermined by the successful challenge from a more authentic populist, the socialist Labour Party leader Jeremy Corbyn, whose motto in the 2017 election – 'For the many, not the few' – won Labour their biggest share of the vote since 1945. It is, of course, far easier for left-wingers to claim the mantle of being 'for the people', as acting for the poorer majority at the expense of the wealthy few is consistent with a commitment to equality and social justice. For them the problems begin when elected, as the Greek socialist party Syriza discovered when they failed to persuade European banks to allow them to finance their anti-austerity policies

(Varoufakis 2016). Socialist governments will need powerful movements of protest to provide the muscle that can prevent anti-social sabotage by the capitalist class (Stubbington 2017), and in prioritizing victory at the ballot box over building social movements on the streets and workplaces they run the risk of undermining their ability to deliver the reforms they promise.

Conclusion

Trump's travails and the rise of Jeremy Corbyn are testament to the importance of protest movements in shaping our future. The 'common-sense' nostrums of our globalized neoliberal world tend to marginalize the electoral possibilities of 'extremists' of the right and left, preferring to believe that all will gather in the middle ground. These ideas, dominant for 30 years or more in the US and Europe, have been shaken by a series of setbacks such as the 2016 'Brexit' referendum and far-right gains in France, Austria and Germany in 2017, alongside growing anti-racist protests and big votes for the likes of open socialists Bernie Sanders and Jeremy Corbyn. It is impossible to predict where tomorrow's victories and defeats will occur, and for whom, but we can be sure that protest movements will be shaping the streets and the workplaces of the future. They are also the concern of criminologists because they are often directed against the 'social harm' (Pemberton 2015) meted out by capitalism and a call for 'social justice'.

References

Akram, S. (2014) 'Recognising the 2011 United Kingdom riots as political protest: a theoretical framework based on agency, habitus and the preconscious', *British Journal of Criminology*, 54 (3), 375–392.

Associated Press/University of Chicago (2017) 'The December 2017 AP-NORC Center Poll', at http://www.apnorc.org/PDFs/AP-aNORC%20December%202017/AP%20Custom%20Poll%20Topline%20December_Trump.pdf (accessed 6.7.18).

Badiou, Alain (2012) *The Rebirth of History: Times of Riots and Uprisings*, London: Verso.

Baker, Stephanie Alice (2012) 'Policing the riots: new social media as recruitment, resistance and surveillance', in Briggs, Daniel (ed.) *The English Riots of 2011: A Summer of Discontent*, Hook: Waterside Press, pp. 169–192.

Bauman, Z. (2011) 'The London riots – on consumerism coming home to roost', *Social Europe Journal*, at http://www.social-europe.eu/2011/08-interview-zygmunt-bauman-on-the-uk-riots (accessed 6.7.18).

Beck, Colin J. (2015) *Radicals, Revolutionaries, and Terrorists*, Cambridge: Polity.

Bingham, Clara (2017) *Witness to the Revolution: Radicals, Resisters, Vets, Hippies, and the Year America Lost Its Mind and Found Its Soul*, New York: Random House.

Blasting News (2018) 'Trump inauguration activists found not-guilty on all charges' (21 December), at https://us.blastingnews.com/opinion/2017/12/trump-inauguration-activists-found-not-guilty-on-all-charges-002244147.html (accessed 28.2.19).

Briggs, Daniel (ed.) (2012) *The English Riots of 2011: A Summer of Discontent*, Hampshire: Waterside Press.

Brotherton, David (2014) 'The criminalisation of Zucotti Park and its lessons for the UK riots', in Pritchard, D. and Pakes, F. (eds) *Riot, Unrest and Protest on the Global Stage*, Basingstoke: Palgrave Macmillan, pp. 222–236.

Burgess, Ernest W. (1967) [1925] 'The growth of the city: an introduction to a research project', in Park, Robert and Ernest Burgess (eds) *The City*, Chicago: University of Chicago Press, pp. 47–62.

Callinicos, Alex (2011) 'The return of the Arab revolution', *International Socialism Journal* 130, at http://isj.org.uk/the-return-of-the-arab-revolution/#130analysis_5 (accessed 6.7.18).

Clement, Matt (2012a) 'Rage against the market: Bristol's Tesco riot', *Race and Class*, 53 (3), 81–90.

Clement, Matt (2012b) 'The urban outcasts of the British city', in Atkinson, W., Roberts, S. and Savage, M. (eds) *Class Inequality in Austerity Britain: Power, Difference and Suffering*, Basingstoke: Palgrave Macmillan, pp. 111–127.

Clement, Matt (2014) 'Mobs versus markets', in Pritchard, David and Pakes, Francis (eds) *Riot, Unrest and Protest on the Global Stage*, Basingstoke: Palgrave Macmillan, pp. 33–51.

Clement, Matt (2016) *A People's History of Riots, Protest and the Law: The Sound of the Crowd*, London: Palgrave Macmillan.

Clover, Joshua (2016) *Riot. Strike. Riot*, London: Verso.

Cohen, Stan (2011) *Folk Devils and Moral Panics: The Creation of the Mods and Rockers*, London: Routledge.

Daily Mail (2016) 'Confident Trump makes final pitch to devoted voters' (8 November), at http://www.dailymail.co.uk/news/article-3913920/Get-did-thing-Confident-Trump-makes-final-pitch-devoted-voters-just-24-hours-left-predicts-big-league-wins-blue-states.html (accessed 6.7.18).

Daily Mail (2017) 'Six anti-Trump inauguration day protesters not guilty' (22 December), at http://www.dailymail.co.uk/wires/afp/article-5207055/Six-anti-Trump-inauguration-day-protesters-not-guilty.html (accessed 6.7.18).

Davidson, Neil (2017) 'Choosing or refusing to take sides in an era of right-wing populism', *International Socialist Review* 106, at https://isreview.org/issue/106/choosing-or-refusing-take-sides-era-right-wing-populism (accessed 6.7.18).

Della Porta, Donatella (2017) 'Afterwords: old and new repertoires of contention', in Favretto, Ilaria and Itcaina, Xabier (eds) *Protest, Popular Culture and Tradition in Modern and Contemporary Western Europe*, London: Palgrave Macmillan, pp. 249–260.

Farmanfarmalan, Roxane (2014) 'Policing the Arab Spring: discordant discourses of protest and intervention', in Pritchard, D. and Pakes, F. (eds) *Riot, Unrest and Protest on the Global Stage*, Basingstoke: Palgrave Macmillan, pp. 277–300.

Götz, Norman (2015) '"Moral economy": its conceptual history and analytical prospects', *Journal of Global Ethics*, 11 (2), 147–162.

Hall, Steve (2018) 'Interview on ultra-realist criminology', at http://www.injustice-film.com/2018/01/02/interview-prof-steve-hall-ultra-realist-criminology/ (accessed 6.7.18).

Harman, Chris (1988) *The Fire Last Time: 1968 and After*, London: Bookmarks.

Kettle, Martin and Hodges, Lucy (1982) *Uprising! The Police, the People and the Riots in Britain's Cities*, London: Pan.

Klein, Axel (2012) 'More police, less safety?: policing as a central factor in the outbreak of riots and public disturbancies', in Briggs, Daniel (ed.) *The English Riots of 2011: A Summer of Discontent*, Hook: Waterside Press, pp. 127–146.

Lea, John (2013) 'Book review: Dan Briggs (ed.) *The English Riots of 2011: A Summer of Discontent*', *Theoretical Criminology*, 17, 417–420.

Lea, John and Young, Jock (1982) 'The riots in Britain 1981: urban violence and political marginalisation', in Cowell, D., Jones, T. and Young, J. (eds) *Policing the Riots*, London: Junction Books, pp. 23–40.

Marx, Karl (1971) [1859] *A Contribution to the Critique of Political Economy*, London: Lawrence and Wishart.

Matza, David (1969) *Becoming Deviant*, New York: Prentice Hall.

Minton, Anna (2017) *Big Capital: Who is London For?* London: Penguin.

Molyneux, John (2011) *Will the Revolution be Televised?*, London: Bookmarks.

Newburn, Tim, Deacon, Rachel, Diski, Beka, Cooper, Kerris, Grant, Maggie and Burch, Alex (2016) '"The best three days of my life": pleasure, power and alienation in the 2011 riots', *Crime, Media, Culture*, 14 (1), pp. 41–59.

Parenti, Michael (2003) *The Assassination of Julius Caesar: A People's History of Ancient Rome*, New York: The New Press.

Pemberton, Simon (2015) *Harmful Societies: Understanding Social Harm*, Bristol: Policy Press.

Platts-Fowler, D. (2013) '"Beyond the loot": social disorder and urban unrest', *Papers from the British Criminology Conference 2013*, 17–32.

Pritchard, David (2014) 'Unrest and inequalities: comparing welfare states', in Pakes, F. and Pritchard, D. (eds) *Riot, Unrest and Protest on the Global Stage*, Basingstoke: Palgrave Macmillan, pp. 191–221.

Reel News (2011) 'Tottenham rebellion', at http://reelnews.co.uk/issue-29-sept-2011/ (accessed 6.7.18).

Reicher, Steve (2011) 'Mass action and mundane reality: crowd analysis and the social sciences', *Contemporary Social Science*, 6 (3), 433–449.

Rogers, Nicholas (1977) 'Resistance to oligarchy: the city opposition to Walpole and his successors', in Stevenson, John (ed.) *London in the Age of Reform*, Oxford: Basil Blackwell, pp. 1–20.

Rose, David (2004) 'They created Winston Silcott, the beast of Broadwater Farm. And they won't let this creation lie down and die', *The Observer*, 18 January, at https://www.theguardian.com/politics/2004/jan/18/ukcrime.race (accessed 9.11.18).

Simon, David R. (2018) *Elite Deviance*, 11th edition, New York: Routledge.

Slater, Tony (2015) 'The neoliberal state and the 2011 English Riots: a class analysis', in Thörn, H., Mayer, M., Semhede, O. and Thörn, C. (eds) *Urban Uprisings: Challenging Neoliberal Urbanism in Europe*, Basingstoke: Palgrave Macmillan, pp. 121–148.

Stubbington, Tommy (2017) 'City waves red flag of warning at march of Comrade Corbyn', *Sunday Times*, 1 October, at https://www.thetimes.co.uk/article/city-waves-red-flag-of-warning-at-march-of-comrade-corbyn-p8lfd26ps (accessed 14.11.18).

Sutterluty, F. (2014) 'The hidden morale of the 2005 French and the 2011 English Riots', *Thesis Eleven*, 12 (1), 38–56.

Thompson, E. P. (1991) *Customs in Common*, London: Merlin.

Treadwell, James, Briggs, Daniel, Winlow, Simon and Hall, Steve (2013) 'Shopocalypse now: consumer culture and the English riots of 2011', *The British Journal of Criminology*, 53, (1), 1–17.

Varoufakis, Yanis (2016) *And the Weak Suffer What They Must?: Europe, Austerity and the Threat to Global Stability*, London: Bodley Head.

Winlow, Simon, Hall, Steve and Treadwell, James (2017) *The Rise of the Right: English Nationalism and the Transformation of Working-Class Politics*, Bristol: Policy Press.

Winlow, Simon, Hall, Steve, Treadwell, James and Briggs, Dan (2015) *Riots and Political Protest: Notes From the Post-Political Present*, London: Routledge.

Younge, Gary (2011) 'These riots were political: they were looting not shoplifting', *The Guardian*, 14 August, at https://www.theguardian.com/commentisfree/2011/aug/14/young-british-rioters-political-actions (accessed 9.11.18).

Žižek, Slavoj (2011) 'Shoplifters of the world unite', *London Review of Books*, 19 August, at https://www.lrb.co.uk/2011/08/19/slavoj-zizek/shoplifters-of-the-world-unite (accessed 9.11.18).

11 The socio-material cultures of global crime: artefacts and infrastructures in the context of drug smuggling

Craig Martin

Introduction

In December 2015, Australian police and security services intercepted £500 million worth of methylamphetamine smuggled into Australia (*The Guardian*, 2016). Although such figures are far from uncommon and speak to a growing trend in the smuggling of illegal narcotics across international borders (UNODC, 2010), what makes this case somewhat more intriguing – but also sensationalist – is the method of smuggling used by the criminal gang. Media reports showed a table neatly laid out with boxes of women's brassieres, alongside bags of glue pots. At first glance these appear simply to be average commodities; things we take for granted. Closer inspection of the product packaging on the bras reveals more. The box states these are 'TPU magic water bag push-up bras'. In this case 'magic water' takes on something of a more sinister tone. For the 'magic water' inserts used in the push-up bras are in fact a liquid form of methylamphetamine, totalling 190 litres. The glue pots, discovered in later police raids, also contained 530 litres of the liquid form of the drug. On the surface, as a colourless gel the 'magic water' in the bras and the liquid form of methylamphetamine are seemingly indistinct. The intrigue in this example – and the aspect this chapter investigates – lies in the use and repurposing of everyday commodities for the trafficking of illegal drugs. As normalized goods these are ostensibly invisible in terms of their sheer ubiquity and embeddedness within the distributive networks of commodity capitalism.

Critical to this chapter is the employment of everyday artefacts by drug smugglers as a form of concealment and disguise. In this example there is apparently nothing untoward in the transshipment of bras and tubs of artists' glue; this juxtaposition of commodities is at the very heart of the global economy, and, as the chapter argues, such artefacts are central to the operative reach and 'distributedness' of global criminal activity, in this case drug trafficking. Key to the latter point is the co-option, or harnessing of, both the material forms of the commodities themselves, i.e. the 'magic water' inserts and the glue, alongside the infrastructures which facilitate the distribution of these commodities, such as containerized shipments in this instance, individual tourist mobilities, or vehicles crossing international borders in other cases. Although this particular attempt to smuggle illicit narcotics was unsuccessful, their interception offers some revealing insights into the practices employed by traffickers, most notably the ingenuity in adapting the products, alongside knowledge of the transport infrastructures and supply chains of international freight transit. However, as this chapter asserts, it is not only the intentionality of the traffickers that is evident here, it is the potentiality of the artefacts themselves as well as the infrastructures which underpin their mobilities. That is, I wish to suggest here that the commodities themselves, the magic water push-up bras, the glue pots, the container in which they were shipped play a critical role in the perpetration of the crime.

In doing so the chapter resonates with the ongoing debates raised by the non-human turn in the cultural and social sciences: like much of the broader work in this area (Bennett, 2010) it does not privilege one over the other; instead, it makes a fundamental claim that things play a critical role in the actions of global organized crime. As such, I employ the term socio-material to emphasize the social force and potentiality that such things possess (Law, 2009). Above all, a central postulation is that the material entities described above and through the brief example at the end of the chapter offer an insight into the vast panoply of actors that form the complex networks of global criminal activity. I make the case that material cultures can tangibly shape the forms and geographies of smuggling in particular by providing platforms and spaces for the global distribution of illicit goods. In part I suggest that this is produced by the invisibility and under-governance of artefacts due to the sheer quantities in circulation at any one time.

Building on these points the chapter aims to foster further debates on the importance of socio-material cultures to our understanding of global organized crime, as well as the broader 'complex processes of global material culture' (Cukier and Sheptycki, 2012: 5). It offers an insight into these wider contexts of the socio-material culture of global crime by adopting a multi-disciplinary perspective, utilizing literature from criminology (see Hobbs, Chapter 3 this volume; Laverick, 2017), economic geography (Hall, 2012, 2018), science and technology studies (Latour, 2009), and material culture studies (Tilley, 2006). The potential being that the intermingling of a range of discourses can provide new perspectives from which to consider the complexity of global criminal activity, critically the relationship between various human and nonhuman actors, and most notably the force of socio-material infrastructures and the circulation of artefacts. By addressing one specific area of global organized crime I also hope that research across other areas – such as money laundering (Ruggiero, 1998: 121), counterfeiting and IP crime (see Large, Chapter 8 this volume), environmental crimes (Block, 2002), trafficking in peoples (Campana and Varese, 2016) and wildlife (van Uhm, 2016) – can examine the socio-material cultures of artefacts and infrastructures. Finally, the chapter deals with one particular aspect of drug trafficking, that of the harnessing of legal freight networks, and as such does not deal with the vast range of trafficking practices which encompass contemporary global organized criminal activities (see Caulkins et al., 2009; Dorn et al., 2005: iv).

Network-approaches to global organized crime

By its very nature global crime has a geography, a 'situatedness' in physical and increasingly virtual environments, grounded in the lived realities of those peoples, places and things which constitute the activities of criminality. Although Paoli (2016: 4) warns us of the rather elusive quality of organized crime as a definitional term, Seigel and Nelen (2008: 1) note how global organized crime is also formed by a range of social, economic, historical and cultural contexts. However, the origins of organized crime are primarily considered by their socio-economic conditions of emergence. For Lupsha, organized crime is markedly American in origin, in that it is premised on the foundations of individualism, property, competitiveness and 'freedom of action' (Lupsha, 1981: 6), key paradigms of American society. Tellingly, for discourses on the imbrication of the legal and illegal (Abraham and van Schendel, 2005), just as these principles have underpinned the rise of capitalism, they have also determined the development of organized crime. Lupsha goes further still in highlighting the imbrication of legal business structures with organized crime practices (see also Hudson, Chapter 2 this volume):

> Organized crime consists of activity by a group of individuals who consciously develop roles and specializations, patterns of interaction, spheres of responsibility and accountability, and who, with continuity over time, engage in a variety of illegal and illicit endeavors (enterprises) involving the use of large amounts of capital, nonmember associates, and the corruption of public officials and their agents, directed toward the achievement of greater capital accumulation in the form of untaxed monies and goods of value which are then processed through legitimate "fronts" and "buffers" to "launder" this black income into white (legitimate economic) earnings. (Lupsha, 1981: 22–23)

Crucially, the processes which for Lupsha define organized crime – specialist roles and division of labour, accountability, capital flows, and ultimately capital accumulation – are akin to the organizational infrastructure of legal financial and commercial activities. While these definitions of the dynamic complexities of organized criminality go some way towards highlighting the socio-economic structural qualities they are also rather abstract, and as such lack a sense of the lived experiences of organized criminality.

One way in which these complex forces can be addressed in a more meaningful way is to look at the configuration of the groups themselves, and in particular to think about them in a different spatial manner. Over the previous 20 years there has been a shift away from viewing organized crime groups as vertically integrated with a top-down hierarchical structure. For Kenney (2007) such organizational forms have typically been associated with the Colombian drug trafficking cartels, most infamously under the stewardship of now cult figures such as Pablo Escobar. The infamous nature of the cartels emanates from what Kenney terms the 'cartel myth' (2007: 234) – Kenney's interviews with traffickers involved in the Colombian drugs trade highlighted the role of independent groups made up of family, friends and associates rather than hierarchically controlled large-scale groups (also see Naylor,

1997; Williams, 1998). One of the primary issues with this image of the cartel as a vertically integrated organization lies with the apparent 'tightness' and control of the organization itself, an aspect that has now been debunked in favour of a richer appreciation of the loose ties that bind together the drugs trade in particular. Rather, the drug trafficking context in Colombia mirrors a range of other organized criminal activities (weapons smuggling, people trafficking, prostitution) whereby 'flexible exchange *networks* expand and retract according to market opportunities and regulatory constraints' (Kenney, 2007: 235, my emphasis).

The network approach has played a significant role in understanding the organizational dynamics of global organized crime (Bouchard and Amirault, 2013). As Kenney notes, one of the critical factors which networked configurations exhibit is flexibility: with vertically integrated forms of organization – which are effectively command and control structures – there is an inherent weakness in the linkages which constitute the grouping. If one of the key members of the group is arrested, for example, a significant gap is left in the structure. For Williams (1998: 154) network forms of organization have been at the forefront of criminal organizations owing to this flexibility, which enables rapid changes in approaches to criminal activity in response to new interdiction techniques for example. In network formations such inherent structural weaknesses are negated through the horizontal nature of the network, i.e. there are other members of the network who can take on specific roles, or new ones can be 'plugged in'. Key to the spatial configuration of networks are the nodes which connect the network together, including 'individuals, organizations, firms, or even computers' (Williams, 1998: 155). Rather than tightly bonded links that determine bureaucratic, hierarchical structures, the nodes which form the network are loosely coupled and semi-autonomous: if one of the nodes such as an individual is no longer operative the node can easily be substituted.

The flexibility of organized crime networks stems also from the inherent 'distributedness' of network configurations. Although networks can be localized on a national scale for example, they are not necessarily bounded geographically (Hall, 2012: 182). The nodes themselves can be located outside of specific geographical governance, particularly in relation to communication and transportation channels. The distributed quality of crime networks is such that although there are cores and peripheries (Williams, 1998: 155–156) there is extensive reach beyond national borders, a key determinant of global organized crime. For my argument in this chapter the extensiveness of reach is generated by a range of different actors, including those identified by Williams above. So rather than individuals forming the entirety of a network it is populated by a wide range of actors, including the human and crucially the nonhuman. In Williams' reading this includes computers, but clearly in light of advances in the understanding of networks, particularly from early work in science and technology studies (Latour and Woolgar, 1986), the extent of the interplay between humans and nonhumans is much greater. We could include the computers as well as the infrastructure underpinning their operation: power networks, or generators; the design of the interfaces; the software; upgrades. The actors are almost limitless.

Mirroring the development on licit global infrastructures, a fundamental facet of the structural configuration of global organized crime networks is the infrastructure that facilitates flexibility and distributed reach. These infrastructures of communication and mobility have propelled a range of changes in the constitution of cross-border organized crime, notably increased interaction and integration of activities (see UNODC, 2004). Such processes of licit integration have created new spaces and opportunities for cross-border criminal activities, in part a result of 'under-governed areas' in certain nation states (Patrick, 2011: 135). However, while lack of governance may be key to drug production, weak state governance is not as central to drug trafficking in the same way, where 'the evidence suggests that drug traffickers value geographical convenience, *exploitable infrastructure*, and easy access to global markets at least as highly as they do the benefits of state weakness' (Patrick, 2011: 150, my emphasis). It is to the interaction between human and nonhuman actors through the exploitation of socio-material infrastructures and artefacts that I focus on in the following sections.

Global organized crime's nonhuman actors

The literature on global organized crime deals with the interplay between the global and the local in a similar vein to other cognate debates on the spatial scales at which globalization operates. For while stereotypical images of the networked geographies of global criminality may posit an idea of a deterritorialized flow of illicit goods, Hobbs (2013: 220) notes the relations between cross-border crime and the actual manifestation of criminal activity on streets, in houses, or in cars. Global crime is enacted amidst the minutiae of everyday life, each folded into the other. This intermingling of geographical scales is similarly crucial to the socio-material cultures of global crime – for as this section outlines, there is an important imbrication between human and nonhuman actors in the taking-place of global organized crime. Hobbs' argument that the tangible qualities of transnational crime are manifest in the lived experiences of those perpetrating crime, as well as those affected by it, is highlighted further when he writes of tobacco bootlegging in the 1990s. Jason, a lead bootlegger, speaks of his actions: 'So I'm paying for hotel rooms, renting six big French cars, spending twenty grand a week on the goods, paying the lads a grand each tax-free on a weekly basis, and on average I'm making nine grand clear profit a week' (cited in Hobbs, 2013: 220–221). This short description raises important issues about the daily experience of cigarette bootlegging, notably the intricacies of interactions between the networked actors – in this instance the bootleggers responsible for bringing tobacco in from Luxemburg and beyond, but equally the cars and the hotel rooms. These human and nonhuman actors form the infrastructure of organized criminal activity. The networked infrastructure is configured by the human bootleggers of course, as well as the hotel rooms and vehicles which form further nodes in the network. Indeed, the bootleggers are reliant on these nonhuman entities.

While there have been significant developments in the spatial understanding of global crime there has been comparatively little research into the multiplicity of the actors that form the various nodes in the networks. I now turn to the way in which nonhuman actors play a significant role in the function of criminal networks. Recasting the perspective from which illicit criminal networks are studied will enable a richer appreciation of the complexity of illicit interactions. This approach follows other precedents in the study of global organized crime, notably from economic sociology where recent work on illegal markets challenges assumptions on the principal role of individual human actors (Beckert and Dewey, 2017). The United Nations Office on Drugs and Crime (UNODC, 2010) similarly argues that efforts to intercept and arrest perpetrators of transnational crimes such as people smuggling or drug trafficking are somewhat futile as the illegal market itself remains in place after individuals have been imprisoned:

> Today, organized crime seems to be less a matter of a group of individuals who are involved in a range of illicit activities, and more a matter of a group of illicit activities in which some individuals and groups are presently involved. If these individuals are arrested and incarcerated, the activities continue, because the illicit market, and the incentives it generates, remain. (UNODC, 2010: 3)

As with the dominance of licit market dynamics, the market – in this case illicit – proliferates and determines all. By repositioning the central role of illicit activities the UNODC's report suggests that markets themselves may be disrupted. While I do not address the illicit markets of drug smuggling in the same manner as economic sociologists, I do suggest that recasting our view of global organized crime networks and looking at their socio-material cultures from a socio-cultural perspective offers a further means of understanding how these networks operate over and above a solely human-centred perspective.[1] In a similar vein the UNODC offers an interesting view on why the study of human actors has proliferated, suggesting that 'law enforcement officials tend to conceive of TOC [transnational organized crime] as groups of *people*, because the tools they possess – the powers of arrest and seizure – can only be levelled against individuals' (UNODC, 2010: 1, my emphasis). Of course, vehicles can be seized, drug shipments intercepted, or goods impounded, but the people responsible for doing so are the ones prosecuted. Such a legislative process should not detract from the role that 'things' play in criminal acts, be they organized, global or otherwise. Human criminal actors cannot operate without the support of nonhuman artefacts and infrastructures, such as vehicles, firearms, buildings, IT and communications technology, to identify just a few. These are the material 'tools' which facilitate crime. These socio-material entities shape organized crime: for example, a building utilized for the storage of illegal firearms has a determinant effect in shaping how the firearms will be used in the perpetration of further criminal activity. In this case it may be that through dint of the building's

---

1 Although this chapter focuses on the socio-material cultures of crime an important backdrop to the theoretical discussions around the nonhuman is the expansiveness of the nonhuman as a conceptual category – in this case markets themselves are clearly 'things'.

apparent normality, its invisibility, it masquerades as a front for legitimate usage as a warehouse. The building has potential as a harbinger of illegality (see Manaugh, 2016).

The wider recalibration of viewpoint clearly chimes with much recent work across a range of disciplines dealing with the nonhuman or more-than-human turn, notably within Actor Network Theory (Latour, 2005), material geographies (Cook and Tolia-Kelly, 2010), political theory (Bennett, 2010; Braun and Whatmore, 2010) and material culture studies (Tilley, 2006). To focus on the material culture, the 'stuff' (Boscagli, 2014), of global crime is to recognize how the things which permeate global organized crime networks are not wholly subservient to human intentionality; rather, matter has agential potential that co-constitutes criminality. While here is not the place to restage the entire intellectual foundations of the nonhuman turn, one of the key arguments to emerge from the broader context of 'new materialisms' (Coole and Frost, 2010) is the idea of things being inherently forceful. That is, they are full of force, full of potential, possessing an energy to disrupt preconceived notions of objects as passive carriers of human will. The co-constitutive nature of the intermingling of the human and nonhuman is critical, for there is reliance on nonhuman matter to enforce criminal action, these are the tools of bootleggers, counterfeiters, traffickers, money launderers and others. More specifically with drug trafficking, the work of Decker and Townsend Chapman (2008) offers a valuable perspective from which to consider this in more depth. In their interviews with convicted drug traffickers they identify a broad range of the actors involved in the production and supply of illegal drugs. Tellingly, their description of a typical Colombian drug smuggling organization shows a range of actors, including: an office of supply; office of finance; brokers in Colombia; an office of transportation; transporters responsible for distribution to brokers in the United States, as well as independent transporters supplying to US contacts; a US distribution office; and buyers (Decker and Townsend Chapman, 2008: 36). Although the diagram depicting the structure of the network does not specifically identify nonhuman actors, the interviews and surrounding discussions are populated with a myriad of human and nonhuman actors: telephones; go-fast speed boats; false compartments in fishing vessels; bait, food, beer, lobsters, fish and the attendant fishing paraphernalia to make the lobster vessels appear legitimate. Decker and Townsend Chapman (2008: 71) call these the 'props' of drug trafficking.

Taken at face value these are mundane, everyday things. They are the stuff of social interactions, hence my use of the term socio-material. In the same way these designed artefacts facilitate licit socio-cultural practices (Michael, 2000), they are also parallel objects of illicit activity: they produce social relations and events, albeit illicit. And as I outline in the final section, it is their very ubiquity that affords them an important place in the socio-material infrastructures of global organized crime networks. Just as Thrift (2000) writes of the proclivity to frame the geopolitical through the lens of large-scale entities such as the tensions over territorial access to the South China Sea (Buszynski and Roberts, 2015), so he argues that 'little things' – like files, paperwork or emails, for example – do much of the work of enforcing geopower. Although the large-scale forms such as the territorial waters of the South China Sea itself have significant impact and affect, crucially, the mundane things which form the backdrop to contemporary social life are equally as forceful. As Law suggests, 'there is no overall social, natural, or conceptual framework or scale within which events take place: as webs grow they tend to grow their own metrics' (Law, 2009: 147). There is no normative hierarchical domination cascading down in scale – the interaction between these different human and nonhuman actors is manifest through multiple, overlapping and emergent relations. This is notable when we consider the specific instances of how the socio-material artefacts and infrastructures enrolled in criminal networks are operationalized through their inherently networked distribution and reach, aspects I now discuss through a brief example of drug smuggling.

Socio-material artefacts and infrastructures: the case of disguised wooden shipping pallets

In her study of illicit global mobilities Gargi Bhattacharyya (2005) argues that organized crime is dependent on legitimate economic structures: it relies on alternate modes of transnational business activity, but financial practices nonetheless. She notes how organized crime 'has a necessarily symbiotic relationship with the formal economy and makes its profits from providing an alternative route through the interstices of "legitimate" transnational business' (Bhattacharyya, 2005: 63). In this final section I develop this notion of reliance by suggesting that there is a dependency at play in the utilization of licit practices. I do so by considering an almost parasitic form of reliance by drug traffickers on existing socio-material artefacts and infrastructures associated with the mobility of everyday commodities (also see Martin, 2015). As noted, a significant facet of the networked structure of global organized crime is its distributed reach across geopolitical boundaries, to which the socio-material artefacts and infrastructures play a pivotal role in shaping the actions of criminal actors. This is particularly telling in relation to Bhattacharyya's assertions. For one sees how the legitimate infrastructures of commodity distribution, tourist travel or transport mobilities become key distributive channels for the circulation of illegal things, in this case narcotics. As discussed below the material entities which one expects to see circulating at the transnational level become decisive props in drug smuggling, notably in relation to their under-governance.

The trafficking of illegal drugs consists of a complex and multifaceted set of approaches. For the sake of brevity, I suggest these practices fall into two categories, both of which are reliant on socio-material artefacts and infrastructures:

1. *Shadow networks and supply chains*: for example, use of standard boats, planes and road vehicles specifically for transshipment through distribution channels specific to the trafficking; or the design of narcosubs (Ramirez and Bunker, 2015).
2. *Harnessing of legitimate transportation networks and supply chains*: for

example, drugs couriers using commercial air, land and sea transport routes; concealment and disguise of drugs in legal freight shipments; adaptation of existing boats such as fishing vessels to make them appear as if embedded in legitimate trade activity (Decker and Chapman, 2008: 70–71); or the use of postal and courier networks.

Again, here for the purpose of expediency I address the latter of these categories by investigating the disguise of drugs in freight shipments.[2] Examples abound of the harnessing of licit freight shipments, notably in the use of shipping containers, including the misrepresentation of contents through false declarations; and commonly through the tactical use of 'double layering', where illegal shipments of narcotics or other contraband are hidden behind legal commodities. If the container is opened the immediate impression is that of a straightforward shipment of particular goods. This notion of the 'front' is a particularly resonant one in relation to Bhattacharyya's recognition of how illicit activities rely on the guise of being licit. Revealingly, it has a long legacy in relation to the histories of smuggling. For example, Alfred Rive's 1929 essay, 'A Short History of Tobacco Smuggling', describes the shipment of contraband tobacco disguised to look like the roping typically used in shipping operations – to the untrained eye this is simply a common piece of shipping paraphernalia, the 'tools of the trade' embedded in the context of shipping (Rive, 1929). There is nothing apparently untoward.

Nearly 90 years later, an almost identical case of material disguise is evident in a case from late 2015. Here, traffickers attempted to smuggle 1.4 tonnes of compressed cocaine into the Port of Valencia in Spain, disguised to look like 40 wooden shipping pallets holding bags of charcoal shipped in containers from Colombia (Harley and Hedgecoe, 2015). All this was carried out through the guise of a supposedly legitimate charcoal importation business, until Spanish police intercepted the container at the port. Akin to the methods employed by the methylamphetamine smugglers outlined at the start of the chapter and Rive's disguised tobacco, this case is equally as telling on a number of levels.

Firstly, and most importantly for my overarching argument, it highlights the inherent material potentiality of the compressed cocaine powder itself, in tandem with the material knowledge and innovation utilized by smugglers. Richard Hooker, a forensics expert, describes the process through which the smugglers were able to disguise the compressed cocaine powder to appear like the pallets as well as the charcoal itself:

To make the cocaine look like wooden pallets they have dissolved the white cocaine powder with a solvent or glue. It has then been placed into moulds shaped like pallets to

---

2 Caulkins et al.'s research into smuggling technologies employed to smuggle narcotics into the United Kingdom shows that by far the most widely used method was the use of individual air couriers, followed by couriers using other forms of transport, then 'operations that involved corrupt vehicle operators' (Caulkins et al., 2009: 71). By comparison the concealment of drugs in legitimate freight was fourth in the list of approaches.

set. When the resin dries out it then solidifies. If you mix it with a dye it then gives the wood effect and gives the appearance of dark wood. Once the dealers get it they can then re-dissolve it and reverse the process to extract the cocaine. The same process can also be used to make it look like pieces of charcoal by using charcoal powder. (Hooker, cited in Harley and Hedgecoe, 2015)

Although this case of drug trafficking was intercepted it still displays some key points with regard to my assertions regarding the potentiality of socio-material artefacts and infrastructures within global crime networks: while the six men arrested are clearly the instigators of the criminal action it also evident that this was made more tangible through the potentiality of the material, that is the affordances (Gibson, 1986) of the compressed cocaine powder when coupled with the solvent and dye. Held within the combination of these materials lies the potential for illicit innovation by way of disguise. Knowledge of material potential and the potentiality of the material itself cannot be separated.

Secondly, this also speaks to the the imbrication of the human and the nonhuman in the co-constitution of the networks of global criminal activity, one is not possible without the other: the smugglers; the 'cooks' responsible for extracting the cocaine; the cocaine itself; the glue or solvent; the dye; the moulds; the charcoal; the charcoal sacks; the shipping container; the technical apparatus for dissolving the cocaine and extracting. All play a fundamental role in the shape of criminal actions.

Thirdly, material potentiality as a form of force is only actionable through embeddedness within the socio-material infrastructure of licit freight distribution. The impression given by transporting a container full of charcoal sacks on wooden pallets is that they are simply part of the commercial and logistical supply chain infrastructure of this charcoal business. The likelihood of successfully transshipping the 1.4 tonnes of compressed cocaine powder is determined by the networked nature of the freight distribution channels and crucially the distributed reach of global container shipping where commodities are regularly transshipped between Colombia and Spain.[3] As noted previously in relation to Patrick's (2011: 150) assertions, we can see the inherent relationship between the convenience of geographical ties, infrastructure that is exploitable, and a global market that is easily accessible through the charcoal import company as a front for the drug trafficking operation.

Finally, related directly to distributed reach, the socio-material infrastructures of legal global trade exhibit an inherent weakness in terms of under-governance. Shipping containers, pallets and other similar paraphernalia are part of the backdrop of commodity capitalism: the inability to examine every shipment without curtailing the global flows of goods and peoples is one of the many structural fallibilities of the securitization of global organized crime. For in a similar way to

---

3   An important historical-geographical context is evident in the long-standing trading relationship between Colombia and Spain, in part a result of the colonization of Colombia by the Spanish.

Patrick's (2011: 135) arguments concerning the exploitation of under-governed states by illicit actors, so we can see in this case that another form of exploitation of under-governance is at play: given the predominance and extensiveness of global trade the socio-material artefacts and infrastructures which form it are a critical facet of its exploitation by global criminal actors. I close this section by arguing that just as geographical under-governance opens up spaces where the securitized gaze is restricted (see Scott, 2010), so a correlative notion of under-governed objects and infrastructures is apparent in how disguised or adapted artefacts circulate in the context of drug smuggling. The key difference between territorial under-governance and an object-centred version is that these territories are isolated from spaces of transnational integration. By contrast, the artefacts and infrastructures of transnational drug smuggling are highly integrated, albeit by harnessing the licit circulatory power of freight distribution in this specific case. These artefacts are under-governed in the sense that governing every commodity in circulation is to defy the flexibility of the distributive logic of capitalism.

Conclusions

This chapter set out to address the panoply of actors that form the complexity of drug trafficking within the broader contexts of contemporary global organized crime. Somewhat inevitably this has been a relatively brief consideration of the role that socio-material artefacts and infrastructures in particular play in the perpetration of drug smuggling. The short example at the end highlights how human and nonhuman actors coalesce together, notably in terms of the material potentiality of the compressed cocaine powder itself, coupled with the ingenuity and expertise of the smugglers. Crucially, it also shows how such trafficking activities are embedded within the infrastructures of licit freight mobilities, in part a result of the inherent fallibility of the security of global supply chains.

This chapter is an initial attempt to build a broader research agenda into the relationships between nonhuman, socio-material forms and illicit activities, including the study of organized crime and other criminal actions. Given the breadth of these aims it is something of a vast undertaking, but my hope is that the chapter offers some potential registers of how this might be undertaken. In particular, one needs to look at the intersections between the materialities of artefacts and infrastructures and the networked formations of the geographies of transnational circulation. One must also be mindful of how artefacts operate in relation to larger-scale infrastructures, often at the expense of control, hence my previous assertion regarding under-governance. By recognizing the networked nature of transport infrastructures and the place of socio-material artefacts within them three key points emerge: firstly, it enriches our understanding and appreciation of how powerful apparently banal artefacts such as wooden pallets can become; secondly, it highlights the ingenuity of criminal actors; and, thirdly, by recognizing the previous two a more robust agenda for tackling such actions may emerge. Ultimately, the chapter has sought to demonstrate how the acknowledgement of the socio-material dimension of drug smuggling might offer valuable new lines of research enquiry into the study of global organized crime from a multi-disciplinary perspective.

References

Abraham, I. and W. van Schendel (2005), 'Introduction: The Making of Illicitness', in W. van Schendel and I. Abraham (eds), *Illicit Flows and Criminal Things: States, Borders, and the Other Side of Globalization*, Bloomington, IN: Indiana University Press, pp. 1–37.

Beckert, J. and M. Dewey (eds) (2017), *The Architecture of Illegal Markets: Towards an Economic Sociology of Illegality in the Economy*, Oxford: Oxford University Press.

Bennett, J. (2010), *Vibrant Matter: A Political Ecology of Things*, Durham, NC: Duke University Press.

Bhattacharyya, G. (2005), *Traffick: The Illicit Movement of People and Things*, London: Pluto Press.

Block, A. (2002), 'Environmental Crime and Pollution: Wasteful Reflections', *Social Justice*, 29(1/2), 61–81.

Boscagli, M. (2014), *Stuff Theory: Everyday Objects, Radical Materialism*, London: Bloomsbury Academic.

Bouchard, M. and J. Amirault (2013), 'Advances in Research on Illicit Networks', *Global Crime*, 14(2–3), 119–122.

Braun, B. and S.J. Whatmore (eds) (2010), *Political Matter: Technoscience, Democracy, and Public Life*, Minneapolis: University of Minnesota Press.

Buszynski, L. and C.B. Roberts (eds) (2015), *The South China Sea Maritime Dispute: Political, Legal and Regional Perspectives*, Abingdon: Routledge.

Campana, P. and F. Varese (2016), 'Exploitation in Human Trafficking and Smuggling', *European Journal on Criminal Policy and Research*, 22(1), 89–105.

Caulkins, J.P., H. Burnett and E. Leslie (2009), 'How Illegal Drugs Enter an Island Country: Insights from Interviews with Incarcerated Smugglers', *Global Crime*, 10(1–2), 66–93.

Cook, I. and D. Tolia-Kelly (2010), 'Material Geographies', in D. Hicks and M.C. Beaudry (eds), *The Oxford Handbook of Material Culture Studies*, Oxford: Oxford University Press, pp. 99–122.

Coole, D. and S. Frost (eds) (2010), *New Materialisms: Ontology, Agency, and Politics*, Durham, NC: Duke University Press.

Cukier, W. and J. Sheptycki (2012), 'Globalization of Gun Culture: Transnational Reflections on Pistolization and Masculinity, Flows and Resistance', *International Journal of Law, Crime and Justice*, 40, 3–19.

Decker, S.H. and M. Townsend Chapman (2008), *Drug Smugglers on Drug Smuggling: Lessons from the Inside*, Philadelphia, PA: Temple University Press.

Dorn, N., M. Levi and L. King (2005), *Literature Review on Upper Level Drug Trafficking*, London: HMSO.

Gibson, J.J. (1986), 'The Theory of Affordances', in *The Ecological Approach to Visual Perception*, New Jersey: Lawrence Erlbaum Associates, pp. 127–143.

Hall, T. (2012), 'The Geography of Transnational Organized Crime: Spaces, Networks and Flows', in F. Allum and S. Gilmour (eds), *Routledge Handbook of Transnational Organized Crime*, Abingdon: Routledge, pp. 173–185.

Hall, T. (2018), *The Economic Geographies of Organized Crime*, New York: Guilford Press.

Harley, N. and G. Hedgecoe (2015), 'Six Britons arrested after police find £240m cocaine disguised as wooden pallets at Spanish port', accessed 10 October 2017 at http://www.telegraph.co.uk/news/uknews/crime/12047146/Cocaine-disguised-as-wooden-pallets-seized-in-Spanish-port.html

Hobbs, D. (2013), *Lush Life: Constructing Organized Crime in the UK*, Oxford: Oxford University Press.

Kenney, M. (2007), 'The Architecture of Drug Trafficking: Network Forms of Organisation in the Colombian Cocaine Trade', *Global Crime*, 8(3), 233–259.

Latour, B. (2005), *Reassembling the Social: An Introduction to Actor-Network-Theory*, Oxford: Oxford University Press.

Latour, B. (2009), 'A Collective of Humans and Nonhumans: Following Daedalus's Labyrinth', in *Pandora's Hope: Essays on the Reality of Science Studies*, Cambridge, MA: Harvard University Press, pp. 174–215.

Latour, B. and S. Woolgar (1986), *Laboratory Life: The Construction of Scientific Facts*, Princeton, NJ: Princeton University Press.

Laverick, W. (2017), 'Transnational Crime', *Policing & Society*, 27(3), 324–340.

Law, J. (2009), 'Actor Network Theory and Material Semiotics', in B.S. Turner (ed.), *The New Blackwell Companion to Social Theory*, Oxford: Blackwell, pp. 141–158.

Lupsha, P.A. (1981), 'Individual Choice, Material Culture and Organized Crime', *Criminology*, 19(1), 3–24.

Manaugh, G. (2016), *A Burglar's Guide to the City*, New York: Farrar, Straus and Giroux.

Martin, C. (2015), 'Smuggling Mobilities: Parasitic Relations, and the Aporetic Openness of the Shipping Container', in T. Birtchnell, S. Savitzky and J. Urry (eds), *Cargomobilities: Moving Materials in a Global Age*, New York: Routledge, pp. 65–86.

Michael, M. (2000), *Reconnecting Culture, Technology and Nature: From Society to Heterogeneity*, London: Routledge.

Naylor, R.T. (1997), 'Mafias, Myths, and Markets: On the Theory and Practice of Enterprise Crime', *Transnational Organized Crime*, 3(3), 1–45.

Paoli, L. (2016), 'Towards a Theory of Organized Crime: Some Preliminary Reflections', in G.A. Antonopoulos (ed.), *Illegal Entrepreneurship, Organized Crime and Social Control*, Cham: Springer, pp. 3–17.

Patrick, S. (2011), 'Transnational Crime', in *Weak Links: Fragile States, Global Threats, and International Security*, Oxford: Oxford University Press, pp. 135–173.

Ramirez, B. and R.J. Bunker (2015), *Narco-Submarines: Specially Fabricated Vessels used for Drug Smuggling Purposes*, U.S. Army Foreign Military Studies Office.

Rive, A. (1929), 'A Short History of Tobacco Smuggling', *Economic History*, 1(4), 554–569.

Ruggiero, V. (1998), 'Transnational Criminal Activities: The Provision of Services in the Dirty Economies', *International Journal of Risk, Security and Crime Prevention*, 3(2), 121–129.

Scott, J.C. (2010), *The Art of Not Being Governed: An Anarchist History of Upland Southeast Asia*, Yale, CT: Yale University Press.

Seigel, D. and H. Nelen (2008), 'Introduction', in D. Seigel and H. Nelen (eds), *Organized Crime: Culture, Markets and Policies*, New York: Springer, pp. 1–3.

The Guardian (2016), 'Australian Police Seize Huge Haul of Meth Hidden in Gel Bra Inserts', accessed 16 February 2016 at https://www.theguardian.com/australia-news/2016/feb/15/australian -police-seize-estimated-1bn-worth-of-methamphetamine

Thrift, N. (2000), 'It's the Little Things', in K. Dodds and D. Atkinson (eds), *Geopolitical Traditions: Critical Histories of a Century of Geopolitical Thought*, London: Routledge, pp. 380–387.

Tilley, C. (ed.) (2006), *Handbook of Material Culture*, London: SAGE.

UNODC (United Nations Office on Drugs and Crime) (2004), *United Nations Convention against Transnational Organized Crime and the Protocols Thereto*, New York: United Nations.

UNODC (United Nations Office on Drugs and Crime) (2010), *The Globalization of Crime: A Transnational Organized Crime Threat Assessment*, Vienna: UNODC.

van Uhm, D.P. (2016), *The Illegal Wildlife Trade: Inside the Worlds of Poachers, Smugglers and Traders*, Cham: Springer.

Williams, P. (1998), 'The Nature of Drug-Trafficking Networks', *Current History*, April, 154–159.

12 Sport and crime in a global society

Nicholas Groombridge

Introduction

Some sports are very particular to their country of origin, and, like sumo in Japan or kabaddi for Sikhs, may have deeper cultural roots and resonance than even baseball in the USA. Yet these sports can be seen to bear relationships to other sports around the world. However, some sports and sports events might be seen to have global reach already while some are actively seeking it. Moreover, some countries are now targeting success in sports formerly not associated with them. Association football has a global following and presence. The USA may resist it and is currently seeking to export American football to England, soccer's home. Perhaps the most global sport might be athletics (track and field) but the largest global media events are the Summer Olympics and the FIFA World Cup. All these, and cycling's Tour de France – the largest free-to-view sporting event in the world – and many individual sports and sportspeople, have become associated with crime often called 'fouling', 'simulating', 'cheating' or 'doping'. Yet many still promote sport as crime prevention or even as a development tool in nation-building and peacekeeping. Both sport and crime are gendered and gendering. Women's crime and women's sport are both sidelined. Sex trafficking is sometimes linked to global mega-sporting events and sportspeople are traded legally and illegally. As sport seeks to grow globally the opportunities for crime, and challenges for justice, grow too. Andrews and Ritzer (2007) distinguish between the 'glocal' (Robertson, 1995) and the 'grobal', 'the imperialistic ambitions of nations, corporations, organizations, and the like and their desire, indeed need, to impose themselves on various geographic areas' (2007: 137) in their critique of Rowe (2003). He had argued sport may be inimitable to a full cultural globalization because of its national/cultural attachments. Andrews and Ritzer disagree, suggesting a greater interplay and they reject 'heroic' praise of local sports (persons). Taking from both, some 'glocal' resistance might be provided by nation states and sports, but irrespective of arguments about globalization is now engaging with new global realities that include harm and crime.

Global sport connections

All of the topics in this volume seem more serious than sport. Sport is a topic dismissed by many simply as play, or, worse, a distraction from the revolution (Brohm, 1987); for its barbarity (Perelman, 2012); identified as Foucauldian 'bio-power' (Miller, 2009); and critiqued by feminists as the site, and cause, of male violence (Nelson, 1995). There are more positive accounts of play; for instance, Kane (2005) reminds us of the value of play generally and of non-Western traditions of sport that are ludic. Two chapters in this volume address war and criminology. Some may recall Orwell's nostrum that international 'sport is war minus shooting' (see Beck, 2013) and it is important to note he was speaking not just of 'sport'. Huizinga noted, 'Ever since words existed for fighting and playing, men have been wont to call war a game' (1949: 89).

Sport is increasingly global and transnational so the concerns of Hobbs and Hudson in this volume are germane to the argument of this chapter. Moreover, sport, like much else, is now moving online (eSports) and into cyberspace, so Yar's chapter has relevance too. Stephenson specifically mentions state-sponsored doping of athletes and most sport has had issues with the sort of corruption other contributors discuss. Replica football kits may be more fashion than sport but they too are frequently counterfeited (see the chapter by Jo Large for a discussion of the global trade in counterfeit goods).

The argument is made in Groombridge (2016) that sport is a social construction much like life, and largely coincident with it, so subject to all the same issues – both good and bad. Sport is not a realm separate from life and many of the aspects of sport are constructed from the same materials as crime, particularly in respect of violence and the construction of gender – though not all sports involve violence, or much physicality.

For tax and grant-receiving purposes the card game bridge has been trying to win recognition as a sport. The English Bridge Union has recently been disappointed by the High Court; it had sought to argue that Bridge is more physically demanding than rifle shooting which is recognized as a sport (Rahman, 2015). The European Court of Justice has upheld the judgment (Boffey, 2017). Perhaps the court should have considered the game's competitiveness and recent 'cheating' scandals (Jourdain, 2015). Groombridge (2016) cynically argues that one of the defining marks of sport is cheating.

Sport, crime and criminology

Sport and sportspeople are studied by sociology and profitably represented by lawyers. Before we turn to the global research agenda for criminology in sport and around sport we might briefly examine how some sports historians have addressed some of the issues in this chapter and elsewhere in this volume. *The*

Oxford Handbook of Sports History (Edelman and Wilson, 2017) contains only four mentions of 'crime'. In this they are similar to the grand texts aimed at criminology students (Newburn, 2013).[1] One mention is that historically sports tournaments were known to attract crime, and another mention notes a fear of crime for the then forthcoming Rio Olympics. The remaining two, in Carvalho's (2017) chapter, note the journalistic yoking of crime and sport to sell newspapers. Groombridge (2017) notes the same link made in many films and other elements of popular culture.

However, more specific terms that chime with the concerns of this volume can be found. Thus 'corruption' is more often mentioned and often in respect of doping, anti-doping or the condemnation, but also the frequent embrace of, doping to further state, corporate or individual interests. Such hypocrisy may require some athletes to be scapegoated, labelled even, which the critical criminologist might recognize as criminalization. The BBC's constant use of the term 'drug cheat' (BBC, 2017) when talking about athlete Justin Gatlin was challenged by their own commentator Michael Johnson. He noted that Gatlin was singled out as a 'villain' despite many other 'cheats'. A Foucauldian take on doping is also possible. Henning (2013) found non-elite athletes self-surveilled themselves. Finley and Finley (2006) went so far as to speak of a war against athletes. They have a background in sport yet liken the 'doping' and 'cheating' of athletes – but also playing while injured – to the actions of exploited workers within a business.

This introductory material serves to examine what sport might be, why it matters to criminology and how it relates to the other contributions in this book. Now we turn to look at some of the growing literature which might now be claimed for global sports criminology but has its origins in other disciplines and concerns.

Doping and corruption

There is much media, and some fan, hand-wringing, plus task forces and commissions globally and locally attempting to control the often-intertwined issues of corruption and doping. There are some broadly criminological/legal texts specifically addressed to such matters: Paoli and Donati (2014) look at doping; Brooks et al. (2013) at corruption and Haberfeld and Abbott (2014) even more specifically at match fixing. Such is the speed of development in this area, with regular disclosures, that even such recent work can seem dated, hence the frequent resort to media sources in this chapter.

Haberfeld and Abbott (2014) mostly examine match fixing in soccer, and Ralf Mutschke of FIFA provides a preface which concludes, 'Football's strength comes from its integrity'! A former German police officer, Mutschke, has now left FIFA

---

1   And all editions of *The Oxford Handbook of Criminology*.

and his role in policing match fixing has been outsourced. Even when in post Declan Hill was not impressed by Mutschke. Hill is the author of *The Fix: Soccer and Organised Crime* (2008) and *The Insider's Guide to Match-Fixing in Football* (2013) and blogged about the suspicions of a fix that were widely aired before the match between Nigeria and Scotland (Hill, 2017). However, that led to no action by FIFA.

Paoli and Donati (2014)[2] open out their research in Italy to examine the many actors (players) involved in doping and anti-doping and touch on wider European and global issues – particularly in respect of the International Olympic Committee (IOC) and the World Anti-Doping Agency. While volleyball, basketball and rugby are all mentioned, their main concern is soccer. Their focus excludes cricket and US professional sports. Their prologue serves up a number of 'antipasti', one of which involved cross-border activities – a coach attempting to flee back to Austria and several athletes doing so and immediately retiring. Apparently, the IOC had sought assurances from the Italian authorities of a light touch during the Winter Olympics in Turin 2006. Yet the Carabinieri raided the Austrian Nordic ski team which led to bans and eventually to a partially successful trial six years later. The mere possession of means to dope was not illegal in Italy but such a law was passed in Austria thereafter. Three officials of the Austrian Ski Federation were acquitted but two athletes and a trainer were convicted.

Sumner crystallizes why thinking on these matters cannot be left to lawyers but requires a critical criminological approach. She argues against what she calls a 'harm reduction' approach and proposes, 'the criminalisation of doping in sport in the UK as part of a growing global movement towards such criminalisation at national level' (2017: 1). She is right to note the global issues but is too easily persuaded towards deterrence and criminal justice solutions. For her, doping is a matter of fraud. This makes sense from a purely legalistic perspective, but she then allows herself to promote the more nebulous and distinctly non-legal concept of 'the spirit of sport'.

It is in this spirit that she discusses Chris Froome's victory in the Tour de France. She imagines: 'Sports fans watching wanted to rejoice in his magnificent achievement. However, his victory was over-shadowed by stories in the press implying his win was not a clean win, but one assisted by doping' (2017: 1). Whereas my concern, as a sports fan, is that he has no personality and his victories have come from the relentless dominance of his Sky team in which money is the performance-enhancing drug. Sumner (2017) takes the Austrian legislation mentioned above as an exemplar; but such an approach of individualized guilt misses the extent to which teams and federations are behind many of these successes and failures. The structural, state and corporate aspects of wrongdoing and harm may pass the academic lawyer and sports fan by, but the critical criminologist should be able to find much to research in global sport.

---

2 See also the special edition of the journal *Trends in Organized Crime* (volume 18, issue 3, September 2015).

Some sports – like golf, tennis or cricket – are seen to be 'cleaner' than others but an Internet search of any of these sports combined with 'cheating', 'doping' or 'corruption' reveals many stories. Fraser (2005) explores the extent to which, 'the man in white is always right'. His way in as a lawyer was through the complex subjectivity of the LBW (leg before wicket) means of a batsman being dismissed in cricket. Others have noted that in 1932 an article in *The Cricketer* could claim that 'Cricket stands for law and order . . . The umpire gives you out: out you must go. The man in the white coat is a symbol of constitutional government' (Williams, 2012: 12). Yet W. G. Grace,[3] the exemplar of gentlemanly cricket, played right up to, and sometimes beyond, what the rules allowed, and only the Australians called him out on his 'cheating' and 'gamemanship' (Tomlinson, 2015). Often with the collusion of the authorities he blurred the line between amateur and professional. Huggins estimates Grace earned £120,000 (2004: 129) over his career, including a final testimonial game which raised £9,000.

More recently a small cricket team in Wales received global attention when, quite legally, within the laws of the game, they declared their last match on 18 for 1, enabling their opponents to win the match easily but not the league due to the allocation of points for wins and bonus points for wickets taken or runs scored. The team was awarded the championship but subsequently demoted (Bull, 2017). This illustrates the problem facing criminalizers like Sumner (2017), in that the spirit of the game cannot be guaranteed by its laws, though the laws of cricket allow a good deal of discretion and speak of the 'spirit of the game'. Much of the debate about the team's unsporting behaviour focused on this. Other declarations have seemed sporting but have been found to have gambling/corruption behind them.

In the 2000 fifth test between South Africa (SA) and England, Hansie Cronje, the SA captain made what many thought to be a 'sporting' declaration – that is, a declaration that might give the opposition a chance to reach the SA run total and tie or win the match, or force a draw. The England team went on to win that test, its only one on that tour. Most of the first four days had been lost to rain. On the last day, Cronje proposed that he would declare the SA first innings at 248–8 and that both teams should then declare their next innings, leaving England to chase a total of 249 in its second innings. Spectators and commentators are used to teams grinding out a draw in such circumstances, so this 'innovation' was welcomed by many as being in the 'true spirit of the game'.[4] But later that summer it became clear that Cronje had made his 'sporting' offer for corrupt purposes on behalf of betting interests, and that he had taken bribes before.

Consideration of fraud is the way into this subject for Brooks et al. (2013) and they rightly claim their work as a pioneering contribution to the sociology of sport. Here their work is claimed for criminology. While much media attention is on

3 1848–1915; playing career 1865 to 1908 and record-breaking statistics in batting and bowling.

4 Fraser (2005) makes the nice point that the England captain Nasser Hussein's declaration was actually a 'forfeiture' and, therefore, his actions were illegal, even if in the spirit of the game.

the wrongdoing of individual athletes – though slightly modified by accusations against the Russian State – Brooks et al. (2013) are clear that sport has a structural problem. They are worth quoting at some length.

> These structural matters range from: organisational corruption (for example, vote-rigging and influence peddling); selective myopia regarding the use of performance-enhancing substances, or a naive view that sport is 'clean': a belief that if gambling is made illegal then the sport is free from its influence; and limited powers to 'police' a sport beyond breaches of a 'sporting code of conduct'. (2013: 170)

They conclude with the need for independent, cross-sport, transnational random drug testing but accept that the 'war on gambling' (not their term) is not won by simple bans. This disparity is worthy of criminological attention but again they suggest international cooperation which raises issues many criminologists are aware of. The commercial pressures to take legitimate gambling sponsorship are enormous and horse racing exists for gambling, but commerce may also demand cleaner partners. For instance, the Football Association announced an end to all sponsorship deals with betting companies in 2017 (Kelner, 2017).

Another way in for criminologists is through the consideration of transnational policing of 'mega-events' like the World Cup or the Olympics; for instance, Bowling and Sheptycki (2012) and, in a similar vein, Fussey et al. (2012) note that such policing had the nature of 'cleansing' about it. They treat the venues for such sporting mega-events as 'theme parks', emphasizing the spectacle of such global sports capitalism. Unruly sports like skateboarding are to be kept out as firmly as beggars and terrorists. Kim (2017) sees such events as among the 'discontents' of the would-be modern global city.

As this selective review indicates, much of the work revolves around the topics of doping/anti-doping and corruption. Sometimes state or corporate corruption uses doping/anti-doping but as Brooks et al. (2013) show – and Haberfeld and Abbott (2014) and Hill (2008, 2013) note – local, regional and criminal interests are in play too. In part, the intention here has been to weave the extant work into criminology's research agenda but also to urge a less comfortable, official, corporatist approach. For instance, Haberfeld and Abbott (2014) and contributors take a very official 'criminal justice' line, which even an uncritical criminology might suggest was doomed to failure. A critical one might suggest that 'failure' was the intention.

Uncomfortable for sport should be the accusations of encouraging violence against women or encouraging the sex trade and human trafficking.

Sporting slavery and sex

In his bid to leave Manchester United Football Club, Christiano Ronaldo claimed he was a 'slave' (Herbert, 2008). At the time he was being paid £120,000 a week.

More recently, Lily Abdullayeva claimed she too was treated like a 'sporting slave'. The Ethiopian athlete says she had prize money stolen and was tricked into taking performance-enhancing drugs after moving to Azerbaijan (Kelner, 2017).

Abdullayeva was a successful athlete. Those starting out face other problems, such as boys trafficked or defrauded by 'agents' who promise them glittering careers in European football (Hawkins, 2015). Unusually Al Bangura, who was trafficked for sex, did eventually play in the English Premier League for Watford from 2005 to 2009 (Kotecha and Bell, 2015). Legal, but reeking of racism and colonialism, we find the plight of Fijian rugby union players lured to New Zealand and elsewhere (Kanemasu and Molnar, 2013). Though not trafficked, Kitson (2017) tells us of Sireli Temo, a 30-year-old Fijian playing for Tarbes in the French third division who killed himself. He had been injured and was remitting money home to support a wife and two children. Kitson also interviewed a campaigner who said that over 600 South Pacific Islanders were in similar circumstances in Europe.

Moving from harms suffered by individual athletes we find the contention that mega-sports events are associated with forced prostitution and modern slavery. This is a highly contested area but the Global Alliance Against Traffic in Women (2011) takes a sceptical perspective, noting claims, for example, that 40,000 foreign sex workers/trafficked women would arrive in South Africa in the run-up to the 2010 World Cup. They found that these claims were unfounded and suggest that business actually decreased for sex workers during this period. It should be noted that a distinction should be made between women who respond to the market signal, to use an economic term, and freely go where they believe there is money, and those who are tricked/forced into going, either with or without the promise of money for sex work. Moreover, most criminologists would be reluctant to place too much emphasis on the police finding no trace of trafficking in such circumstances.

Having examined some of the crimes associated with sport we can examine the more direct claims that sport is a cause of or factor in crime, or, conversely, that it can prevent crime or aid in desistance from crime.

Cause of, or cure for, crime

A muscular Christianity, now secularized, suggests sport as a 'cure' for crime, assisting prevention and/or desistance (see Nichols, 2007; Meek, 2012, 2014; Chamberlain, 2013, for assessments). At the time of writing, one example is current England international cricketer Moeen Ali's contention that the sport kept him from drugs (McRae, 2017). This might also be seen as an aspect of the Eliasian 'civilizing process'. Elias himself (1994: 157) makes only the scantest of references to sport conjoined with comments on bathing, both having a 'relative degree of freedom to develop' in a 'society in which a high degree of restraint is taken for granted'. Babiak (2016) notes in an Eliasian way that boxing's tamed violence was seen to be 'unmanly' but came to be sufficiently established to be parodied in film and theatre.[5]

The mission statement of Fight for Peace[6] reads, 'We use boxing and martial arts combined with education and personal development to realize the potential of young people in communities affected by crime and violence.' The 'appeal of sport' is seen to bring offenders and those 'at risk' to projects, and the 'positive values' of sport seen to work, but they recognize that wider developmental programmes reinforce learning. Much is made of the evaluations of their work, but they cannot unpick the relative or respective contributions of the sport and wider programmes nor of the external environment. Any downside has no place in such promotional material. Armstrong and Hodges-Ramon (2015) are highly critical of such 'naivety' and Groombridge (2016) is sceptical. However, government and sports bodies remain convinced.[7]

For every boxer who claims that without the sport he would have ended up in prison, for instance Luis Collazo (Davies, 2014), we might find a list like 'the 10 best boxers who ended up in prison' (King, 2012). The list was compiled by King, prompted by the case of Floyd Mayweather, who served a 90-day sentence in a county jail rather than a federal or state prison. The offence is not mentioned, and the writer is 'thankful' that an upcoming fight with Paquiano can go ahead as scheduled. You need to look elsewhere to discover that Mayweather was sentenced for 'domestic violence and battery' against the mother of three of his four children (Mitchell, 2015). The media has covered incidents of violence against five different women over 14 years by Mayweather. But note also the work of Argentinian boxer Sergio Martinez who campaigns to end violence against women, inspired by the poor example of his countryman Carlos Monzon (Zaimov, 2013). Monzon, a world middleweight champion, was accused of domestic violence against two wives and mistresses and served 11 years in prison for the murder of his second wife.

King's list includes Jack Johnson and reminds us of the criminalization of black men too. Johnson's conviction in 1912 for the interstate trafficking of a prostitute should serve as a warning to naive interventions in the area of 'human trafficking'. The Mann Act was inspired by panic about 'white slavery' and Gaskew (2012) is clear that racism was behind the first ever use of the Act, in a case against Johnson. Johnson's popularity with white women was deemed to be immoral and arguments relating to the women's consent were set aside. He served a year in prison in 1920, having surrendered to federal authorities after time in Canada and Europe. The US Senate urged a presidential pardon (*Sports Illustrated*, 2015) and in a populist move

---

5 See Groombridge (2017) on wider sport and crime intersections in popular culture.

6 See their website http://fightforpeace.net (accessed 1 March 2018).

7 See the website of The National Alliance of Sport for the Desistance of Crime http://www.nasdc.org/power-of-sport/sport-desistance/ (accessed 1 March 2018).

President Trump granted a pardon in May 2018, enabling him to be pictured with Lennox Lewis and Sylvester Stallone.[8]

Moving from the wrongdoings of individual sportsmen to those of spectators we find what might be called the 'Super Bowl effect' or the 'Old Firm' effect. The charge is that domestic violence increases over the NFL Super Bowl weekend or in Scotland when old and sectarian rivals Glasgow's Rangers and Celtic play each other. Both claims are frequently repeated by the media. Academics have been divided over methodology (that is to count and timescale) and interpretation of any association found, with confounding factors being alcohol, drug use, holidays and even the anticipated result (see Crowley et al., 2014). However – former broad-caster turned academic – Adubato (2016) found a correlation in Philadelphia with domestic violence and the games played by the local team. She suggests that the presentation of the game (such as the frequent use of 'hard hits' montages) and even associated adverts may also be associated factors. She notes too that White et al.'s (1992) work on this was ridiculed as feminist, anti-sport (and therefore un-American?). Katz and White (1993) set out their (mis)match with media which they likened to an offensive blitz, with them cast as the opposing quarterback.

Finally, we might mention Hope Solo to remind us that women play sport and may also be offenders. Solo was goalkeeper of the US women's soccer team, and in 2014 faced charges of assaulting her sister and 17-year-old nephew in a drunken, violent outburst. Clear gender issues arise, particularly in respect of Solo's alleged taunts of her nephew (6 feet, 8 inches tall, and weighing in at 270lbs) that he was a 'pussy' and of one of the arresting officers that he was 'a 14-year-old boy'. It should also be noted that in the US media the incident was framed as 'domestic violence'. The case has yet to come to trial due to extensive legal arguments.

Moving the agenda forward

As we have seen, many sports have very local origins, but many are now seeking to go global or at least to extend their international connections and markets. Many of the problems of harm and crime that beset them in the national sphere are exacerbated on going global, or on attempting to do so. Sports crimes and harms often play out in the public sphere before a large live audience and watched by many high definition cameras, yet they are deeply contested. Was that a foul or is the player simulating injury? Much of this is condemned in moral terms as 'cheat-ing'. Yet it might be seen as violence or fraud. The intentions of the actors may not be obvious though their actions are. Less obvious are the actions of gambling syndicates or state or corporate players intent on winning a game, 'predicting' an event, winning the right to stage games or even deliberately to lose. All, however,

---

8 *The Guardian* Sports (24 May 2018), 'Trump Grants Posthumous Pardon to Heavyweight Champion Jack Johnson', https://www.theguardian.com/sport/2018/may/24/trump-pardons-jack-johnson-heavyweight-champion (accessed 25 February 2019).

should be of interest to criminologists. They should not let sport's claims of sovereignty – or their love of it – spare it from critical examination.

Clearly some obvious, though overlapping, areas for research are: doping; anti-doping; corruption and exploitation. As we have seen, all are researched (work from law, sociology, history and economics are all cited here) and are given increasing media coverage but a critical criminological eye is required. Although discussed above no suggestions are made here for addressing the violence by fans towards their partners (the 'Super Bowl effect'); the growth or otherwise of the sex trade; or fans' behaviour towards each other – 'hooliganism'. They are prone to ideological and methodological arguments and also seem to be well covered, and, while related to sport, do not take sport as a central theme. But the global aspects – with potential local and sporting differences – of this violence associated with sports fans cannot be ignored. Hopkins and Treadwell (2014) place football hooligans within a wider context of harms and wrongdoing in football more generally. Work on non-soccer-related violence is more rare but exists. Thus, Lewis (2007) examines fan violence in North America and links such 'celebratory' events to riots more generally. The fear of such violence, and now terrorism, conditions the policing of mega-events (Fussey et al., 2012). Fans may deliberately seek to stop a game, but Brooks et al. (2013) note that on 16 June 1917 bookmakers occupied the field in the hope that a match between the Boston Red Sox and the Chicago White Sox would be cancelled.

The term 'drug cheat' masks the involvement of many others in the individual athlete's 'choice' to resort to apparently performance enhancing drugs.[9] Sponsors, national governing bodies and the state all add pressure towards 'deviance' or crime. Moreover, anti-doping does far more than seek to catch 'cheats' – it represents a surveillance regime of athletes that can be turned against them at any time: capriciously, corruptly or to prove it works by sacrificing a lesser or troublesome athlete.

The Tour de France is mentioned in this chapter's introductory section but its manifold problems are too extensive to catalogue here save to note that most of the themes of this chapter all play out in the sport. It now crosses borders; towns bid for inclusion in the itinerary; drugs are used; police and sporting organizations 'police' the event; allegations are now arising of 'technical doping' through the use of hidden motors – and all of this under the scrutiny of a worldwide media and close pressing fans.

Both doping and anti-doping may be carried out as part of a wider corruption and, as the case of Lily Abdullayeva shows, this may be part of a wider exploitation/ modern slavery. Smaller local sports cannot so much resist as find themselves ignored. Some, however, have big enough local markets to attract big crimes. Thus sumo, which is big in Japan, has its problems with gambling (as does baseball for which Japan is less well known) and corruption more generally (Duggan and Levitt,

---

9 There is debate about the effectiveness of some drugs and as with all drugs there is the possibility of fake pharma (Hall and Antonopoulos, 2016).

2002; Manzenreiter, 2014). Even kabaddi has not escaped accusations of cheating. The requirement to chant 'kabaddi' while 'raiding' the opposition's area has been replaced by a 30-second time limit because of cheating. Moreover, attempts have been made to globalize the sport with the Bollywood touch of the Indian Premier League of cricket (Wellings, 2014). Accusations of cheating between local teams in India recently led to a fight and a shooting (*Millennium Post*, 2017).

Sport is too often ignored in criminology as a site of crime, harm and criminalization at the local level. Sport hides in plain sight, with its many problems bemoaned – from fan violence to cheating and doping – without reference to their crime and crime-like connotations. Sport is always gendered and as we have seen is often racialized and colonialized (Kanemasu and Molnar, 2013). Sport's increased global reach requires that criminology 'steps up to the plate'. This may require some wrestling with the media and sports fans (Katz and White, 1993).

References

Adubato, B. (2016), 'The Promise of Violence: Televised, Professional Football Games and Domestic Violence', *Journal of Sport and Social Issues*, 40(1): 22–37.

Andrews D. L. and Ritzer, G. (2007), 'The Grobal in the Sporting Glocal', *Global Networks*, 7(2): 113–153.

Armstrong, G. and Hodges-Ramon, L. (2015), 'Sport and Crime', *Oxford Handbooks Online*. DOI: 10.1093/oxfordhb/9780199935383.013.87

Babiak, P. M. (2016), '"The Manly Art": The Burlesque Boxing Match in Nineteenth-Century Knockabout Comedy', *Nineteenth Century Theatre and Film*, 43(1): 21–42.

BBC (2017, 6 August), 'World Championships 2017: Justin Gatlin Booed During Gold Medal Ceremony', BBC Sport website, http://www.bbc.co.uk/sport/athletics/40842008 (accessed 7 September 2017).

Beck, P. J. (2013), '"War Minus the Shooting": George Orwell on International Sport and the Olympics', *Sport in History*, 33(1): 72–94.

Boffey, D. (2017, 26 October), 'Not the Real Deal: EU Court Rejects Claim that Bridge is a Sport', *The Guardian* online, https://www.theguardian.com/sport/2017/oct/26/not-real-deal-eu-court-rejects-claim-bridge-sport?CMP=share_btn_link (accessed 27 October 2017).

Bowling, B. and Sheptycki, J. (2012), *Global Policing*, London: Sage Publications.

Brohm, J.-M. (1987), *Sport: A Prison of Measured Time*, London: Pluto Press.

Brooks, G., Aleem, A. and Button, M. (2013), *Fraud, Corruption and Sport*, London: Palgrave Macmillan.

Bull, A. (2017), 'Was a Headline-making Village Team's Declaration against the Spirit of Cricket?', *The Guardian* website, 5 September 2017, https://www.theguardian.com/sport/2017/sep/05/the-spin -carew-vilage-spirit-cricket?utm_source=esp&utm_medium=Email&utm_campaign=The+Spin+ 2016&utm_term=242411&subid=99320&CMP=EMCSPTEML942 (accessed 14 September 2017).

Carvalho, J. (2017), 'Communications and Journalism', in Edelman, R. and Wilson, W. (eds) *The Oxford Handbook of Sports History*, New York: Oxford University Press.

Chamberlain, J. M. (2013), 'Sports-based Intervention and the Problem of Youth Offending: A Diverse Enough Tool for a Diverse Society?', *Sport in Society: Cultures, Commerce, Media, Politics*, 16(10): 1279–1292.

Crowley, A., Brooks, O. and Lombard, N. (2014), *Football and Domestic Abuse: A Literature Review Report*, No. 6/2014, Glasgow: Scottish Centre for Crime and Justice Research.

Davies, G. A. (2014, 30 April), '"Without Boxing, I Would have Gone to Prison, No Question", says Amir Khan's Opponent Luis Collazo', *The Telegraph*, www.telegraph.co.uk/sport/othersports/

boxing/10798626/Without-boxing-I-would-have-goneto-prison-no-question-says-Amir-Khans-opponent-Luis-Collazo.html (accessed 11 October 2015).

Duggan, M. and Levitt, S. D. (2002), 'Winning isn't Everything: Corruption in Sumo Wrestling', *American Economic Review*, 92(5): 1594–1605.

Edelman, R. and Wilson, W. (eds) (2017), *The Oxford Handbook of Sports History*, New York: Oxford University Press.

Elias, N. (1994), *The Civilising Process: Sociogenetic and Psychogenetic Investigations*, Oxford: Blackwell.

Finley, P. S. and Finley, L. L. (2006), *The Sports Industry's War on Athletes*, Westport, CT: Praeger.

Fraser, D. (2005), *Cricket and the Law: The Man in White is Always Right*, Abingdon: Routledge.

Fussey, P., Coaffee, J., Armstrong, G. and Hobbs, D. (2012), 'The Regeneration Games: Purity and Security in the Olympic City', *British Journal of Sociology*, 63(2): 260–284.

Gaskew, T. (2012), 'Mann Act', in Miller, Wilbur R. (ed.) *The Social History of Crime and Punishment in America: An Encyclopedia*, Thousand Oaks, CA: Sage Publications.

Global Alliance Against Traffic in Women (2011), 'What's the Cost of a Rumour? A Guide to Sorting out the Myths and the Facts about Sporting Events and Trafficking', www.gaatw.org/publications/WhatstheCostofaRumour.11.15.2011.pdf (accessed 23 July 2015).

Groombridge, N. (2016), *Sports Criminology: A Critical Criminology of Sports and Games*, Bristol: Policy Press.

Groombridge, N. (2017), 'Sports Crime and Popular Culture', *Oxford Research Encyclopedia of Criminology and Criminal Justice*, available at http://oxfordindex.oup.com/view/10.1093/acre fore/9780190264079.013.277

Haberfeld, M. J. and Abbott, J. (2014), 'Introduction: Match Fixing as a Modality of Sports Related Crimes', in Haberfeld, M. R. and Sheehan, D. (eds) *Match-Fixing in International Sports: Existing Processes, Law Enforcement, and Prevention Strategies*, Cham: Springer.

Hall, A. and Antonopoulos, G. (2016), *Fake Men Online: The Internet and the Transnational Market in Illicit Pharmaceuticals*, London: Palgrave Macmillan.

Hawkins, E. (2015), T*he Lost Boys: Inside Football's Slave Trade*, London: Bloomsbury Publishing.

Henning, A. D. (2013), '(Self-)Surveillance, Anti-Doping, and Health in Non-Elite Road Running', *Surveillance & Society*, [S.l.] 11(4): 494–507.

Herbert, I. (2008), 'Ronaldo: "I am a slave"', *The Independent* website, 10 July 2008, http://www.inde pendent.co.uk/sport/football/transfers/ronaldo-i-am-a-slave-864958.html (accessed 20 September 2017).

Hill, D. (2008), *The Fix: Soccer and Organised Crime*, Ontario: McClelland and Stewart.

Hill, D. (2013), *The Insider's Guide to Match-Fixing in Football*, Toronto: Anne McDermid and Associates.

Hill, D. (n.d.), 'More Revelations, the Nigerian Goalkeeper and Ralf Mutschke, Brazilian Fixing How to Win Money on the Gambling Market and Hoyzer the Hero', http://declanhill.com/revelations-nigerian-goalkeeper-ralf-mutschke-brazilian-fixing-win-money-gambling-market-hoyzer-hero/ (accessed 7 September 2017).

Hopkins, M. and Treadwell, J. (eds) (2014), *Football Hooliganism, Fan Behaviour and Crime: Contemporary Issues*, Basingstoke: Palgrave Macmillan.

Huggins, M. (2004), *The Victorians and Sport*, New York: Palgrave Macmillan.

Huizinga, J. (1949), *Home Ludens: A Study of the Play-Element in Culture*, Abingdon: Routledge.

Jourdain, P. (2015), 'International Bridge Champions Accuse Teammates of Cheating', *The Telegraph*, 25 August 2015, https://www.telegraph.co.uk/news/worldnews/middleeast/israel/11824257/Internat ional-bridge-champions-accuse-teammates-of-cheating.html

Kane, P. (2005), *The Play Ethic*, London: Pan Macmillan.

Kanemasu, Y. and Molnar, G. (2013), 'Collective Identity and Contested Allegiance: A Case of Migrant Professional Fijian Rugby Players', *Sport in Society: Cultures, Commerce, Media, Politics*, 16(7): 863–882.

Katz, J. and White, G. F. (1993), 'Engaging the Media: A Case Study of the Politics of Crime and the Media', *Social Justice*, 20: 57–68.

Kelner, M. (2017), 'FA Announces End to all Sponsorship Deals with Betting Companies', *The Guardian*, 22 June 2017, https://www.theguardian.com/football/2017/jun/22/fa-announces-end-to-sponsorship-deals-with-betting-companies (accessed 14 September 2017).

Kim, Y. H. (2017), 'The Global City and its Discontents', in Short, J. R. (ed.), *A Research Agenda for Cities*, Cheltenham, UK and Northampton, MA, USA: Edward Elgar.

King, A. (2012, 6 January), '10 Best Boxers who Went to Prison', Bleacher Report, http://bleacherreport.com/articles/1013180-10-best-boxers-who-went-to-prison (accessed 11 October 2015).

Kitson, R. (2017) 'Workers' Welfare Becomes First Casualty of Pacific Islands Gold Rush', *The Guardian* website, 18 November 2016, https://www.theguardian.com/sport/2016/nov/18/pacific-islands-rugby-union-fiji-samoa-tonga (accessed 20 September 2017).

Kotecha, S. and Bell, S. (2015), 'Former Premier League Footballer was Trafficked for Sex', BBC website, 20 November 2015, http://www.bbc.co.uk/news/uk-34849619 (accessed 20 September 2017).

Lewis, J. M. (2007), *Sports Fan Violence in North America*, Lanham, MD: Rowman and Littlefield.

Manzenreiter, Wolfram (2014), 'Cracks in the Moral Economy of Sumo: Beasts of Burden, Sport Heroes, National Icons and Living Gods in Disgrace', *International Journal of the History of Sport*, 31(4): 459–473.

McRae, D. (2017), Moeen Ali: 'If it Wasn't for Cricket I Don't Know What I'd be Doing Now', *The Guardian*, 1 August 2017, https://www.theguardian.com/sport/2017/aug/01/moeen-ali-england-cricket-racism-islam (accessed 3 August 2017).

Meek, R. (2012), 'The Role of Sport in Promoting Desistance from Crime: An Evaluation of 2nd Chance Project Rugby and Football Academies at Portland Young Offender Institution', Second Chance. Report available at http://eprints.soton.ac.uk/210815/1/Meek_2nd_Chance_Portland_Evaluation_Final_Report.pdf (accessed 19 February 2016).

Meek, R. (2014), *Sport in Prison: Exploring the Role of Physical Activity in Penal Practices: Exploring the Role of Physical Activity in Correctional Settings*, Abingdon: Routledge.

Millennium Post (2017) '18-year-old Shot at Over Kabaddi Score', 11 September 2017, *Millennium* Post, http://www.millenniumpost.in/delhi/18-year-old-shot-at-over-kabaddi-score-261572 (accessed 20 September 2017).

Miller, T. (2009), 'Michel Foucault and the Critique of Sport', in Carrington, B. and McDonald, I. (eds) *Marxism, Cultural Studies and Sport*, Abingdon: Routledge.

Mitchell, K. (2015, 28 April), 'Storm Grows over Mayweather's Violent Past', *The Guardian*, www.theguardian.com/sport/blog/2015/apr/26/floyd-mayweather-espnreport-violence (accessed 11 October 2015).

Nelson, M. B. (1995), *The Stronger Women Get, The More Men Love Football: Sexism and the American Culture of Sports*, San Diego, CA: Harcourt Brace.

Newburn, T. (2013), *Criminology*, Abingdon: Routledge.

Nichols, G. (2007), *Sport and Crime Reduction: The Role of Sports in Tackling Youth Crime*, Abingdon: Routledge.

Paoli, L. and Donati, A. (2014), *The Sports Doping Market: Understanding Supply and Demand, and the Challenges of their Control*, New York: Springer.

Perelman, M. (2012), *Barbaric Sport: A Global Plague*, London: Verso.

Rahman, Khaleda (2015), 'Judge Says Card Game Bridge is More Physical than Rifle Shooting and Rules Bid to Get Recognised as a Sport for Lottery Funding Can go Ahead', *Daily Mail* (27 April 2015), www.dailymail.co.uk/news/article-3057633/Judge-says-cardgame-bridge-physical-rifle-shooting-rules-bid-recognised-sport-lottery-fundingahead.html#ixzz3gbeTgzX4 (accessed 11 October 2015).

Robertson, R. (1995), 'Glocalization: Time–Space and Homogeneity–Heterogeneity', in Featherstone, M., Lash, S. and Robertson, R. (eds) *Global Modernities*, London: Sage, pp. 25–44.

Rowe, D. (2003), 'Sport and the Repudiation of the Global', *International Review for the Sociology of Sport*, 38: 281–294.

Sports Illustrated (2015), 'US Senate Passes Amendment Urging Pardon for Boxer Jack Johnson', *Sports Illustrated*, 16 July 2015, www.si.com/boxing/2015/07/16/jack-johnson-boxer-us-senateamend-ment-mccain-reid# (accessed 11 October 2015).

Sumner, C. (2017), 'The Spirit of Sport: The Case for Criminalisation of Doping in the UK', *International Sports Law Journal*, 16: 217–227.

Tomlinson, R. (2015), *Amazing Grace: The Man who was WG*, London: Little, Brown.

Wellings, L. (2014), 'Kabaddi Striving for a Global Audience. The 900-year-old Sport from India Vies for Global Reach as World Kabaddi League Takes off in London with Great Hopes', 16 August 2014, Al Jazeera, http://www.aljazeera.com/sport/features/2014/08/kabaddi-striving-global-audi ence-2014816128056710.html (accessed 20 September 2017).

White, G. F., Katz, J. and Scarborough, K. E. (1992), 'The Impact of Professional Football Games upon Violent Assaults on Women', *Violence and Victims*, 7: 157–171.

Williams, J. (2012), *Cricket and England: A Cultural and Social History of Cricket in England*, Abingdon: Routledge.

Zaimov, S. (2013), 'Pope Francis to Meet Boxing Champion Sergio Martinez; Talk Anti-bullying, Violence against Women', *Christian Post*, 9 October 2013, www.christianpost.com/news/pope-francis-to-meet-boxing-champion-sergio-martineztalk-anti-bullying-violence-against-women-1063 21/#qSXGC862T68UouCS.99 (accessed 11 October 2015).

Index